Insights from the Masters

A Compilation

Insights from the Masters

A Compilation

Fiona C. Odgren

AXIS MUNDI
BOOKS

Winchester, UK
Washington, USA

First published by Axis Mundi Books, 2016
Axis Mundi Books is an imprint of John Hunt Publishing Ltd., Laurel House, Station Approach,
Alresford, Hants, SO24 9JH, UK
office1@jhpbooks.net
www.johnhuntpublishing.com
www.axismundi-books.com

For distributor details and how to order please visit the 'Ordering' section on our website.

Text copyright: Fiona C. Odgren 2015

ISBN: 978 1 78535 338 3
Library of Congress Control Number: 2015956005

A CIP catalogue record for this book is available from the British Library.

Design: Stuart Davies

Printed in the USA by Edwards Brothers Malloy

We operate a distinctive and ethical publishing philosophy in all
areas of our business, from our global network of authors to
production and worldwide distribution.

CONTENTS

Dedicated to my late, beloved husband Klas-Goran ("George") Odgren, who was the first to introduce me to the uplifting teachings of Ageless Wisdom.

The proceeds of this book will be donated to *The Theosophical Order of Service in Canada*, which funds three major projects: *The Tibetan Delek Hospital* in Dharamsala, Northern India, the educational sponsorship of children from pre-school to collegiate levels and the support of special projects at *The Golden Link College* in the Philippines, and the funding of animal welfare initiatives at *The Besant Animal Welfare Dispensary* at Adyar, Chennai, India.

Acknowledgments

This compilation could not have come to fruition without the advice, help, encouragement and expertise of certain people in my life. To these I am extremely grateful.

Denise Mcdermott King, writer and Homeopath, provided unlimited help and guided me through the literary process. Sandra and W. Robert Earle for offering their professional computer skills, as well as Sue Prescott, author and American theosophist, who assisted with proof reading and offered constructive suggestions. Ted Davy, author and long-term editor of *The Canadian Theosophist*, provided useful suggestions and information with regard to the earlier editions of *The Mahatma Letters*. I am also in debt to my ever-helpful neighbor, Ken Garvin, who was always available for solving computer crises!

To the above and others not mentioned, who provided help in one way or another, I offer profound thanks.

Grateful acknowledgements are also in order to those professionals in the theosophical publishing field who gave invaluable guidance and assistance: Delacy Sarantos of the Theosophical Publishing House, Wheaton, Illinois and Will Thackara, of the Theosophical University Press, California, for permission to use the second edition and *the Combined Chronology*; also Daniel Entin of The Nicholas Roerich Museum, who provided permission for use of the Nicholas Roerich painting, *The Path to Shambhala*, for the cover.

My greatest thanks go to the Masters Koot Hoomi and Morya for their constant compassion and service to humanity.

Foreword

During the years 1880 to 1885 an extraordinary body of correspondence took place between two Himalayan Masters and two influential British men living and working in India. Alfred Percy Sinnett was the talented, highly respected editor of a leading Anglo-Indian newspaper, *The Pioneer,* published in Allahabad, India. Arthur Octavian Hume was an eminent government official, also well known for his research in the field of natural science, in particular the study of ornithology. Both men had met H.P. Blavatsky (later to be known as H.P.B. by her friends) and Col. Henry Steel Olcott, founders of the Theosophical movement, and were interested in the ideas and development of the newly formed organization.

These letters were destined to become, along with *Isis Unveiled, The Secret Doctrine,* and *The Key to Theosophy,* an essential seminal work of the Theosophical movement worldwide. They have unquestionably challenged, stimulated, and inspired genuine seekers and students of the Ancient Wisdom everywhere for nearly a century. Fascination for this correspondence has not diminished over the years, indeed; rather the opposite is occurring, as interest in spirituality is increasing exponentially in the Western world.

The majority of the letters are addressed to Sinnett; but, there are also a number of significant ones to his friend and co-theosophist, Hume. The subjects cover a wide range of topics, philosophical and otherwise. Most importantly for theosophists today, they include certain aspects of esoteric knowledge which they were trying to make intelligible to these two Englishman. Especially relevant for seekers today, intent on doing more service in the world, they address ethical and moral values necessary for spiritual development. The Mahatmas were hoping these two men, with their education and intelligence, would help

1

make these teachings more available to others through writing articles for *The Theosophist*. For those interested in the "human face" of the Theosophical movement in the 1880s, the letters also provide specific and historically fascinating details of incidents and a broad range of personalities who played a part in the drama of those early days.

Very few of the letters written by Sinnett and Hume to the Masters exist today, but fortunately for serious students of the Ageless Wisdom, nearly all of the letters from the Mahatmas were carefully preserved by Sinnett. Following his death, they became the property of his friend and theosophist, Maud Hoffman and were later presented to the curator of the British Museum in London. Recognizing the exceptionally high caliber and tone of the letters, he agreed for them to be safely preserved and housed in this prestigious institution. In recent times they have been re-located to the British Library, London, UK, in close proximity to the British Museum. This made it possible for theosophists, the world over, to experience first-hand the originals of these remarkable missives.

How these two renowned, British, society gentlemen came to be involved in a correspondence with two Mahatmas for several years, is an intriguing saga in itself. Their interest in communicating with these advanced souls, was sparked initially by their friendship with the enigmatic Russian lady, H.P.B., and the distinguished American, Col. Henry Steel Olcott, who had arrived in India in 1879 from New York (at the advice of the Master Morya) to establish the headquarters of the theosophical movement on the great sub-continent.

The Masters involved in this correspondence were members of the Himalayan brotherhood and were known as Koot Hoomi or K.H., and Morya or simply M. Their precise location was not known but there are several references to the Tibetan town of Shigatse, with its renowned monastery connected to the Panchen Lama, and also to areas in Ladakh "Little Tibet," which is now under the jurisdiction of India.

It needs to be emphasized, they were full-bodied men in physical form and not some kind of ethereal entities dreamed up by Blavatsky. Koot Hoomi was a Kashmiri Brahmin by birth, but his family came from Northern India. At the time of the correspondence, both he and Morya had strong links to the esoteric Gelugpa division of Tibetan Buddhism and described themselves as "Buddhists." Koot Hoomi had been educated at several European universities and was fluent in both English and French. On occasion, Morya would speak of him as "my Frenchified K.H." Koot Hoomi was actually his Tibetan mystical name and the name that he allowed to be used by Blavatsky and aspiring chelas (disciples), his real name never being divulged. He signed most of his letters to Sinnett and Hume with the initials K.H. but in some of the early letters he signed his full mystical name – Koot Hoomi Lal Singh.

Morya was Blavatsky's personal spiritual Teacher, whom she had met numerous times in her life. He had saved her life on more than one occasion and she recalled having visions of him as a child. She came to actually meet him for the first time in London, in 1851, when he was part of an entourage invited to have an audience with Queen Victoria. He was a Rajput prince by birth and was described once by Blavatsky as being "one of the old warrior race of the Indian desert." He was exceptionally tall (six feet, eight inches) and splendidly built – a superb type of manly beauty. K.H. sometimes referred to him as "my bulky brother." Morya also usually signed his name with his initial. He was not highly proficient in the English language and spoke of himself as "using words and phrases lying idly in my friend's brain," meaning of course the brain of Koot Hoomi.

The Mahatmas, or Masters, which came to be the term used by Blavatsky and the members of the theosophical movement, are men and women who have mastered the mental, emotional, and physical aspects of their being and are in touch with their inner divinity; however, they have chosen to forego Nirvana in order to continue to assist humanity. They are part of a body of advanced souls known in some spiritual writings as *The Great White Brotherhood*, also as *The Spiritual Hierarchy*, who from ancient times have been watching over the spiritual evolvement of humanity and other forms of life on this planet. Blavatsky once described Them as follows: "They are living men, not spirits. Their knowledge and learning are immense and their personal holiness of life is still greater – still they are mortal men."

Sinnett and Hume witnessed some remarkable phenomena on a number of occasions. H.P.B. and Olcott had been invited to visit the Sinnetts in the British hill town of Simla and the Humes in Rothney Castle on Jacko Hill. These extraordinary events are well documented in Olcott's *Occult Diaries* and Sinnett's book *The Occult World*. H.P.B. attributed these happenings to the two Mahatmas. Eventually, Sinnett's unbridled interest in these matters culminated in him asking H.P.B. whether it would be possible for him personally to correspond with one of the Mahatmas. Sinnett was seriously interested in the mysteries of life: how did humans originate; the truths with regard to creation and evolution; what happens after death; how to become a Mahatma and so forth. His motive was to engage in a dialogue in which he could pose certain questions to the Mahatmas, about esoteric knowledge not generally available.

Sinnet's request was processed by H.P.B., who at first approached her own Teacher, Morya, but he adamantly refused. Other Mahatmas were also asked but to no avail. Eventually Koot Hoomi agreed to undertake a limited correspondence. Later, due to rather unusual circumstances, Morya came to be involved. Koot Hoomi retreated for three months for his own spiritual advancement, and out of profound love and respect for his spiritual brother, Morya agreed to maintain the correspondence for the time of his absence.

Koot Hoomi's first letter was written in answer to two letters sent by the eager Sinnett, addressed to "An Unknown Brother." Sinnett was so elated to receive this first letter, that he hastened to discuss it with his friend, A.O. Hume. This must have aroused Hume's interest considerably for he too decided to write a letter to the Mahatma, which was also answered rather promptly.

Explanation needs to be made with regard to the process of the transmission of the correspondence, both to and from the Mahatmas. The Mahatmas were, for the most part, residing in remote areas where it was impossible to use a regular postal service. There were some instances when the Master K.H. was passing through cities in Northern India, such as Amritsar and Bombay and on these occasions he would give Sinnett an actual address to which he could send his letter. Very often Sinnett would give his letter to H.P.B. and she would use her esoteric abilities to get in touch with the Master and within a short time the letter would be received, by means we can scarcely under-stand with the rational mind. H.P.B. wrote about the difficulties of this process as follows:

> I have never, before beginning the service for you and Mr. Hume, transmitted and received a letter to, and from Masters, except for myself. If you had any idea of the difficulties, or the modus operandi you would not have consented to be in my place. And yet I never refused …. (*Mahatma Letter 138*, p. 444)

She continues:

> I have often facilitated phenomena of letter-transmission by easier but still occult means. Only as none of the Theosophists, except occultists, know anything of either difficult or easy means of occult transmission nor are they acquainted with occult laws, everything is suspicious to them. Take for instance this illustration as an instance: transmission by mechanical thought transference (in contradistinction with the conscious).

The former is produced by calling first the attention of a chela or the Mahatma. The letter must be open and every line of it passed over the forehead, holding the breath and never taking off the part of the letter from the latter until a bell notifies it is read and noted. The other mode is to impress every sentence of the letter still mechanically on the brain, and then send it phrase by phrase to the other person on the other end of the line. This is of course if the sender permits you to read it, and believes in your honesty .... (*Mahatma Letter 138*, pp. 470–471)

In many cases, the reply would come back seemingly miraculously in the same envelope in which Sinnett had sent the original letter with the Master's name crossed over and Sinnett's in its place. Otherwise the envelope was totally untampered with.

Further comments are also required in considering the methods and process the Masters used in replying and transmitting their letters. Many of the letters from the Mahatmas were not written in the conventional way but rather "impressed and precipitated." This was an extremely involved process that was explained by Master K.H. in Mahatma Letter six.

H.P.B. has commented with regard to "precipitation" that one would have to be clairvoyant to understand this process. For a time during the correspondence, due to certain circumstances, the Mahatmas were forbidden by their superiors to use the "precipitation" method and had to write their letters out in longhand, but later the permission was restored. The actual work of sending the letters involved the Master using an "electro-magnetic connection" with one of his chelas who would then act as an amanuensis. On some occasions, Damodar K. Mavalankar (a theosophist and chela of the Master K.H.) was used as the link. Writes H.P.B. on this subject:

When the Master wants a letter to be written in this way, he draws the attention of the chela whom he selects for the task by causing an astral bell ... to be rung near him just as the dispatching telegraph office signals to the receiving office before writing the message. The thoughts arising in the mind of the Mahatma are then clothed in word, pronounced mentally, and forced along the astral currents he sends towards the pupil to impinge on the brain of the latter. Thence they are borne by the nerve-currents to the palms of his hand and the tips of his fingers, which rest on a piece of magnetically prepared paper. As the thought-waves are thus impressed on the tissue, materials are drawn to it from the ocean of akasa ... by an occult process, out of place here to describe, and permanent marks are left. (*The Theosophist*, Vol. V, p. 64)

It needs to be mentioned also that some letters arrived in totally mysterious ways and certainly not always when H.P.B. was present. For instance, Sinnett would find a reply to his letter sitting on the hall table of his home in Allahabad. And on more than one occasion, replies came falling down onto his breakfast table, seemingly manifested out of thin air. The chela, Damodar K. Mavalankar also experienced, on several occasions, letters arriving in inexplicable ways from his teacher, the Master K.H.

On a few occasions, replies came though the regular mail, included in letters written to Sinnett from friends abroad. There is also an example of a letter (Mahatma Letter 31) that came through the regular mail, bearing a French stamp and not included in someone else's letter. In his book *The Mahatmas and Their Letters*, Geoffrey A. Barborka suggests that the letter was transmitted by the Master K.H. from a remote valley in the region of Terich-Mir, a mountain in the Hindu Kush mountains close to Afghanistan, to an adept and member of the Fraternity somewhere in France. This adept then supposedly affixed a French stamp and mailed it by regular post to Sinnett, who at the time was staying in London.

Many students of Theosophy and the Ageless Wisdom today

cherish the idea that the Masters involved with these letters are still existing and influencing humanity in one way or another. In later spiritual writings, such as the books of Alice A. Bailey (which are purported to have been inspired by Djwhal Khul, (Djual Khool) the Tibetan Master, and written in the 1930s and 40s) further and interesting information can be found with regard to these two Mahatmas. At the time of these letters, Djwhal Khul was a chela of the Master K.H. and sometimes he is referred to by the nickname: "The Disinherited One," adopted in a humorous vein by the Mahatmas. There is even more than one letter penned by him on behalf of K.H., notably when the latter was preparing to reassume his duties after his retreat.

In the book *Initiation Human and Solar* by Alice A. Bailey, it is intimated the Master K.H. is concerned with vitalizing certain of the ancient great philosophies and has a special interest in the philanthropic agencies of the world. His work with the Himalayan Brotherhood is particularly devoted to the stimulation and awakening of love-wisdom in the consciousness of humanity and in expanding the concept of the great fundamental fact of brotherhood in humanity. As regards the Master Morya, it is stated he has a special interest and role to play with regard to various esoteric groups and the political climate of the world.

In 1923, Alfred Trevor Barker, a British theosophist, with the encouragement of Maud Hoffman, made the letters available to the general public in book form entitled *The Mahatma Letters to A.P. Sinnett*. It is this original, and the second and third editions, with which many students of Theosophy are familiar. But they pose certain problems for study purposes, due to the fact the letters were compiled according to seven major headings, instead of being chronologically presented: *The Occult World Series, Philosophical and Theoretical Teachings, Probation and Chelaship, The Phoenix Venture and the Condition of India, Spiritualism and Phenomena, The London Lodge*, and, *Miscellaneous Letters*.

To compensate for the confusion posed by the non-sequential

editions of the letters, in 1939, American theosophist, Margaret Conger published a *Combined Chronology*. This was the result of exhaustive research and comprised a table of dates and explanatory notes giving the order of the letters as they were written and received.

However, it was not until 1998 that a fully comprehensive chronological version became available. This was produced by Vincente Hao Chin Jr. of the Theosophical Society in the Philippines and it included excellent informative editorial notes as prefaces to each letter. For many this made the content of the letters much more accessible and understandable. More students were therefore encouraged to study the letters in depth. Then in 2012, the eminent American theosophist, Joy Mills, took on the mammoth task of publishing a commentary on the letters entitled *Reflections on an Ageless Wisdom*. As far as I am aware, no other such definitive commentary has been attempted. This work sparked further enthusiasm and, as a result, more lodges and groups became engaged in the study of *The Mahatma Letters*.

It needs to be mentioned also that there were letters which for some reason were not presented in A.T. Barker's editions. They comprise two significant letters which rightly belong to the original series: *The First Letter of the Master K.H. to A.O. Hume* (1880) and the so-called *View of the Chohan on the T.S.* (1882). The first one was the Master K.H.'s response to Hume's proposal to form an Anglo-Indian branch of the Theosophical Society in Simla. The second is a summary by the Master K.H. of the views expressed by his chief – the Chohan – with regard to the mission and role of the Theosophical Society in the world. Fortunately, both these letters were added to the 1973 re-printing of Margaret Conger's *Combined Chronology*. They are also to be found as Appendices in Vicente Hao Chin Jr.'s 1998 chronological version.

There is another letter of the Master K.H. addressed to A.O. Hume (1881/1882) which also was not included in the earlier editions but interestingly it appeared in the Theosophist, June

1907 and was also later published in the book *Letters from the Masters of the Wisdom* 1881/1888 by Annie Besant. Furthermore, there were some additional "Cosmological Notes" found in A.P. Sinnett's manuscript book that should also have been included in the earlier editions of the letters. In these, the Masters provide profound answers to difficult questions posed by Sinnett and Hume. Happily though, they were made available by A.T. Barker in 1925 as an Appendix to his reproduction of *Letters of H.P. Blavatsky to A.P. Sinnett.*

Let it be noted that this compilation has been based on the second edition of *The Mahatma Letters to A.P. Sinnett,* and I have also included valuable material from all the above specially mentioned letters.

We need to recognize some of the teachings of the letters had never been presented openly to Western students and the general public before this time, simply because they were too esoteric and were a part of a knowledge which was only usually divulged to aspirants who had undergone certain austere disciplines and initiations, in either the Ancient Mystery Schools or in specific monastic institutions of the East.

At the time of this correspondence, the only theosophical work already published was Blavatsky's *Isis Unveiled,* followed by *The Secret Doctrine* presented in 1889. No wonder some of the teachings included in the letters posed endless questions and confusion in the minds of the recipients. The Mahatmas were in the throes of experimenting with the most appropriate language and means for presenting these previously well-closeted concepts to western minds. A formidable task indeed!

It is my hope this compilation, covering a variety of themes, will not only be a beneficial companion study to *The Mahatma Letters* for students of Theosophy, but will also inspire others to explore these remarkable letters.

Fiona C. Odgren

Adepts and Masters

(1) The adept is the rare efflorescence of a generation of enquirers; and to become one, he must obey the inward impulse of his soul, irrespective of the prudential considerations of worldly science and sagacity. *ML 2, p. 6*

(2) But my first duty is to my Master. And duty, let me tell you, is for us stronger than friendship, or even love; as without this abiding principle, which is the indestructible cement that has held together, for so many millennium, the scattered custodians of nature's grand secrets – our Brotherhood, nay, our doctrine itself – would have crumbled long ago into unrecognizable atoms. *ML 62, p. 351*

(3) Nothing, my friend – even apparently absurd and reprehensible actions – is ever done by us without a purpose.
ML 57, p. 332

(4) Both if you labor under the strange impression that we can, and even do care for anything that may be said or thought of us. Disabuse your minds, and remember that the first requisite in even a simple fakir, is that he should have trained himself to remain as indifferent to moral pain as to physical suffering. Nothing can give US *personal* pain or pleasure. And what I say is rather to bring you to understand US than *yourselves*, which is the most difficult science to learn. *ML 29, p. 224*

(5) We never whine over the inevitable but try to make the best of the worst. And though we neither push nor draw into the mysterious domain of occult nature those who are unwilling, we never shrink from expressing our opinions freely and fearlessly, yet we are ever ready to assist those who come to us even to –

agnostics who assume the negative position of *"knowing nothing but phenomena and refuse to believe in anything else." ML 4 pp. 16-17*

(6) Realize my friend that the social affections have little, if any, control over any true adept in the performance of his duty.
L 43, p. 259

(7) And to begin with let him rid himself of the *maya* that any man living can set up "claims" upon adepts. He may create irresistible *attractions* and compel their attention, but they will be spiritual, not mental or intellectual. And this bit of advice applies and is directed to several British theosophists, and it may be well for them to know it. Once separated from the common influence of Society, *nothing* draws us to any outsider save his evolving spirituality. **ML 59, p. 341**

(8) I can come nearer to you, but you must draw me by a purified heart and a gradually developing will. Like the needle the adept follows his attractions. **ML 45, p. 266**

(9) I hope that at least you will understand that we (or most of us) are far from being the heartless, morally dried up mummies some would fancy us to be. "Mejnour" (the adept hero of Bulwer Lytton's occult novel, *Zanoni*) is very well where he is – as an ideal character of a thrilling – in many respects truthful story. Yet, believe me, few of us would care to play the part in life of a desiccated pansy between the leaves of solemn poetry.

We may not be quite the "boys" – to quote Olcott's irreverent expression when speaking of us – yet none of our degree are like the stern hero of Bulwar's romance. While the facilities of observation secured to some of us by our condition certainly give a greater breadth of view, a more pronounced and impartial, as a more widely humaneness ... we might justly maintain that it is the business of "magic" to humanize our natures with compassion, for the whole of mankind as all living beings, instead of concentrating and limiting our affections to one predilected race – yet few of us (except such as have attained the final negation of Moksha) can so far enfranchise ourselves from the influence of our earthly connection as to be insusceptible in various degrees to the higher pleasures, emotions, and interests of the common run of humanity. *ML 8, p. 32*

(10) Even an adept, when acting in his body, is not beyond mistakes due to human carelessness. *L 55, p. 324*

(11) Believe me, there comes a time in the life of an adept, when the hardships he has passed through are a thousand fold rewarded. In order to acquire further knowledge, he has no more to go through a minute and slow process of investigation and comparison of various objects, but is accorded an instantaneous, implicit insight into every first truth. ... the adept sees and feels and lives in the very source of all fundamental truths – the Universal Spiritual Essence of Nature, Shiva the Creator, the Destroyer, and the Regenerator. *ML 31, p. 241*

(12) And I wish I could impress upon your minds the deep conviction that we do not wish Mr. Hume or you to prove conclusively to the public that we really exist. Please realize the fact that so long as men doubt, there will be curiosity and enquiry, and that enquiry stimulates reflection, which begets effort; but let our secret be once thoroughly vulgarized and not only will skeptical society derive no great good but our privacy would be constantly endangered and have to be continually guarded at an unreasonable cost of power. *ML 29, p. 227*

(13) Realize, my friend that the social affections have little, if any control over any true adept in the performance of his duty. In proportion as he rises towards perfect adeptship the fancies and

antipathies of his former self are weakened: as K.H., in substance, has explained to you, he takes all mankind into his heart and regards them in the mass. *ML43, p. 259*

(14) You ought to have learned by this time our ways. We *advise* – and never *order*. But we *do* influence individuals. *ML 48, p.271*

(15) Alone the adepts, i.e., the embodied spirits – are forbidden by our wise and intransgressible laws, to completely subject to themselves another and a weaker will – that of freeborn man. The latter mode of proceeding is the favourite one resorted to by the "Brothers of the Shadow," the Sorcerers, the Elementary Spooks, and, as an isolated exception – by the highest Planetary Spirits, those who can no longer err. *ML 9, p. 40-41*

(16) It is a familiar saying that a well matched couple "grow together," so as to come to a close resemblance in features as well as in mind. But so you know that between adept and chela – master and pupil – there gradually forms a closer tie; for the psychic interchange is regulated scientifically, whereas between husband and wife, unaided nature is left to herself. As the water in a full tank runs into an empty one which it is connected with; and as the common level will be sooner or later reached, according to the capacity of the feed pipe, so does the knowledge of the adept flow to the chela; and the chela attains the adept level according to his receptive capacities.

At the same time, the chela being an individual, a separate evolution, unconsciously imparts to the master the quality of his accumulated mentality. The master absorbs *his* knowledge; and if it is a question of language he does not know, the master will get the chela's linguistic accumulations just as they are – idioms and all – unless he takes the trouble to sift and remodel the phrases when using. Proof M (Morya) who does not know English and has to use Olcott's or the O.L.'s language (H.P.B.'s). So you see, it

is quite possible for *me* to catch H.P.B.'s or any other chela's ideas about you, without meaning to do any injustice; for whenever we find such ideas – unless trifling – we never proceed to judge and render our sentences merely on the testimony of such borrowed light; but always ascertain independently and for ourselves, whether the ideas so reflected in us are right or wrong.
Letter to A.O. Hume – The Theosophist, June 1907, pp. 702-706

(17) We cannot alter Karma, my "good friend" or we might lift the present cloud from your path. But we do all that is possible in such material matters. No darkness can stay forever. Have hope and faith and we may disperse it. *ML 97, p. 433*

(18) We are not gods, and even they, our chiefs – they *hope*. *L 28, p. 210*

(19) An adept – the highest as the lowest – is one only *during the exercise of his occult powers.* Whenever these powers are needed, the sovereign will unlocks the door to the *inner* man (the adept,) who can emerge and act freely but on condition that his jailor – the *outer* man – will be either completely or partially paralysed, as the case may require: viz. either (a) mentally and physically: (b) mentally – but not physically: (c) physically but not entirely mentally: (d) neither – but with an akashic film interposed between the *outer* and the *inner* man. *ML 24B, p. 180*

(20) We have to fight our own battles, and the familiar adage – "the adept *becomes* he is not *made*" is true to the letter. Since every one of us is the *creator* and producer of the *causes* that lead to such or some other *results,* we have to reap but what we have sown. *Our chelas are helped but when they are innocent of the causes that lead them into trouble;* when such causes are generated by foreign, outside influences. Life and the struggle for adeptship would be too easy, had we all scavengers behind us, to sweep

away the *effects* we have generated through our own rashness and presumption. *ML 54, pp. 309-310*

(21) Ah, Sahibs, Sahibs! If you could only catalogue and label us and set us up in the British Museum, then indeed might your world have the absolute, the desiccated truth. *ML 29, p. 227*

(22) One does not cease entirely, my dear friend, to be a *man* nor lose one's dignity for being an *adept*. In the latter capacity, one no doubt remains in every case indifferent to the opinion of the outside world. The former always draws the line between *ignorant surmise* and – deliberate, *personal insult*. *ML 93, p. 427*

(23) The smallest exercise of occult powers then, as you will now see, requires an effort. We may compare it to the inner muscular effort of an athlete preparing to use his physical strength. As no athlete is likely to be always amusing himself at swelling his veins, in anticipation of having to lift a weight, so no adept can be supposed to keep his will in constant tension and the inner in full function, when there is no immediate necessity for it. When the *inner* man rests, the adept becomes an ordinary man, limited to the physical senses and the functions of his physical brain. Habit sharpens the intuition of the latter, yet is unable to make them super sensuous. The inner adept is ever ready, ever on the alert, and that suffices for our purposes.

At moments of rest then, his faculties are at rest also. When I sit at meals, or when I am dressing, reading or otherwise occupied, I am not thinking even of those near to me, and Djual Khool can easily break his nose to blood, by running in the dark against a beam, as he did the other night – (just because instead of throwing a "film" he had foolishly paralysed all his outer senses while talking to a distant friend) – and I remained placidly ignorant of the fact. *I was not thinking of him* – hence my ignorance. From the aforesaid, you may well infer that an adept is an ordinary mortal at all moments of his daily life, but those – when the inner man is acting. *ML 24B, p. 180*

(24) Lying is a refuge of the weak, and we are sufficiently strong, even with all the shortcomings you are pleased to discover in us, to dread truth very little; nor are we likely to lie, only because it is to our interest to appear wise concerning matters of which we are ignorant. Thus, perchance it might have been prudent to remark that you knew that we did not really possess the power of reading minds, unless we brought ourselves *thoroughly en rapport* with and concentrated an undivided attention on the person whose thoughts we wanted to know – since that would be an undeniable *fact* .... *ML 30, pp. 228-229*

(25) We of the Indo-Tibetan hovels never quarrel ... Quarrels and even discussions we leave to those who, unable to take in a situation at a glance, are thereby forced before making up their final decision to anything to analyse and weigh one by one, and over and over again every detail. Whenever we – at least those of us who are *dikshita* (initiates) seem, therefore to a European not "quite sure of our facts" it may be often due to the following peculiarity. That which is regarded by most men as a "fact" to us may seem but a simple RESULT, an afterthought unworthy of our attention, generally attracted but to *primary facts*. Life, esteemed Sahibs, when even indefinitely prolonged, is too short to burden our brains with flitting details – mere shadows. When watching the progress of a storm, we fix our gaze upon the producing Cause and leave the clouds to the whims of the breeze which shapes them. Having always the means on hand – whenever absolutely needed – of bringing to our knowledge minor details, we concern ourselves but with the main facts. Hence we can hardly be absolutely wrong – as are often accused by you, for our conclusions are never drawn from secondary data but from the situation as a whole. *ML 29, p. 218*

(26) Guided by his Guru, the chela first discovers this world, then its laws, then their centrifugal evolutions into the world of matter. To become a perfect adept takes him long years, but at last he becomes the master. The hidden things have become patent, and mystery and miracle have fled from his sight forever. The secret chemical, electric or odic properties of plants, herbs, roots, minerals, animal tissue, are as familiar to him as the feathers of your birds are to you. No change in the etheric vibrations can escape him. He applies his knowledge, and behold a miracle! And he who started with the repudiation of the very idea that miracle is possible is straightaway classed as a miracle worker, and either worshipped by the fools as a demi-god or repudiated by still greater fools as a charlatan. *ML 22, p. 144*

(27) The adept does not create anything new, but only utilises and manipulates materials which nature has in store around him; a material which throughout eternities has passed through all the forms; he has but to choose the one he wants and recall it into objective existence. Would not this sound to one of your "learned" biologists like a madman's dream?
K.H.'s First Letter to A.O. Hume, Combined Chronology by M. Conger, p. 31

(28) I am also of the opinion that few candidates imagine the degree of inconvenience – nay suffering and harm to himself – the said initiator submits to for the sake of his pupil. The peculiar physical, moral, and intellectual conditions of neophytes and adepts alike vary much, as anyone will easily understand; thus, in each case, the instructor has to adapt his conditions to those of the pupil and the strain is terrible, for to achieve success we have to bring ourselves into a *full* rapport with the subject under training. And as the greater the powers of the adept the less he is in sympathy with the natures of the profane, who often come to him saturated with the emanations of the outside world, those

animal emanations of the selfish, brutal, crowd that we so dread – the longer he was separated from that world and the purer he has himself become, the more difficult the self-imposed task.

Then – knowledge can only be communicated gradually; and some of the highest secrets – if actually formulated even in your well-prepared ear – might sound to you as insane gibberish, notwithstanding all the sincerity of your present assurance that "absolute trust defies misunderstanding." This is the real cause of our reticence. This is why people so often complain, with a plausible show of reason, that no new knowledge is communicated to them, though they have toiled for it for two, three or more years. Let those who really desire to learn abandon all and come to us, instead of asking or expecting us to go to them. But how is this to be done in your world and atmosphere?
ML 49, pp. 283-284

Atlantis and Lemuria

(1) The sinking of Atlantis (the group of continents and isles) began during the Miocene period – as certain of your continents are now observed to be gradually sinking – and it culminated – first, in the final disappearance of the continent, an event coincident with the elevation of the Alps: and second with that of the last of the fair Islands mentioned by Plato. The Egyptian priests of Sais told his ancestor, Solon, that Atlantis (i.e. the only remaining large island) had perished 9,000 years before their time. This was not a fancy date, since they had for millennium preserved most carefully their records. But then, as I say, they spoke but of the "Poseidonis" and would not reveal, even to the great Greek legislator, their secret chronology.

As there are no geological reasons for doubting, but on the contrary, a mass of evidence for accepting the tradition, science has finally accepted the existence of the great continent and Archipelago and thus vindicated the truth of one more "fable." It now teaches, as you know, that Atlantis, or the remnants of it, lingered down to post-tertiary times, its final submergence occurring within the palaeozoic ages of American history! Well, truth and fact ought to feel thankful, even for such small favours in the previous absence of any, for so many centuries.

The deep-sea explorations – especially those of the Challenger, *have* fully confirmed the reports of geology and paleontology. The great event – the triumph of our *"Sons of the Fire Mist,"* the inhabitants of "Shamballah" (when yet an island in the central Asian Sea) over the selfish but not entirely wicked magicians of Poseidonis occurred just 11,446 (years) ago. Read in this connection the incomplete and partially veiled tradition in *Isis,* Volume I, pp. 588-94 *(Isis Unveiled)* and some things may become still plainer to you. The corroboration of tradition and history brought forward by Donnelly I find in the main correct;

but you will find all this and much more in Isis. *ML 23A, p. 155*

(2) M. (Morya) thinks *for your purposes* I better give you a few more details upon Atlantis, since it is greatly connected with *evil* if not with its origin ... I am unable to give you purely scientific information, since we can never agree entirely with Western conclusions; and ours will be rejected as "unscientific." Yet both geology and paleontology bear witness to much we have to say. Of course, your science is right in many of her generalities, but her premises are wrong, or at any rate – very faulty. For instance, she says that while the new America was forming, the ancient Atlantis was sinking and gradually washing away; but she is neither right in her given epochs nor in the calculations of the duration of that sinking. The latter – is the future fate of your British Islands, the first on the list of victims that have to be destroyed by fire (submarine volcanoes) and water; France and other lands will follow suit. When they reappear again, the last seventh Sub-race of the sixth Root race of present mankind will be flourishing on "Lemuria" and "Atlantis," both of which will have reappeared also (their reappearance following immediately the disappearance of the present isles and continents) and very few seas and *great waters* will be found then on our globe, waters as well as land appearing and disappearing and shifting periodically and each in turn. *ML 23A, p. 156*

(3) The approach of every new "obscuration" is always signalled by cataclysms – of either fire or water. But apart from this, every "Ring" or Root Race has to be cut in two, so to say, by either one or the other. Thus having reached the apex of its development and glory the fourth Race – the Atlanteans were destroyed by *water,* you find now but their degenerated, fallen remnants, whose sub-races, nevertheless, aye – each of them had its palmy days of glory and relative greatness. What they are now – you will be some day, the law for cycles being one and immutable.

When your race – the fifth – will have reached its zenith of *physical* intellectuality, and developed the highest civilisation (remember the difference we make between *material* and *spiritual* civilisations) unable to go any higher in its own cycle, its progress towards absolute evil will be arrested, as its predecessors, the Lemurians and Atlanteans, the men of the third and fourth root races, were arrested in their progress towards the same by one of such cataclysmic changes; its great civilization destroyed, and all the sub-races of that race will be found going down their respective cycles, after a short period of glory and learning. *ML 23A, pp. 156-157*

(4) See the remnants of the Atlanteans – the old Greeks and Romans (the modern belong all to the fifth Race) see how great and how short, how evanescent were their days of fame and glory! For they were but sub-races of the seven off-shoots of the "root race." No mother Race, any more than her sub-races and off-shoots, is allowed by the one Reigning Law to trespass upon the prerogatives of the Race or Sub-race that will follow it; least of all – to encroach upon the knowledge and powers in store for its successor. "Thou shalt not eat of the fruit of Knowledge of Good and Evil of the tree that is growing for thy heirs" we may say with more right than would be willingly conceded us by the Humes of your sub-race. This "tree" is in our safe-keeping, entrusted to us by the Dhyan Chohans, the protectors of our race and the Trustees for those that are coming. *Ml 23A, p. 157*

(5) In the Eocene Age – even in its "very first part" – the great cycle of the fourth Race men, the Atlanteans, had already reached its highest point, and the great continent, the father of nearly all the present continents, showed the first symptoms of sinking – a process that occupied it down to 11,446 years ago, when its last island, that, translating its vernacular name, we may call with propriety *Poseidonis*, went down with a crash. By the bye, *whoever*

wrote the review of Donnelly's *Atlantis* is right: Lemuria can no more be confounded with the Atlantic Continent than Europe with America. Both sank and were drowned with their high civilizations and "gods," yet between the two catastrophes a short period of about 700,000 years elapsed; "Lemuria" flourishing and ending her career, just at about that trifling lapse of time before the early part of the Eocene Age, since its race was the *third*. Behold, the relics of that once great nation in some of the flat-headed aborigines of your Australia! No less right is the review in rejecting the kind attempt of the author to people India and Egypt with the refuse of Atlantis.

No doubt your geologists are very learned; but why not bear in mind that, under the continents explored and fathomed by them, in the bowels of which they have found the "Eocene Age" and forced it to deliver them its secrets, there may be, hidden deep in the fathomless, or rather *unfathomed* ocean beds, other, and far older continents whose stratums have never been geologically explored; and that they may some day upset entirely their present theories, thus illustrating the simplicity and sublimity of truth is connected with inductive "generalization" in opposition to their visionary conjectures. Why not admit – true, no one of them has ever thought of it – that our *present continents* have, like Lemuria and "Atlantis," been *several times already* submerged and had the time to reappear again, and bear their new groups of mankind and civilization; and that, at the first great geological upheaval, at the next cataclysm – in the series of periodical cataclysms that occur from the beginning to the end of every Round, our already *autopsized* continents will go down, and the Lemurias and Atlantises come up again. *ML 23A, p. 151*

Blavatsky and Olcott

(1) One or two of us hoped that the world had so advanced intellectually, if not intuitionally, that the Occult doctrine might gain an intellectual acceptance, and the impulse given for a new cycle of occult research. Others – wiser as it would now seem – held differently, but consent was given for the trial. It was stipulated, however, that the experiment should be made independently of our personal management; that there should be no abnormal interference by ourselves.

So, casting about, we found in America the man to stand as a leader – a man of great moral courage, unselfish, and having good qualities. He was far from being the best, but (as Mr. Hume speaks in H.P.B.'s case) – he was the best one available. With him we associated a woman of most exceptional and wonderful endowments. Combined with them, she had strong personal defects but just as she was, there was no second to her living fit for this work. We sent her to America, brought them together – and the trial began. From the first both she and he were given to clearly understand that the issue lay entirely with themselves. And both offered themselves for the trial for certain remuneration in the far distant future – as K.H. would say – soldiers volunteer for a Forlorn Hope. For six-and-a-half years they have been struggling against such odds as would have driven off anyone who was not working with the desperation of one who stakes life and all the prizes on some distant supreme effort. *ML 44, p. 263*

(2) I am painfully aware of the fact that the habitual incoherence of her statements – especially when excited – and her strange ways make her, in your opinion, a very undesirable transmitter of our messages. Nevertheless, kind Brothers, once that you have learned the truth; once told, that this unbalanced mind, the seeming incongruity of her speeches and ideas, her nervous excitement,

all that in short which is so calculated to upset the feelings of sober minded people, whose notions of reserve and manners are shocked by such strange outbursts of what they regard as her temper, and which so revolt you – once that *you know* that nothing of it is due to any fault of hers, you may perchance, be led to regard her in quite a different light.

Notwithstanding that the time is not quite ripe to let you entirely into the secret; and that you are hardly yet prepared to understand the great Mystery, even if told of it, owing to the great injustice and wrong done, I am empowered to allow you a glimpse behind the veil. This state of hers is intimately connected with her occult training in Tibet, and due to her being sent out alone into the world to gradually prepare the way for others.

After nearly a century of fruitless search, our chiefs had to avail themselves of the only opportunity to send out a European *body,* upon European soil, to serve as a connecting link between that country and our own. You do not understand? Of course not. Please then, remember, what she tried to explain, and what you gathered tolerably well from her, namely the fact of the seven principles in the *complete* human being.

Now, no man or woman, unless he be an initiate of the "fifth circle," can leave the precincts of *Bod-Lhas* (Divine Rulers – Ed.) and return back into the world in his integral whole – if I may

25

use the expression. *One* at least of his seven satellites has to remain behind for two reasons; the first to form the necessary connecting link, the wire of transmission – the second as the safest warranter that certain things will never be divulged. She is no exception to the rule, and you have seen another exemplar – a highly intellectual man – who had to leave one of his skins behind; hence is considered highly eccentric. The bearing and status of the remaining six depend upon the inherent qualities, the psycho-physiological peculiarities of the person ....
ML 26, pp. 203-204

(3) And now, do you want to know how far she is guilty? Know then that if she ever became guilty of real *deliberate* deception, owing to that "zeal," it was when in the presence of phenomena produced she kept constantly denying – except in the matter of such trifles as bells and raps – that she had anything to do with their production *personally*. From your "European standpoint" it is downright deception, a big thundering *lie*; from our *Asiatic* standpoint, though an imprudent, blamable zeal, an untruthful exaggeration ... meant for the benefit of the "Brothers," – yet withal, if we look into the motive – a sublime self-denying, noble and meritorious – not *dishonest* – zeal.

Yes; in that, and in that alone, she became constantly guilty of deceiving her friends. She could never be made to realize the utter uselessness, the danger of such a zeal; and how mistaken she was in her notions that she was adding to our glory, whereas, by attributing to us very often phenomena of the most childish nature, she but lowered us in the public estimation and sanctioned the claim of her enemies that she was "but a medium!" But it was of no use. In accordance with our rules, M. was not permitted to forbid her such a course, in so many words. She had to be allowed full and entire freedom of action, the liberty of *creating causes* that became in due course of time her scourge, her public pillory. *ML 54, pp. 311-312*

(4) Her impulsive nature – as you have correctly inferred in your reply – is always ready to carry her beyond the boundaries of truth, into the regions of exaggeration; nevertheless without a shadow of suspicion that she is thereby deceiving her friends, or abusing their great trust in her. The stereotyped phrase: "It is not I; I can do nothing by myself ... it is all they – the Brothers ... I am but their humble and devoted slave and instrument" is a downright fib.

She can and did produce phenomena owing to her natural powers, combined with several long years of regular training, and her phenomena are sometimes better, more wonderful and far more perfect than those of some high, initiated chelas, whom she surpasses in artistic taste and purely Western appreciation of art – as for instance in the instantaneous production of pictures: witness her portrait of the "fakir" Tiravalla ... and compared with my portrait by Djual Khool. Notwithstanding all the superiority of his powers, as compared to hers; his youth as contrasted with her old age; and the undeniable and important advantage he possesses, of having never brought his pure, unalloyed magnetism in direct contact with the great impurity of your world and society – yet do what he may, he will never be able to produce such a picture, simply because he is unable to conceive it in his mind and Tibetan thought. *ML 54, p. 312*

(5) Thus while fathering upon us all manner of foolish, often clumsy and *suspected* phenomena, she has most undeniably been *helping* us in many instances, saving us sometimes as much as two-thirds of the power used, and when (we) remonstrated – for often we are unable to prevent her doing it on her end of the line – answering that she had no need of it, and that her only joy was to be of some use to us. And thus she kept on killing herself inch by inch, ready to give – for our benefit and glory, as she thought – her life-blood drop by drop, and yet invariably denying before witnesses that she had anything to do with it. Would you call this

sublime, albeit foolish self-abnegation – "dishonest"? We do not; nor shall we ever consent to regard it in such a light.
ML 54, pp. 312-313

(6) Such is the true history and facts with regard to her "deception" or, at best – "*dishonest* zeal." No doubt she has merited a portion of the blame; most undeniably she is given to exaggeration in general, and when it becomes a question of "puffing up" those she is devoted to, her enthusiasm knows no limits. Thus she has made of M. an Apollo of Belvedere, the glowing description of whose physical beauty made him more than once start in anger, and break his pipe while swearing like a true – Christian; and thus, under her eloquent phraseology, I myself had the pleasure of hearing myself metamorphosed into an "angel of purity and light" – shorn of his wings. We cannot help feeling at times angry with, oftener – laughing at, her. Yet the feeling that dictates all this ridiculous effusion is too ardent, too sincere and true, not to be respected or even treated with indifference. *ML 54, p. 313*

(7) I do not believe I was ever so profoundly touched by anything I witnessed in all my life, as I was with the poor old creature's ecstatic rapture, when meeting us recently, both in our natural bodies, one – after three years, the other – nearly two years absence and separation in flesh. Even our phlegmatic M. was thrown off his balance by such an exhibition – of which he was chief hero. He had to use his *power*, and plunge her into a profound sleep, otherwise she would have burst some blood vessel including kidneys, liver and her "interiors" – to use our friend Oxley's favourite expression – in her delirious attempts to flatten her nose against his riding mantle, besmeared with the Sikkim mud!

We both laughed; yet could we feel otherwise but touched? Of course, she is utterly unfit for a *true adept*: her nature is too passionately affectionate and we have no right to indulge in *personal* attachments and feelings. You can never know her as we do, therefore – none of you will ever be able to judge her impartially or correctly. You see the surface of things; and what you would term "virtue," holding but to appearances, we – judge but after having fathomed the object to its profoundest depth, and generally leave the appearances to take care of themselves. *ML 54, p. 314*

(8) In your opinion, H.P.B. is, at best, for those who like her despite herself – a quaint, strange woman, a psychological riddle; impulsive and kindhearted, yet not free from the vice of untruth, We, on the other hand, under the garb of eccentricity and folly – we find a profounder wisdom in her inner Self than you will ever find yourselves able to  perceive. In the superficial details of her homely, hard-working, common-place, daily life and affairs, you discern but unpracticality, womanly impulses, often absurdity and folly; we, on the contrary, light daily upon traits of her inner nature, the most delicate and refined, and which would cost an uninitiated psychologist years of constant and keen observation, and many an hour of close analysis and efforts to draw out of the depth of that most subtle of mysteries – human mind – and one of her most complicated machines, – H.P.B.'s mind – and thus learn to know her true *inner* Self. *ML 54, p. 314*

(9) However crazy an enthusiast, I pledge to you my word of honour, she was never a *deceiver*; nor has she ever willfully

uttered an untruth, though her position becomes often untenable, and that she has to conceal a number of things, as pledged by her solemn vows. *ML 54, pp. 314-315*

(10) Try to believe more than you do in the "old lady." She *does* rave betimes; but she *is* truthful and does the best she can for you. *ML 106, pp. 443-444*

(11) Even if Madame B. might "be induced" to give the A. I. (Anglo-Indian) Society any "practical instruction," I am afraid *she has remained too long a time outside the adytum to be of much use for practical explanations. However, though it does not depend on me, I will see what I can do in this direction. But I fear she is sadly in need of a few months of recuperative villegiatura on the glaciers, with her old Master, before she can be entrusted with such a difficult task.* Be very cautious with her in case she stops with you on her way down home. Her nervous system is terribly shaken and she requires every care. *ML 5, p. 21*

(12) ... I must say she suffers acutely and I am unable to help her; for all this is effect from causes which *cannot* be *undone* – occultism in theosophy. She has now to either conquer or die. When the hour comes, she will be taken back to Tibet. Do not blame the poor woman, blame me. She is but a "shell" at times and I, often careless in watching her ... Do not feel despondent. Courage, my good friend and remember you are working off by helping her your own law of retribution, for more than one cruel fling she receives is due to K.H.'s friendship for you, for his using her as the means of communication. But – Courage. *ML 41, pp. 256-257*

(13) ... imperfect as may be our visible agent – and often most unsatisfactory and imperfect she is – yet she is the best available at present, and her phenomena have for about half a century

astounded and baffled some of the cleverest minds of the age.
ML 2, pp. 9-10

(14) Of these two persons, one has already given three-fourths of
a life, the other six years of manhood's prime to us, and both will
so labour to the close of their days, though ever working for their
merited reward, yet never demanding it, nor murmuring when
disappointed. *ML 2, p. 9*

(15) Again I might cite the case of Olcott (who, had he not been
permitted to communicate face to face – and without any intermediary – with us, might have subsequently shown less zeal and
devotion but more discretion) and his fate up to the present ...
Olcott – would you say – is an enthusiast, a stubborn, unrea-
soning mystic, who goes headlong before him, blindfolded, and
who will not allow himself to look forward with his own eyes.
While you (Sinnett) are a sober, matter-of-fact man of the world,
the son of your generation of cool thinkers; ever keeping fancy
under the curb, and saying to enthusiasm: "Thus far shalt thou
go and no farther." ... Perhaps you are right – perhaps not. "No
lama knows where the *ber-chhen* will hurt him until he puts it
on," says a Tibetan proverb. *ML 8, p. 28*

(16) All quick thinkers are hard to impress – in a flash they are
out and away in "full cry," before half understanding what one
wants to have them think. This is our trouble with both Mrs. B.
and O. The frequent failure of the latter to carry out the suggestions he sometimes receives – even when written, is almost
wholly due to his own active mentality preventing his distin-
guishing our impressions from his own conceptions. And Missus
B.'s trouble is (apart from physical ailment) that she sometimes
listens to two or more of our voices at once; e.g. this morning,
while the "Disinherited" (Djual Khool) ... was talking with her
on an important matter, she lent an ear to one of ours (probably

the Master Hilarion – Ed.) who is passing through Bombay from Cyprus, on his way to Tibet – and so got both in an inextricable confusion. *Women* do lack the power of concentration. *ML 8, p. 36*

(17) It is not politic that H.S. Olcott should be exclusively your guest during his whole stay in Britain; his time should be divided between yourself and others of various opinions – should they wish to invite him for a short time. He will be accompanied by Mohini whom I have chosen as my chela and with whom I sometimes communicate directly. Treat the boy kindly, forgetting he is a Bengalee, and only remembering *he is now my chela.* Do what you can to dignify Olcott's office; for he represents the entire Society, and by reason of his official position, if for no other, stands with Upasika (H.P.B.) closest to ourselves in the chain of Theosophical work. *ML 84, p. 397*

(18) It's quite useless to say anything more about Olcott's eccentricity and the inferiority of America to England; all this is real in your point we recognise and knew long ago; but you do not know how that mere superficial prejudice glares in your eyes, like the reflection of a thin taper on deep water. Take care lest we should some day take you at your thought and put you (Sinnett) in Olcott's place, after taking him to our own, as he has longed to have us do these several years. Martyrdom is pleasant to look at and criticise, but hard to suffer. There never was a woman more unjustly abused than H.P.B. *ML 47, p. 273*

(19) If you still care to renew the occult teachings, save first our post-office (H.P.B.) H.P.B. – I say again, is not to be approached any longer without her full consent. She has earned so much, and has to be left alone. She is permitted to retire for three reasons (1) to disconnect the T.S. from her phenomena ... (2) to help it by removing the chief cause of the hatred against it; (3) to try and restore the health of the body, so it may be used for some years

longer. *ML 55, p. 325*

(20) Those two (H.P.B. and Olcott) are, say, far from perfect – in some respects – quite the opposite. But they have that in them (pardon the eternal repetition but it is being as constantly overlooked) which we have but too rarely found elsewhere – UNSELFISHNESS, and an eager readiness for self-sacrifice for the good of others; what a "multitude of sins" does not this cover! It is but a truism, yet I say it, that in adversity alone, can we discover the real man. It is a true manhood when one boldly accepts one's share of the collective Karma of the group one works with, and does not permit oneself to be embittered, and to see others in blacker colours than reality, or to throw all blame upon some, one, "black sheep," a victim, specially selected. Such a true man as that we will ever protect and, despite his short-comings, assist to develop the good he has in him. Such a one is sublimely *unselfish*; he sinks his personality in his cause and takes no heed of discomforts or personal obloquy unjustly fastened upon him. *ML 66, p. 370*

Buddha

(1) ... Buddha – a sixth-round being, as he had run so successfully the race in his previous incarnations as to out-run even his predecessors. But then such a man is to be found one in a *billion* of human creatures. He differed from other men as much in his physical appearance as in spirituality and knowledge. Yet even he escaped further incarnations but on this earth; and when the last of sixth-round men of the third ring is gone out of this earth, the Great Teacher will have to get reincarnated on the next planet. Only, and since He sacrificed Niravanic bliss and rest for the salvation of his fellow creatures, He will be re-born in the highest – the *seventh* ring of the upper planet. Till then He will *overshadow* every decillenium, a chosen individual (let us rather say and add *"has* overshadowed already") a chosen individual who generally overturned the destinies of nations. *ML 17, p. 117*

(2) Read the Mahavagga and try to understand, not with the prejudiced Western mind but the spirit of intuition and truth what the Fully Enlightened one says in the 1st Khandhaka. Allow me to translate it for you.

"At the time the blessed Buddha was at Uruvela, on the shores of the river Nerovigara, as he rested under the Bodhi tree of wisdom after he had become Sambuddha. At the end of the seventh day, having his mind fixed on the chain of causation, he spake thus: 'from Ignorance spring the samkharas of threefold nature – productions of body, of speech, of thought. From the samkharas springs consciousness, from consciousness springs name and form, from this spring the six regions (of the six senses, the seventh being the property of but the enlightened) from these spring contact from the sensation; from this springs thirst (or desire, kama, tanha) form thirst attachment, existence, birth, death, old age and death, grief, lamentation, suffering, dejection and despair. Again by the destruction of ignorance, the samkharas are destroyed, and their consciousness, name and form, the six regions, contact, sensation, thirst, attachment (selfishness), existence, birth, old age, death, grief, lamentation, suffering, dejection, and despair are destroyed. Such is the cessation of this mass of suffering."

Knowing this the Blessed One uttered this solemn utterance:

"When the real nature of things becomes clear to the meditating Bhikshu, then all his doubts fade away since he has learned what is that nature and what its cause. From ignorance spring all the evils. From knowledge comes the cessation of this mass of misery, and then the meditating Brahmana stands dispelling the hosts of Mara like the sun that illuminates the sky."
ML 10, pp. 58-59

(3) Our Lord Buddha – a 6th-round man – would not have appeared in our epoch, great as were his accumulated merits in previous rebirths, but for a *mystery* ... Individuals cannot outstrip the humanity of their round any further than by one remove, for it is mathematically impossible ... And Buddha only forms an exception by virtue of the *mystery*. We have fifth-round men among us because we are in the latter half of our septenary earth ring. In the first half this could not have happened ... and the sixth can only come at rare intervals and prematurely, like Buddhas (only under prepared conditions) .... *ML 15, p. 96*

(4) The victor's crown is only for him who proves himself worthy to wear it; for him who attacks *Mara* single-handed and conquers the demon of lust and earthly passions; and not we but he himself puts it on his brow. It was not a meaningless phrase of the Tathagata that "he who masters *Self* is greater than he who

conquers thousands in battle": there is no such other difficult
struggle. *ML 54, p. 316*

Buddhi

(1) The supreme energy resides in the *Buddhi*; latent – when wedded to *Atman* alone, active and irresistible when galvanized by the *essence* of "Manas" and when none of the dross of the latter commingles with the pure essence to weigh it down by its finite nature. *ML 59, p. 341*

(2) Fathom the nature and essence of the sixth principle of the universe and man and you will have fathomed the greatest mystery in this, our world – and why not – are you not surrounded by it? What are its familiar manifestations, mesmerism, *Od* force, etc. – all different aspects of one force capable of good and evil application. *ML 15, p. 99*

(3) Many prefer to call themselves Buddhists, not because the word attaches itself to the ecclesiastical system built upon the basic ideas of our Lord Gautama Buddha's philosophy, but because of the Sanskrit word "Buddhi" – *wisdom*, enlightenment; and as a silent protest to the vain rituals and empty ceremonials which have in too many cases been productive of the greatest calamities. Such also is the origin of the Chaldean term *Mage*. *ML 85, p. 399*

(4) A madman may remember very clearly some portions of his past life; yet he is unable to perceive anything in its true light, for the higher portion of his *Manas* and his *Buddhi* are paralysed in him, have left him. *ML 23B, p. 173*

(5) To my knowledge and recollection H.P.B. explained to Mr. Hume that man's sixth principle (buddhi) as something purely spiritual could not exist, or have conscious being in the Devachan, unless it assimilated some of the more abstract and

pure of the mental attributes of the fifth principle or animal Soul, its *manas* (mind) and memory **ML 16, p. 103**

(6) Every molecule is part of the Universal Life. Man's soul (his fourth and fifth principle) is but a compound of the progressed entities of the lower kingdom. The superabundance or preponderance of one over another compound, will often determine the instincts and passions of a man, unless these are checked by the soothing and spiritualizing influence of his sixth principle. *ML 14, p. 80*

Chelaship (Discipleship)

(1) True, we have our schools and teachers, our neophytes and shaberons (superior adepts) and the door is always open to the right man who knocks. And we invariably welcome the newcomer; only instead of going over to him he has to come to us. More than that, unless he has reached that point in the path of occultism from which return is impossible, by him having irrevocably pledged himself to our association, we never – except in cases of utmost moment – visit him or even cross the threshold of his door in visible appearance. *ML 2, pp. 8-9*

(2) It is he alone who has the love of humanity at heart, who is capable of grasping thoroughly the idea of a regenerating practical brotherhood, who is entitled to the possession of our secrets. He alone – such a man – will never misuse his powers, as there will be no fear that he should turn them to selfish ends. The man who places not the good of mankind above his own good is not worthy of becoming our *chela* – he is not worthy of becoming higher in knowledge than his neighbour. *ML 38, p. 252*

(3) PROBATION: Something every chela who does not want to remain simply ornamental has ... to undergo for a more or less prolonged period; something that – for this very reason, that it is undoubtedly based upon what you Westerns would ever view as a system of humbug or deception – that I, who knew European ideas better than Morya, have always refused to accept or even to regard any of you two as – chelas. *ML 30, p. 230*

(4) A chela under probation is allowed to think and do whatever he likes. He is warned and told beforehand: "You will be tempted and deceived by appearances; two paths will be open before you, both leading to the goal you are trying to attain; one

easy, and that will lead you more rapidly to the fulfilment of orders you may receive; the other – more arduous, more long; a path full of stones and thorns that will make you stumble more than once on your way; and at the end of which you may, perhaps, find failure after all and be unable to carry out the orders given for some particular small work – but, whereas the latter will cause the hardships you have undergone on it to be all carried to the side of your credit in the long run, the former, the easy path, can offer you but a momentary gratification, an easy fulfilment of the task." *ML 30, pp. 230-231*

(5) The chela is at perfect liberty, *and often quite justified from the standpoint of appearances* – to suspect his Guru of being "a fraud" as the elegant word stands. More than that: the greater, the sincerer his indignation – whether expressed in words or boiling in his heart – the more fit he is, the better qualified to become an *adept*. He is free and will not be held to account for using the most abusive words and expressions regarding his guru's actions and orders, provided he comes out victorious from the fiery ordeal; provided he resist all and every temptation; rejects every allurement, and proves that nothing, not even the promise, that which he holds dearer than life, of that most precious boon, his future adeptship – is able to make him deviate from the path of truth and honesty, or force him to become a *deceiver. ML 30, p. 231*

(6) You have repeatedly offered yourself as a chela, and the first duty of one is to hear without anger or malice anything the guru may say. How can we ever teach or you learn if we have to maintain an attitude utterly foreign to us and our methods – that of two society men? If you really want to be a chela i.e. to become the recipient of our mysteries, you have to adapt yourself to our ways, and we to yours. Until you do so, it is useless for you to expect any more than we can give under ordinary circumstances. *ML 30, p. 231*

(7) The option of receiving him or not as a regular chela – remains with the Chohan. M. (Morya) has simply to have him tested, tempted and examined by all and every means, so as to have his real nature drawn out. This is a rule with us as inexorable as it is disgusting in your Western sight, and I could not prevent it even if I would. It is not enough to know thoroughly what the chela is capable of doing or not doing, at the time and under the circumstances during the period of probation. We have to know of what he may become capable under different and every kind of opportunity. *ML 30, p. 236*

(8) Beware of an uncharitable spirit, for it will rise up like a hungry wolf in your path and devour the better qualities of your nature that have been springing into life. Broaden instead of narrowing your sympathies; try to identify yourself with your fellows, rather than to contract your circle of affinity. ... You laugh at *probations* – the word seems ridiculous as applied to you? You forget that he who approaches our precincts even in thought, is drawn into the vortex of probation. *ML 66, p. 367*

(9) Ah, how long shall the mysteries of chelaship overpower and lead astray from the path of truth, the wise and perspicacious as much as the foolish and the credulous! How few of the many pilgrims who have to start without chart or compass on the shoreless Ocean of Occultism, reached the wished for land. Believe me, faithful friend, that nothing short of full confidence in us, in our good motives if not in our wisdom, in our foresight, if not omniscience – which is not to be found on this earth – can help one to cross over from one's land of dream and fiction to our Truth land, the region of stern reality. Otherwise the ocean will prove shoreless indeed; its waves will carry one no longer on waters of hope, but will turn every ripple into doubt and suspicion; and bitter shall they prove to him who starts on that dismal, tossing sea of the Unknown, with a prejudiced

mind! *ML 64, p. 358*

(10) Nor are we especially anxious to have anyone work for us except with entire spontaneity. We want true and unselfish hearts; fearless and confiding souls. *ML 54, p. 310*

(11) The fact is that to the last and supreme initiation, every chela … is left to his own device and counsel … Before they are allowed to go into the world they – the chelas – are every one of them endowed with more or less clairvoyant powers; and with the exception of that faculty that, unless paralysed and watched, would lead them perchance to divulge certain secrets that must not be revealed – they are left in the full exercise of their powers – whatever these may be – why don't they exercise them? Thus step by step, and after a series of punishments, is the chela taught by bitter experience to suppress and guide his impulses; he loses his rashness, his self-sufficiency and never falls into the same errors. *ML 54, pp. 309-310*

(12) The mass of human sin and frailty is distributed throughout the life of a man who is content to remain an average mortal. It is gathered in and centred, so to say, within one period of the life of the chela – the period of probation … That which is generally accumulating to find its legitimate issue only in the next rebirth of an ordinary man, is quickened and fanned into existence in the chela – especially in the presumptuous and selfish candidate who rushes in without having calculated his forces.
ML 64, pp. 359-360

(13) The keepers of the sacred light did not safely cross so many ages but to find themselves wrecked on the rocks of modern skepticism. Our pilots are too experienced sailors to allow us to fear any such disaster. We will always find volunteers to replace the tired sentries, and this world, bad as it is in its present

transitory period, can yet furnish us with a few men now and then. *ML 28, p. 215*

(14) ... since, as in law, no one – either plaintiff or defendant – has a right to plead ignorance of the law, so in Occult Science, the lay chelas ought to be forced to give the benefit of the doubt to their gurus in cases in which, owing to their great ignorance of that science, they are likely to misinterpret the meaning – instead of accusing them point blank of *contradiction*! *ML 24B, p. 181*

(15) Intuitive as you naturally are – chelaship is yet almost a complete puzzle for you as for my friend Sinnett, and the others, they have scarcely an inkling of it yet. Why must I even now – (to put your thoughts in the right channel) remind you of the three cases of insanity within seven months among "lay chelas," not to mention one's turning a thief? Mr. Sinnett may consider himself lucky that his *lay chelaship* is in "fragments" only, and that I have so uniformly discouraged his desires for a closer relationship as an *accepted* chela. Few men know their inherent capacities – only the ordeal of crude chelaship develops them. (Remember these words: they have a deep meaning.) *ML 67, pp. 371-372*

(16) Why will "would-be" *chelas* with such intense self personalities, force themselves within the enchanted and dangerous circle of probation! *ML 63, p. 357-358*

(17) And now, friend, you have completed one of your minor cycles, have suffered, struggled, triumphed. Tempted, you have not failed, weak you have gained strength, and the hard nature of the lot and ordeal of every aspirant after occult knowledge is now better comprehended by you, no doubt. *ML 55, p. 322*

(18) Your strivings, perplexities and forebodings are equally noticed, good and faithful friend. In the imperishable RECORD

of the Masters *you have written them all*. There are registered your every deed and thought; for though not a chela, as you say to my Brother Morya, not even a "protégé" – as you understand the term – still, you have stepped within the circle of our work, you  have crossed the mystic line which separates your world from ours, and now whether you persevere or not; whether we become later on, in your sight, still more living, *real* entities or vanish out of your mind like so many dream fictions – perchance an ugly nightmare – you are virtually OURS. Your hidden *Self* has mirrored itself in our Akasa; your nature is – yours, your essence is – ours. The flame is distinct from the log of wood which serves it temporarily as fuel; at the end of your apparitional birth – and whether we two meet face to face in our grosser *rupas* – you cannot avoid meeting us in *Real Existence*. **ML 45, pp. 266-267**

(19) Yea, verily good friend, your *Karma* is ours, for you imprinted it daily and hourly, upon the pages of that book where the minutest particulars of the individuals stepping inside our circle are preserved … In thought and deed by day, in soul struggles by night, you have been writing the story of your desires and your spiritual development. This everyone does who approaches us with any earnestness of desire to become our co-worker; he himself "precipitates" the written entries, by the identical process used by us when we write inside your closed letters and uncut pages of books and pamphlets in transit.
ML 45, p. 267

(20) During the past few months especially, when your weary brain was plunged in the torpor of sleep, your eager soul has

often been searching after me, and the current of your thought been beating against my protecting barriers of Akas, as the lapping wavelets against a rocky shore. What that "inner Self" impatient, anxious – has longed to bind itself to, the carnal man, the worldlings' master has not ratified. Sacred indeed, some of them are, and no one would ask you to rupture them. There below lies your long cherished field of enterprise and usefulness. Ours can never be more than a bright phantom world, to a man of thorough "practical sense" and if your case be in some degree exceptional, it is because your nature has deeper inspirations than those of others, who are still more "businesslike," and the fountainhead of whose eloquence is in the brain, not in the heart, which never was in contact with the mysteriously effulgent and pure heart of Tathagata (Buddha). *ML 45, p. 267*

(21) You have often put the question, "Why should the Brothers refuse turning their attention to such worthy, sincere theosophists as C.C.M. (Charles Massey) and Hood, or such a precious subject as S. Moses?" Well, I now answer you very clearly, that we have done so – ever since the said gentlemen came into contact and communication with H.P.B. They were all tried and tested in various ways, and not one of them came up (to) the desired mark. M. Gave a special attention to "Ç.C.M." ... You may say that such a secret way of testing people is *dishonest*; that we ought to have warned him etc. Well, all I can say is, that it may be so from our European standpoint, but that, being Asiatics, we cannot depart from our rules. A man's character, his true inner nature, can never be thoroughly drawn out if he believes himself watched, or strives for an object. Besides Col. O. had never made a secret of that way of ours, and all the British theosophists *ought* to ... know that their body was, since we had sanctioned it, under a regular probation. *ML 54, p. 315*

(22) Take another case, that of Fern. His development, as

occurring under your eye, affords you a useful study and a hint as to even more serious methods, adopted in individual cases to thoroughly test the latent moral qualities of the man. Every human being contains within himself vast potentialities and it is the duty of the adepts to surround the would-be chela with circumstances which shall enable him to take the "right-hand path" – if he has the ability in him.

We are no more at liberty to withhold the chance from a postulant than we are to guide and direct him into the proper course. At best, we can only show him – after his probation period was successfully terminated – that if he does this he will go right: if the other, wrong. But until he has passed that period, we leave him to fight out his battles as best he may, and have to do so occasionally with higher and *initiated* chelas such as H.P.B., once they are allowed to work in the world that all of us more or less avoid. More than that – and you better learn it at once, if my previous letters to you about Fern have not sufficiently opened your eyes – we allow our candidates to be tempted in a thousand various ways, so as to draw out the whole of their inner nature and allow it the chance of remaining conqueror either one way or the other. *ML 54, p. 316*

(23) One who is true and approved today, may tomorrow prove, under a new concatenation of circumstances a traitor, an ingrate, a coward, an imbecile. The reed, bent beyond its limit of flexibility, will have snapped in twain. Shall we accuse it? No, but because we can and *do* pity it, we cannot select it as part of those reeds that have been tried and found strong, hence fit to be accepted as material for the indestructible fan we are so carefully building. *L 54, pp. 316-317*

(24) With the "visible" one (Sinnett) we have nothing to do. He is to us only a veil that hides from profane eyes that other *ego* with whose evolution we are concerned. In the external *rupa* do what

you like, think what you like: only when the effects of that voluntary action are seen in the body of our correspondent – is it incumbent upon us to notice it. *ML 43, pp. 259- 260*

(25) Why is it that doubts and foul suspicions seem to beset every aspirant for chelaship? My friend, in the Masonic Lodges of old times, the neophyte was subjected to a series of frightful tests of his constancy, courage and presence of mind. By psychological impressions supplemented by machinery and chemicals, he was made to believe himself falling down precipices, crushed by rocks, walking spider-web bridges in mid-air, passing through fire, drowned in water and attacked by wild beasts. This was a reminiscence of and a programme borrowed from the Egyptian Mysteries.

The West having lost the secrets of the East, had, as I say, to resort to artifice. But in these days, the vulgarization of science has rendered such trifling tests obsolete. The aspirant is now assailed entirely on the psychological side of his nature. His course of testing – in Europe and India – is that of Raj-yog and its result is – as frequently explained – to develop every germ good and bad in him in his temperament. The rule is inflexible, and not one escapes whether he but writes to us a letter, or in the privacy of his own heart's thought formulates a strong desire for occult communication and knowledge. As the shower cannot fructify the rock, so the occult teaching has no effect upon the unreceptive mind; and as the water develops the heat of caustic lime, so does the teaching bring into fierce action every unsuspected potentiality latent in him. *ML 65, pp. 365-366*

(26) So, my good brother, be not surprised, and blame us not as readily as you have already done, at any development of our policy towards the aspirants, past, present or future.
ML 54, p. 316

(27) Her clairvoyance (Laura Holloway's) is a fact, her selection and chelaship another. However well fitted psychically and physiologically to answer such selection, unless possessed of spiritual, as well as of physical unselfishness, a chela, whether selected or not, must perish, as a chela in the long run. Self personality, vanity and conceit harboured in the higher principles are enormously more dangerous than the same defects, inherent only in the lower physical nature of man. They are the breakers against which the cause of chelaship, in its probationary stage, is sure to be dashed to pieces, unless the would-be disciple carries with him the white shield of perfect confidence and trust in those he would seek out through mount and vale, to guide him safely toward the light of Knowledge. *ML 64, p. 359*

(28) ... there are persons, who without showing any external sign of selfishness, are intensely selfish in their inner spiritual aspiration. These will follow the path, once chosen by them, with their eyes closed to the interests of all but themselves and see nothing outside the narrow pathway filled with their own personality. They are so intensely absorbed in the contemplation of their own supposed "righteousness" that nothing can ever appear right to them outside the focus of their own vision, distorted by their self-complacent contemplation and their judgement of the right and wrong. *ML 64, p. 360*

(29) The methods used for developing lucidity in our chelas may be easily used by you. Every temple has a dark room, the north wall of which is entirely covered with a sheet of mixed metal, chiefly copper, very highly polished, with a surface capable of reflecting in it things as well as a mirror. The chela sits on an insulated stool, a three-legged bench

placed in a flat-bottomed vessel of thick glass, – the lama operator likewise, the two forming with the mirror wall a triangle. A magnet with the North Pole up is suspended over the crown of the chela's head without touching it. The operator, having started the thing going leaves the chela alone gazing on the wall, and after the third time is no longer required. *ML 127, pp. 455-456*

(30) I (K.H.) desired Mad. B. to select among the two or three Aryan Punjabees, who study *Yog Vidya* and are natural mystics, one whom – without disclosing myself to him too much – I could designate as an agent between yourself and us, and whom I was anxious to despatch to you, with a letter of introduction, and have him speak to you of *Yoga* and its practical effects. This young gentleman, who is as pure as purity itself, whose aspirations and thoughts are of the most spiritual, ennobling kind, and who merely through self-exertion is able to penetrate into the regions of the formless worlds – this young man is not fit for – a drawing room.

Having explained to him that the greatest good might result for his country if he helped you to organize a Branch of English mystics, by proving to them *practically* to what wonderful results led the study of Yog, Mad. B. asked him in guarded and very delicate terms to change his dress and turban before starting for Allahabad – for, though she did not give him this reason, they were very *dirty and slovenly*.

You are to tell Mr. Sinnett, she said, that you bring him a letter from our brother K. with whom he corresponds, but, if he asks you anything either of him or the other Brothers, answer him simply and truthfully, that you are not allowed to expatiate upon the subject. Speak of Yog and prove to him what powers you have attained.

This young man, who had consented, wrote later on the following curious letters: "Madam," he said, "you who preach the highest standards of morality, of truthfulness, etc., you would have me play the part of an imposter. You ask me to change my clothes at the risk of giving a false idea of my personality and mystifying the gentleman you send me to. And what if he asks me if I personally know Koot Hoomi, am I to keep silent and allow him to think I do? This would be a tacit falsehood, and guilty of that, I would be thrown back into the awful whirl of transmigration!"

Here is an illustration of the difficulties under which we have to labour. Powerless to send to you a neophyte before you have pledged yourself to us – we have either to keep back or despatch to you one, who at best would shock, if not inspire you at once with disgust! The letter would have been given him by my own hand; he had but to promise to hold his tongue upon matters he knows nothing about and could give but a false idea of, and to make himself look cleaner. Prejudice and dead letter again. For over a thousand years, says Michelet, the Christian saints never washed themselves! For how long will our saints dread to change their clothes for fear of being taken for Marmaliks (barbarians) and the neophytes of rival and cleaner sects! *ML 4, p. 15-16*

Civilization and Races

(1) Be it as it may, we are content to live as we do – unknown and undisturbed by a civilization which rests so exclusively upon intellect. Nor do we feel in any way concerned about the revival of our ancient arts and high civilization, for these are as sure to come back in their time, and in a higher form, as the Plesiosaurus and the Megatherium in theirs. We have the weakness to believe in ever recurrent cycles and hope to *quicken* the resurrection and what is past and gone. We *could not* impede it even if we would. The "new civilization" will be but the child of the old one, and we have but to leave the eternal law to take its own course to have our dead ones come out of their graves; yet we are certainly anxious to hasten the welcome event. Fear not; although we do "cling superstitiously to the relics of the Past" our knowledge will not pass away from the sight of man. It is the "gift of the gods" and the most precious relic of all. *ML 28, pp. 214-215*

(2) In the first half of the fourth race, sciences, arts, literature and philosophy were born, eclipsed in one nation, reborn in another, civilization and intellectual development whirling in septenary cycles as the rest; while it is but in the latter half that the spiritual Ego will begin its real struggle with body and mind, to manifest its transcendental powers. Who will help in the forthcoming gigantic struggle? Who? Happy the man who helps a helping hand. *ML 14, p. 88*

(3) Greeks and Romans were small *sub-races*, and Egyptians part and parcel of our own "Caucasian" stock. Look at the latter and at India. Having reached the highest civilization and, what is more, *learning* – both went down. Egypt as a distinct sub-race disappearing entirely (her Copts are a hybrid remnant.) India – as one of the most powerful off-shoots of the mother Race, and

composed of a number of sub-races – lasting to these times and struggling to take once more her place in history some day. That History catches but a few stray, hazy glimpses of Egypt, some 12,000 years back when, having already reached the apex of its cycle thousands of years before, the latter had begun going down. What does, or can it know of India 5,000 years ago, or of the Chaldees – whom it confounds most charmingly with the Assyrians, making of them one day "Akkadians," at another Turanians and what not? We say then, that your History is entirely at sea. *ML 23B, p. 152*

(4) Civilization is an inheritance, a patrimony that passes from race to race along the ascending and descending paths of cycles. During the minority of a sub-race, it is preserved for it by its predecessor, which disappears, dies out generally, when the former "comes of age." At first most of them squander and mismanage their property, or leave it untouched in the ancestral coffers. They reject contemptuously the advice of their elders and prefer, boy-like, playing in the streets, to studying and making the most of the untouched wealth stored up for them in the records of the Past. Thus during your transition period – the middle ages – Europe rejected the testimony of Antiquity, calling such sages as Heredotus and other learned Greeks – the Father of Lies, until she knew better and changed the appellation into that of "Father of History." Instead of neglecting, you now accumulate and add to your wealth.

As every other race, you had your ups and downs, your periods of honour and dishonour, your dark midnight and – you are now approaching your brilliant noon. The youngest of the fifth race family, you were for long ages the unloved and uncared for, the Cendrillon (Cinderella) in your home. And now, when so many of your sisters have died and others still are dying, while the few of the old survivors, now in their second infancy, wait but for their Messiah – the sixth race (i.e. the sixth sub-race – Ed.) – to resurrect to a new life and start anew with the coming stronger along the path of a new cycle – now that the Western Cendrillon has suddenly developed into a proud wealthy princess, the beauty we all see and admire – how does she act? Less kind hearted than the princess in the tale, instead of offering to her elder and less favoured sister, the oldest now, in fact, since she is nearly "a million years old" and the only one who has never treated her unkindly, though she may have ignored her – instead of offering her, I say, the "kiss of peace" she applies to her the *lex talionis* with a vengeance that does not enhance her natural beauty. This, my good friend and brother, is not a far-fetched allegory but – history. *ML 23B, p. 150*

(5) Do you know that the Chaldees were at the apex of their Occult fame before what you term as the "bronze Age?" That the "Sons of Ad" or the children of the Fire Mist preceded by hundreds of centuries the Age of Iron, which was an old age already when what you now call the Historical period – probably because what is known of it is generally no history but fiction – had hardly begun. We hold – but then what warrant can you give the world that we are right? – that far "greater civilizations than our own have risen and decayed." It is not enough to say as some of your modern writers do – that an extinct civilization existed before Rome and Athens were founded. We affirm that a *series* of civilizations existed *before,* as well as after the Glacial period, that they existed upon various points of the globe, reached the apex of glory and – died. Every trace and memory had been lost of the Assyrian and Phoenician civilizations until discoveries began to be made a few years ago. And now they open a new, though not by far one of the earliest pages in the history of mankind. And yet how far back do those civilizations go in comparison with the oldest? – and even them, history is shy to accept.

Archaeo-geology has sufficiently demonstrated that the memory of man runs back vastly further than history has been willing to accept, and the sacred records of once mighty nations preserved by their heirs are still more worthy of trust. We speak of civilizations of the ante-glacial period; and (not only in the minds of the vulgar and the profane but even in the opinion of the highly learned geologist) the claim sounds preposterous.

What would you say then to our affirmation that the Chinese – I now speak of the inland, true Chinaman, not of the hybrid mixture between the fourth and fifth Races now occupying the throne – the aborigines, who belong in their unallied nationality wholly to the highest and last branch of the fourth Race, reached their highest civilization when the fifth had hardly appeared in Asia, and that its first off-shoot was yet a thing of the future. When was it? Calculate. You cannot think that we, who have such tremendous odds against the acceptance of our doctrine would deliberately go on inventing Races and sub-races (in the opinion of Mr. Hume) were not they a matter of undeniable fact.
ML 23B, pp. 153-154

(6) The group of islands off the Siberian coast discovered by Nordenskjold of the "Vega" was found strewn with fossils of horses, sheep, oxen, etc., among giant bones of elephants, mammoths, rhinoceroses and other monsters, belonging to periods when man – says your science – had not yet made his appearance on earth. How came horses and sheep to be found in the company with the huge "antediluvians?" The horse, we are taught in schools – is quite a modern invention of nature, and no man ever saw its pedactyl ancestor. The group of the Siberian islands may give the lie to the comfortable theory. The region now locked in the fetters of eternal winter uninhabited by man – that most fragile of animals, – will be very soon proved to have had not only a tropical climate – something your science knows and does not dispute, but having been likewise the seat of one of the most ancient civilizations of that fourth race ....
ML 23B, p. 154

(7) I told you before now, that the highest people now on earth (spiritually) belong to the first sub-race of the fifth *root* Race and those are the Aryan Asiatics; the highest race (physical intellectuality) is the last sub-race of the fifth (i.e. the fifth sub-race of the fifth Root Race – Ed.) – yourselves, the white conquerors. The majority of mankind belongs to the seventh sub-race of the fourth *Root race*, the above mentioned Chinamen and their offshoots and branchlets (Malayans, Mongolians, Tibetans, Javanese, etc. etc.) and remnants of other sub-races of the fourth – and the seventh sub-race of the third race. All these … are the direct lineal descendants of highly civilized nations neither the names nor memory of which have survived except in such books as *Popol Vuh* and a few other unknown to Science. *ML 23B, p. 154*

(8) *En passant*, to show you that not only were not the "races" *invented* by us, but that they are a cardinal dogma with the Lama Buddhists and with all who study our esoteric doctrine, I send you an explanation on a page or two in Rhys Davids' *Buddhism*, – otherwise incomprehensible, meaningless and absurd. It is written with the special permission of the Chohan (my Master) and – for your benefit. No Orientalist has ever suspected the truths contained in it, and – you were the first Western man (outside Tibet) to whom it is now explained. *ML 23B, pp. 157-158*

(9) A student of occultism ought not to speak of the "stagnant condition of the fourth Race people" since *history* knows next to nothing of that condition "up to the beginning of modern progress" of other nations but the Western. What do you know of America, for instance, before the invasion of that country by the Spaniards? Less than two centuries prior to the arrival of Cortex there was as great a "rush" towards progress among the *sub-races* of Peru and Mexico as there is now in Europe and the U.S.A. Their sub-race ended in nearly total annihilation through causes generated by itself; so will yours at the end of its cycle.

We may speak only of the "stagnant conditions" into which, following the law of development, growth, maturity and decline every race and sub-race falls into during its transition periods. It is the latter condition your *Universal* History is acquainted with, while it remains superbly ignorant of the condition even India was in, some ten centuries back. Your sub-races are now running toward the apex of their respective cycles, and that History goes no further back than the periods of decline of a few other sub-races, belonging most of them to the preceding fourth race. And what is the area and period of time embraced by its *Universal* eye? – At the utmost stretch a few miserable dozens of centuries. A mighty horizon, indeed! Beyond – all is darkness for it, nothing but hypotheses .... *ML 23B, pp. 149-150*

Creation and Evolution

(1) Nothing in nature springs into existence suddenly, all being subjected to the same law of gradual evolution. Realize but once the process of the *maha* cycle of one sphere and you have realized them all. One man is born like another man, one race evolves, develops, and declines like another and all other races. Nature follows the same groove from the "creation" of a universe down to that of a mosquito. In studying esoteric cosmogony, keep a spiritual eye upon the physiological process of human birth; proceed from cause to effect, establishing as you go along analogies between the birth of man and that of a world. In our doctrine you will find necessary the synthetic method; you will have to embrace the whole – that is to say to blend the *macrocosm* and microcosm together – before you are enabled to study the parts separately or analyze them with profit to your understanding. Cosmology is the physiology of the universe spiritualized, for there is but one law. *ML 13, p. 70*

(2) In Cosmogony and the work of nature, the positive and negative of the active and passive forces correspond to the male and female principles. Your "spiritual efflux" comes not from "behind the veil" but is the male seed falling into the veil of cosmic matter. The active is attracted by the passive principle and the Great Nag, the serpent emblem of eternity, attracts its tail to its mouth, forming thereby a circle (cycles in the eternity) in that incessant pursuit of the negative by the positive. Hence the emblem of the *lingam*, the *phallus* and the *kteis*. The one and chief attribute of the universal spiritual principle – the unconscious but ever active life-giver – is to expand and shed; that of the universal material principle to gather in and fecundate. Unconscious and non-existing when separated they become consciousness and life when brought together. Hence again –

Brahma, from the root "brih," the Sanskrit for "to expand, grow or to fructify," Brahma being but the vivifying *expansive* force of nature in its eternal evolution. *ML 13, p. 71*

(3) As our Pondicherry *chela* significantly says, neither you nor any other man across the threshold has had or ever will have "the complete theory" of Evolution taught him; or get it unless he guesses it for himself. If anyone can unravel it from such tangled threads as are given him, very well; and a fine proof it would indeed be of his or her spiritual insight. Some have come *very near* it. But yet there is always with the best of them just enough error – colouring and misconception; the shadow of *Manas* projecting across the field of *Buddhi* – to prove the eternal law, that only the unshackled Spirit shall see the things of the Spirit without a veil. *ML 59, p. 348*

(4) In the evolution of man there is a topmost point, a bottom point, a descending arc and an ascending arc. As it is "Spirit" which transforms itself into "matter" and (not "matter" which ascends – but) matter which *resolves* once *more into spirit*, of course the first race evolution and the last on a planet (as in each round) must be more ethereal, more spiritual, the fourth or lowest one most physical (progressively of course in each round) and at the same time – *as physical intelligence is the masked manifes-tation of spiritual intelligence* – each evoluted race in the downward arc must be more physically intelligent than its prede-cessor, and each in the upward arc must have a more refined form of mentality commingled with spiritual intuitiveness.
ML 14, p. 86

(5) The difficulty of explaining the fact that "unintelligent Forces can give rise to highly intelligent beings like ourselves," is covered by the eternal progression of cycles, and the process of evolution ever perfecting its work as it goes along. *ML 22, p. 141*

(6) Take the human foetus. From the moment of its first planting, until it completes its seventh month of gestation, it repeats in miniature the mineral, vegetable, and animal cycles it passed through in its previous encasements, and only during the last two develops its future human entity. It is completed but towards the child's seventh year. Yet it existed without any *increase* or *decrease* aeons on aeons before it worked its way onward, through and in the womb of mother nature as it works now in its earthly mother's bosom.

Truly said; a learned philosopher who trusts more to his intuitions than the dicta of modern science, "The stages of man's intra-uterine existence embody a condensed record of some of the missing pages in Earth's history." Thus you must look back at the animal, vegetable and mineral entities. You must take each entity at its starting point in the manvantaric course, as the primordial cosmic atom already differentiated by the first flutter of the manvantaric life breath. For the potentiality which develops finally in a perfected planetary spirit lurks in, is in fact, the primordial cosmic atom. *ML 15, pp. 88-89*

(7) If you can show me one being or object in the universe which does not originate and develop through, and in accordance with blind law, then only will your argument hold good ... The doctrine of evolution is an eternal protest. Evolution means unfolding of the evolute from the involute, a process of gradual growth.

The only thing that could have possibly been spontaneously created is cosmic matter, and primordium with us means not only primogenitureship but eternalism, for matter is eternal and one of the *Hlun dhub* (Self-existing – Ed.) not a *kyen* – a cause, itself the result of some primary cause. Were it so, at the end of every Maha pralaya when the whole cosmos moves into collective perfection and every atom (that you call primordial, and we eternal) emanates from itself a still finer atom – every individual atom containing in itself the actual potentiality of evoluting milliards of worlds, each more perfect and more ethereal –– how is it that there is no sign of such an intelligence outside the self-governed universe?

You take a last hypothesis – a portion of your god sits in every atom. He is divided *ad infinitum*, he remains concealed *in abscondito* and the logical conclusion we arrive at is, that, (as) the Infinite mind of the Dhyan Chohans knows, the newly emanated atoms are incapable of any conscious or unconscious action, unless they receive the intellectual impulse *from them*. Ergo your god is no better than blind matter ever propelled by a blind eternal force or law, which is that matter, god – Perchance.

Cosmological Notes, LBS – First Edition, pp. 384-385

(8) The evolution of the worlds cannot be considered apart from the evolution of everything created or having being on these worlds. Your accepted conceptions of cosmogony – whether from the theological or scientific standpoints – do not enable you to solve a single anthropological, or even ethical problem and they stand in your way whenever you attempt to solve the problem of the races on this planet.

When a man begins to talk about creation and the origin of man, he is butting against the facts incessantly. Go on saying: "Our planet and man were created" – and you will be fighting against *hard facts* forever, analyzing and losing time over trifling details – unable to ever grasp the whole. But once admit that our planet and ourselves are no more *creations* than the iceberg now before me (in our K.H.'s home) but that both planet and man are – states for a given time; their present appearance – geological and anthropological – is transitory and but a condition concomitant of that stage of evolution at which they have arrived in the descending cycle – and all will become plain.

ML 13, pp. 72-73

(9) For, as planetary development is as progressive as human or race evolution, the hour of the Pralaya's coming catches the series of worlds at successive stages of evolution; (i.e.) each has attained to some one of the periods of evolutionary progress – each stops there, until the outward impulse of the next *manvantara* sets it going from that very point – like a stopped time-piece rewound. *ML 12, p. 67*

Cycles

(1) This picture of an eternity of action may appall the mind that has been accustomed to look forward to an existence of ceaseless repose. But their concept is not supported by the analogies of nature, nor – and ignorant though I may be thought of your Western Science, may I not say? – by the teachings of that Science. We know that periods of action and rest follow each other in everything in nature, from the macrocosm with its Solar Systems down to man and its parent-earth, which has its seasons of activity followed by those of sleep; and that in short all nature, like her begotten living forms has her time for recuperation.

So with the spiritual individuality, the Monad, which starts on its downward and upward cyclic rotation. The periods which intervene between each great *manvantarian* "round" are proportionately long to reward for the thousands of existences passed on various globes; while the time given between each "race birth" – or rings as you call them – is sufficiently lengthy to compensate for any life of strife and misery, during that lapse of time passed in conscious bliss after the re-birth (*i.e.* into Devachan – Ed.) of the *Ego*. To conceive of an eternity of bliss or woe, and to offset it to any conceivable deeds of merit or demerit, of a being who may have lived a century or even a millennium in the flesh, can only be proposed by one who has never yet grasped the awful reality of the word Eternity, nor pondered upon the law of perfect justice and equilibrium which pervades nature. *ML 2, p. 68*

(2) The cycles must run their rounds. Periods of mental and moral light and darkness succeed each other, as day does night. The major and minor yugas must be accomplished according to the established order of things. And we, borne along on the mighty tide, can only modify and direct some of its minor currents. If we had the powers of the imaginary Personal God, and the universal

and immutable laws were but toys to play with, then indeed might we have created conditions that would have turned this earth into an Arcadia for lofty souls. But having to deal with an immutable Law, being ourselves its creatures, we have to do what we could and rest thankful.
The First Letter of K.H. to A.O. Hume
Combined Chronology by M. Conger, p. 35

(3) Almost unthinkably long as is a Mahayug, it is still a definite term and within it must be accomplished the whole order of development, or to state it in occult phraseology, the descent of Spirit into matter and its return to the re-emergence. A chain of beads and each bead a world, is an illustration already made familiar to you. You have already pondered over the life impulses beginning with each *Manvantara* to evolve the first of these worlds; to perfect it; to people it successively with all the aerial forms of life.

After completing on the first world seven cycles – or evolutions of development – in each kingdom, as you know – passing forward down the arc – to similarly evolve the next world in the chain, perfect it, and abandon it. Then to the next and the next – until the seven-fold round of world evolutions along the chain is run through and Mahayug comes to its end. Then chaos *again* – the *Pralaya*. As this life-impulse (at the seventh and last round from planet to planet) moves on, it leaves behind it dying and – very soon – "dead planets." *ML 12, pp. 66-67*

(4) The cycle of intelligent existences commences at the highest worlds or *planets* – the term highest meaning here the most spiritually perfect. Evolving from cosmic matter – which is akasa, the primeval not the secondary plastic medium or Ether of science, instinctively suspected, unproven as the rest – man first evolutes from this matter in its most sublimated state, appearing at the threshold of Eternity as a perfectly *Etherial* – not Spiritual Entity,

say – a Planetary Spirit. He is but one remove from the universal and Spiritual World Essence – the *Anima Mundi* of the Greeks, or that which humanity in its spiritual decadence has degraded into a mythical personal God. Hence at that stage, the Spirit-man is at best an active Power, an *immutable*, therefore an *unthinking* Principle (the "immutable" being again used here but to denote that state for the time being, the immutability applying here but to the inner principle, which will vanish and disappear as soon as the spark of the material in him will start on its cyclic work of Evolution and transformation.) In his subsequent descent and in proportion to the increase of matter, he will assert more and more his activity. *ML 9 pp. 45-46*

(5) Now, the congeries of the star worlds, (including our own planet) inhabited by intelligent beings, may be likened to an orb or rather an epicycloid formed of rings like a chain – worlds interlocked together, the totality representing an imaginary endless ring or circle. The progress of man throughout the whole – from its starting to its closing points, meeting on the highest point of the circumference – is what we call the *Maha Yug* or Great Cycle, the *Kuklos*, whose head is lost in a crown of *absolute* Spirit, and its lowest point of circumference in *absolute* matter – to viz. the point of cessation of action of the active principle.

If, using a more familiar term, we call the Great Cycle the *Macrokosm* and its component parts or the inter-linked star worlds *Microkosms*, the occultists' meaning in representing each of the latter as perfect copies of the former will become evident. The Great is the Prototype of the smaller cycles and as such, each star world has in its turn its own cycle of evolution which starts with a purer and ends with a grosser or more material nature. As they descend, each world presents itself naturally more and more shadowy, becoming at the "antipodes" *absolute* matter.
ML 9, p. 46

(6) There are cycles of 7, 11, 21, 77, 107, 11,000, 21,000 etc. so many cycles will make a major and so on. *ML 47, p. 272*

(7) Control your involuntary powers and develop in the right direction your will and you will become a teacher instead of a learner. I would not refuse what I have a right to teach. Only I (Mahatma K.H) had to study for fifteen years before I came to the doctrines of cycles and had to learn simpler things first.
ML 22, p. 144

(8) When the last cycle of man-bearing has been completed by that last fecund earth, and humanity has reached in a mass the stage of Buddhahood and passed out of the objective existence into the mystery of Nirvana – then "strikes the hour;" the seen becomes the unseen, the concrete resumes its pre-cyclic state of atomic distribution.

But the dead worlds left behind by the on-sweeping impulse *do not* continue *dead*. Motion is the eternal order of things and affinity or attraction its handmaid of all works. The thrill of life will again re-unite the atoms, and it will stir again in the inert planet when the time comes. Though all its forces have remained in status quo and are now asleep, yet little by little it will – when the hour strikes – gather for a new cycle of man-bearing maternity, and give birth to something still higher as moral and physical types than during the preceding *manvantara*. And its "cosmic atoms already in a differentiated state" (*differing* – in the producing force, in the mechanical sense of motions *and* effects) remains in status quo, as well as globes and everything else in the process of formation." *ML 12, p. 67*

Death and Dying

(1) It is a widely spread belief among all the Hindus that a person's future pre-natal state and birth are moulded by the last desire he may have at the time of death. But this last desire, they say, necessarily hinges onto the shape which the person may have given to his desires, passions, etc. during his past life. It is for this very reason, viz. – that our last desire may not be unfavourable to our future progress – that we have to watch our actions and control our passions and desires throughout our whole earthly career. *ML 23B, p. 170*

(2) ... remember, both, that we create ourselves our *devachan* as our *avitchi* while yet on earth, and mostly during the latter days and even moments of our intellectual, sentient lives. That feeling which is the strongest in us at that supreme hour, when, as in a dream, the events of a long life, in their minutest details are marshalled in the greatest order in a few seconds in our vision – that feeling will become the fashioner of our bliss or woe, the *life principle* of our future existence. *ML 20C, pp. 127-128*

(3) "The Spirits of very fair, average good people, dying *natural* deaths remain ... in the earth's atmosphere from a few days to a few years," the period depending on their readiness to meet their – *creature*, not their creator; a very abstruse subject you will learn later on when you too are more prepared. *ML 20c, p. 133*

(4) ... no religion with the exception of Buddhism has hitherto taught a practical contempt for this earthly life, while each of them, always with the one solitary exception, has through its hells and damnations inculcated the greatest dread of death. Therefore do we find that struggle for life raging most fiercely in Christian countries, most prevalent in Europe and America. It

weakens in the Pagan lands and is nearly unknown among Buddhist populations. *K.H.'s View of the Chohan Letter Combined Chronology by M. Conger, p. 45*

(5) What grumblings, what criticism on *Devachan* and kindred subjects for their incompleteness and many a seeming contradiction! Oh blind fools! They forget – or never knew that he who holds the keys to the secrets of *Death* is possessed of the keys of *Life*. *ML 65, p. 365*

(6) It is not nature that creates diseases, but man. The latter's mission and destiny in the economy of nature is to die his natural death, brought by old age; save accident, neither a savage nor a wild (free) animal dies of disease. *ML10, p. 57*

(7) Although not "wholly dissevered from their sixth and seventh principles" and quite "potent" in the seance room, nevertheless to the day when they (suicides) would have died a natural death, they are separated from the higher principles by a gulf. The sixth and seventh remain passive and negative, whereas in cases of *accidental death* the higher and the lower groups mutually attract each other. In cases of good and innocent Egos, moreover, the latter gravitates irresistibly towards the sixth and seventh, and thus – either slumbers, surrounded by happy dreams, or sleeps a dreamless, profound sleep until the hour strikes. With a little reflection, and an eye to eternal justice and fitness of things, you will see why. The victim whether good or bad is *irresponsible* for his death, even if the death were due to some action in a previous life or an antecedent birth; was an act, in short, of the Law of retribution, still it was not the *direct* result of an act deliberately committed by the *personal* Ego, of that life during which he happened to be killed. *ML 20C, p. 131*

(8) The experience of dying men – by drowning and other

accidents – brought back to life, has corroborated our doctrine in almost every case. Such thoughts are involuntary and we have no more control over them than we would over the eye's retina, to prevent it perceiving that colour that affects it most. At the last moment, the whole life is reflected in our memory and emerges, from all the forgotten nooks and corners, picture after picture, one event after the other. The dying brain dislodges memory with a strong supreme impulse, and memory restores faithfully every impression entrusted to it during the period of the brain's activity. That impression and thought which was the strongest, naturally becomes the most vivid and survives, so to say, all the rest which now vanish and disappear for ever, to reappear but in Devachan. *ML 23B, p. 170*

(9) No man dies insane or unconscious – as some physiologists assert. Even a madman, or one in a fit of *delirium tremens,* will have his instant of perfect lucidity at the moment of death, though unable to say so to those present. The man may often appear dead. Yet, from the last pulsation, from and between the last throbbing of his heart and the moment when the last spark of animal heat leaves the body – the *brain thinks* and the *Ego* lives in those few brief seconds his whole life over again. Speak in whispers ye who assist at the death-bed and find yourselves in the solemn presence of death. Especially have you to keep quiet just after death has laid her clammy hand upon the body. Speak in whispers, I say, lest you disturb the quiet ripple of thought and hinder the busy work of the Past casting its reflection upon the Veil of the Future. *ML 23B, p. 170*

(10) When man dies, his second and third principles die with him; the lower triad disappears, and the fourth, fifth, sixth and seventh principles form the surviving *Quaternary.* Thenceforth it is a "death" struggle between the Upper and Lower dualities. If the upper wins, the sixth, having attracted itself the quintessence

of Good from the fifth – its nobler affections, its saintly (though they may be *earthly*) aspirations, and the most Spiritualised portions of its mind – follows its divine *elder* (the seventh) into the "gestation" state; and the fifth and fourth remain in association as an empty *shell* – (the expression is quite correct) – to roam in the earth's atmosphere, with half the personal memory gone, and the more brutal instinct fully alive for a certain period – an "Elementary" in short. This is the "angel guide" of the average medium. *ML 16, pp. 103-104*

(11) If, on the other hand, it is the Upper *Duality* which is defeated, then it is the fifth principle that assimilates all that there may be left of *personal* recollection and perceptions of its personal individuality in the sixth. But, with all this additional stock, it will not remain in *Kama-Loka* – "the world of Desire" or our Earth's atmosphere. In a very short time, like a straw floating within the attraction of the vortices and pits of the Maelstrom, it is caught up and drawn into the great whirlpool of human Egos; while the sixth and seventh – now a purely spiritual *individual* MONAD, with nothing left in it of the late personality, having no regular "gestation" period to pass through (since there is no purified *personal* Ego to be reborn), after a more or less prolonged period of unconscious Rest in boundless Space – will find itself reborn in another personality ....

When arrives the period of "Full Individual Consciousness" – which precedes that of *Absolute* Consciousness in the *Paranirvana* – this lost *personal* life becomes as a torn out page in the great *Book of Lives*, without even a disconnected word left to mark its absence. The purified monad will neither perceive nor remember it in the series of its past rebirths – which it would had it gone to the "World of Forms" (*rupa loka*) – and its retrospective glance will not perceive even the slightest sign to indicate that it had been.

The light of *Samma-Sambuddh* –

"... that light which shines beyond our mortal ken
The light of all the lives in all the worlds" –

Throws no ray upon the personal life in the series of lives foregone.

To the credit of mankind, I must say, that such an utter obliteration of an existence from the tablets of Universal Being does not occur often enough to make a great percentage. ... such a thing is ... an exception not the rule. *ML 16, p. 104*

(12) There is a great difference in our humble opinion (between conscious and unconscious suicide). We, who look at it from a standpoint which would prove very unacceptable to Life Insurance Companies, say that there are very few if any of the men who indulge in the above enumerated vices, (e.g. over indulgences; overwork – Ed.) who feel perfectly sure that such a course of action will lead them eventually to premature death. Such is the penalty of *Maya*.

The "vices" will not escape their punishment; but it is the *cause* not the *effect* that will be punished, especially an unforeseen though probable effect. As well call a *suicide* a man who meets his death in a storm at sea, as one who kills himself with "overstudy." Water is liable to drown a man, and too much brain work to produce a softening of the brain, which may carry him away. In such a case no one ought to cross the *Kalapani* nor even to take a bath (for fear of getting faint in it and drowned (for we all know of such cases) nor should a man do his duty, least of all sacrifice himself for even a laudable and highly beneficent cause, as many of us – (H.P.B. for one) – do.

Would Mr. Hume call her a suicide were she to drop dead over her present work? *Motive* is everything and man is punished in a case of direct responsibility, never otherwise. In the victim's case the natural hour of death was anticipated accidentally, while in that of the suicide, death is brought on voluntarily and with a full and deliberate knowledge of its immediate consequences. Thus a man who causes his death in a fit of temporary insanity is not a *felo de se* (suicide) to the great grief and often trouble of the Life Insurance Companies. Nor is he left a prey to the temptations of the Kama Loka but falls asleep like any other victim. *ML 20C, p. 132*

(13) Every just disembodied *four-fold* entity – whether it died a natural or violent death, from suicide or accident, mentally sane or insane, young or old, good, bad, or indifferent ... 'sleeps its akashic sleep in the Kama-loka. This state lasts from a few hours, (rarely less) days, weeks, months – sometimes to several years. All this according to the entity, its mental status at the moment of death, to the character of its death etc. That remembrance will return slowly and gradually toward the end of the gestation, (to the entity or Ego) still more slowly but far more imperfectly and *incompletely* to the *shell*, and *fully* to the Ego at the moment of its entrance into the Devachan. *ML 24B, pp. 186-187*

(14) When life has retired from the last particle in the brain matter, his perceptive faculties become extinct forever, his spiritual powers of cogitation and volition – (all those faculties in short which are neither inherent in, nor acquirable by organic matter) – for the time being. His *Mayavi rupa* may be often thrown into objectivity, as in the cases of apparitions after death; but, unless it is projected with the knowledge of, whether latent or potential, or, owing to the intensity of the desire to see or appear to someone shooting through the dying brain, the apparition will be simply – automatical. It will not be due to any sympathetic attraction, or to any act of volition, and no more than the reflection of a person passing unconsciously near a mirror is due to the desire of the latter. *ML 20C, pp. 128-129*

Devachan

(1) "Who goes to Devachan?" The personal Ego of course, but beautified, purified, holy. Every Ego – the combination of the sixth and seventh principles – which, after the period of unconscious gestation is reborn into the Devachan, is of necessity as innocent and pure as a newborn babe. The fact of his being reborn at all, shows the preponderance of good over evil in his old personality. And while the karma (of evil) steps aside for the time being, to follow him in his future earth reincarnation, he brings along with him but the karma of his good deeds, words, and thoughts into this Devachan. "Bad" is a relative term for us – as you were told more than once before – and the Law of Retribution is the only law that never errs. Hence, all those who have not slipped down into the mire of unredeemable sin and bestiality – go to the Devachan. They will have to pay for their sins, voluntarily and involuntarily, later on. Meanwhile they are rewarded; receive the *effects* of the *causes* produced by them.
ML 16, pp. 100 - 101

(2) Of course it is a *state*, one, so to say, of *intense selfishness*, during which an *Ego* reaps the reward of his *unselfishness* on earth. He is completely engrossed in the bliss of all his personal earthly affections, preferences and thoughts, and gathers in the fruit of his meritorious actions. No pain, no grief nor even the shadow of a sorrow comes to darken the bright horizon of his unalloyed happiness: *for, it is a state of perpetual "Maya."*... Since the conscious perception of one's *personality* on earth is but an evanescent dream, that sense will be equally that of a dream in the Devachan – only a hundred fold intensified. So much so, indeed, that the happy Ego is unable to see through the veil the evils, sorrows and woes to which those it loved on earth may be subjected. It lives in the sweet dream with its loved ones –

whether gone before, or yet remaining on earth; it has them near itself, as happy, as blissful and as innocent as the disembodied dreamer himself; and yet, apart from rare visions, the denizens of our gross planet feel it not. It is in this, during such a condition of complete *Maya* that the Souls or astral Egos of pure, loving sensitives, labouring under the same illusion, think their loved ones come down to them on earth, while it is their own Spirits that are raised towards those in the Devachan. *ML 16, p. 101*

(3) Nature cheats no more the *devachanee* than she does the living, physical man. Nature provides for him far more real bliss and happiness there than she does *here*, where all the conditions of evil and chance are against him, and his inherent helplessness – that of a straw violently blown hither and thither by every remorseless wind – has made unalloyed happiness on this earth an utter impossibility for the human being, whatever his chances and conditions may be. Rather call this life an ugly, horrid nightmare, and you will be right. To call the Devachan existence a "dream" in any other sense but that of a conventional term, well suited to your languages all full of misnomers – is to renounce for ever the knowledge of the esoteric doctrine – the sole custodian of truth. *ML 25, p. 195*

(4) Yes, there are great varieties in the Devachan states ... As many varieties of bliss, as on earth there are shades of perception and of capability to appreciate such reward. It is an ideated paradise, in each case of the Ego's own making, and by him filled with the scenery, crowded with the incidents, and thronged with the people he would expect to find in such a sphere of compensative bliss. And it is that variety which guides the temporary personal *Ego* into the current which will lead him to be reborn, in a lower or higher condition in the next world of causes. Everything is so harmoniously adjusted in nature – especially in the subjective world, that no mistake can be ever committed by

the Tathagata – or Dhyan Chohans – who guide the impulse.
ML 16, p. 102

(5) The question is now sufficiently explained, I believe: the sixth and seventh principles, apart from the rest, constitute the eternal, imperishable, but also *unconscious* "Monad." To awaken in it to life the latent consciousness, especially that of *personal* individuality, requires the monad plus the highest attributes of the fifth ... and it is that which makes the ethereal *Ego* that lives and enjoys bliss in the Devachan. Spirit, or the unalloyed emanations of the ONE – the latter forming with the seventh and sixth principles the highest triad – neither of the two emanations are capable of assimilating but that which is good, pure, and holy; hence, no sensual, material or unholy recollection can follow the purified memory of the *Ego* to the region of Bliss. The Karma for these recollections of evil deeds and thought will reach the Ego when it changes *its personality*, in the following world of causes. The *Monad*, or the "Spiritual Individuality," remains untainted in all cases. "No sorrow or Pain for those born there, (in the *Rupa-Loka* of Devachan) for this is the Pure-Land, All the regions in space possess such lands (*Sakwala*) but this land of Bliss is the most pure." In the *Djana Prasthana Shaster*, it is said, "By personal purity and earnest meditation, we overleap the limits of the World of Desire and enter in the World of Forms."
ML 18, p. 104-105

(6) Most emphatically "the Devachan is *not* solely the heritage of adepts," and most decidedly there is a "heaven" – if you must use this astro-geographical Christian term – for "an immense number of those who have gone before." But "the life of Earth" can be *watched* by none of these, for reasons of the Law of Bliss, plus *Maya*, already given. *ML 16, p. 106*

(7) "Bardo" is the period between death and rebirth – and may

last from a few years to a kalpa. It is divided into three subperiods. (1) when the *Ego*, delivered of its mortal coil, enters into *Kama-Loka* (the abode of Elementaries.) (2) when it enters into its "Gestation State." (3) when it is reborn in the *Rupa-Loka* of Devachan. Sub-period (1) may last from a few minutes to a *number* of years – the phrase "a few years" becomes puzzling and utterly worthless without a more complete explanation; Sub-period (2) is very long, as you say, longer sometimes than you may even imagine, yet proportionate to the *Ego's* spiritual stamina; Sub-period (3) lasts in proportion to the good KARMA, after which the monad is again reincarnated. The *Agama Sutra* saying: – "In all these *Rupa-Lokas*, the Devas (Spirits) are equally subjected to birth, decay, old age and death," means only that an Ego is borne thither, then begins fading out and finally "dies," i.e. falls into that unconscious condition which precedes rebirth; and ends the Sloka with these words: "As the devas emerge from these heavens, they enter the lower world again;" i.e. they leave a world of bliss to be reborn in a world of causes.
ML 16, pp. 105-106

(8) Devachan is a state, not a locality. Kama-Loka, Rupa-Loka, and Arupa-Loka are the three spheres of ascending spirituality in which the several groups of subjective entities find their attractions. In the Kama-Loka (semi-physical sphere) dwell the shells, like victims and suicides; and this sphere is divided into innumerable regions and sub-regions corresponding to the mental states of the comers at their hour of death. This is the glorious "Summer-land" of the Spiritualists, to whose horizons is limited the vision of their best seers – vision imperfect and deceptive because untrained and non-guided by *Alaya Vijnana* (hidden knowledge). Who in the west knows anything of true *Sahalokadhatu*, the mysterious Chiliocosm out of the many regions of which but three can be given out to the outside world, the *Tribhuvana* (three worlds) namely: Kama, Rupa, and Arupa-

Lokas. *ML 25, pp.198-199*

(9) (A. P. Sinnett's Question: Does this state of spiritual beatitude endure for years? For decades? For centuries?)

Answer: For years, decades, centuries and millenniums, often-times multiplied by something more. It all depends upon the duration of Karma. Fill with oil Den's little cup and a city reservoir of water, and lighting both see which burns the longer. The *Ego* is the wick and Karma the oil, the difference in the quantity of the latter (in the cup and the reservoir) suggesting to you the great difference in the duration of various *Karmas*.

ML 16, p. 106

(10) Every effect must be proportionate to the cause. And, as man's terms of incarnate existence bear but a small proportion to his periods of internatal existence in the manvantaric cycle, so the good thoughts, words, and deeds of any one of these "lives" on a globe are causative of effects, the working out of which requires far more time than the evolution of the causes occupied. Therefore when you read in the Jats and other *fabulous* stories of the Buddhist Scriptures that this or the other good action was rewarded by Kalpas of several figures of bliss, do not smile at the absurd exaggeration, but bear in mind what I have said. From a small seed, you know, sprung a tree whose life endures now for 22 centuries: I mean the Anuradha-pura *Bo* tree. *ML 16, p. 106*

(11) *Most* of those, whom you may call, if you like, candidates for *Devachan* – die and are reborn in the Kama-Loka "without remembrance," though (and just because) they do get some of it back in the Devachan. Nor can we call it a full, but only a *partial* remembrance.

You would hardly call "remembrance" a dream of yours; some particular scene or scenes, within those narrow limits you would find enclosed a few persons – those whom you loved best, with an undying love, that holy feeling that alone survives, and – not the slightest recollection of any other events or scenes? *Love* and *Hatred* are the only *immortal* feelings, the only survivors from the wreck of *Ye-dhamma*, or the phenomenal world. Imagine yourself then, in Devachan with those you may have loved with such immortal love; with the familiar, shadowy scenes connected with them for a background and – a perfect blank for everything else relating to your interior, political, literary and social life. And then, in the face of that spiritual, purely cogitative existence, of that unalloyed felicity which, in proportion with the intensity of the feelings that *created* it, lasts from a few to several thousand years, – call it the "personal remembrance of A.P. Sinnett" – if you can. *ML 20, p. 127*

(12) Dreadfully monotonous! – you may think. – Not in the least – I answer. Have you experienced monotony during – say – that moment which you considered *then* and *now* so consider it – as the moment of the highest bliss you have ever felt? Of course not. Well, no more will you experience it there, in that passage through the Eternity in which a million of years is no longer than a second.

There, where there is no consciousness of an external world, there can be no discernment to mark differences, hence no perception of contrasts of monotony or variety; nothing in short, outside that immortal feeling of love and sympathetic attraction whose seeds are planted in the fifth, whose plants blossom luxuriantly in around the fourth, but whose roots have to penetrate deep into the sixth principle, if it would survive the lowest groups. *ML 20C, pp. 127*

(13) The Devachan, or land of "Sukhavati," is *allegorically* described by our Lord Buddha himself. What he said may be found in the *Shan-Mun-yih-Tung*. Says Tathagata:–

"Many thousand myriads of systems of worlds beyond this (ours) there is a region of Bliss called *Sukhavati* ... This region is encircled with seven rows of vast curtains, seven rows of waving trees; this holy abode of Arhats is governed by the Tathagatas (Dhyan Chohans) and is possessed by the Bodhisatwas. It hath *seven* precious lakes, in the midst of which flow crystalline waters having *"seven and one"* properties, or distinctive qualities (the seven principles emanating from the ONE). This, O Sariputra is the 'Devachan.' Its divine Udumbara flower casts a root *in the shadow of every earth*, and blossoms for all those who reach it. Those born in the blessed region are truly felicitous, there are no more griefs or sorrows *in that cycle* for them ... Myriads of Spirits (Lhas) resort there for rest and then *return* to their own regions. Again, O, Sariputra, in that land of joy many born in it are *Avaivartyas....*" etc. etc. **ML 16, pp. 99-100**

(14) Certainly, the new *Ego*, once it is reborn, (in Devachan – Ed.) retains for a certain time – proportionate to its Earth life, a "complete recollection of his life on earth." But it can *never* return on earth, from the Devachan, nor has the latter even omitting all "anthropomorphic ideas of God" – any resemblance to the paradise or heaven of any religion, and it is H.P.B.'s literary fancy that suggested to her the wonderful comparison. **ML 16, p. 100**

(15) Why should it be supposed that Devachan is a monotonous condition only because some moment of earthly sensation is indefinitely perpetuated – stretched, so to say, throughout eons? It is not, it cannot be so. This would be contrary to all analogies and antagonistic to the law of effects, under which results are proportioned to antecedent energies.

To make it clear, you must keep in mind that there are two fields of causal manifestation, to wit: the objective and subjective. So the grossest energies, those which operate in the heavier or denser conditions of matter, manifest objectively in physical life, their outcome being the new personality of each birth, included within the grand cycle of the evoluting individuality. The moral and spiritual activities find their sphere of effects in "Devachan."

For example, the vices, physical attractions – say, of a philosopher, may result in the birth of a new philosopher, a king, a merchant, a rich Epicurean, or any other personality whose make-up was inevitable from the preponderating proclivities of the being in the next birth. Bacon, for inst: whom a poet called – "The wisest, greatest, *meanest* of mankind" – might reappear in his next incarnation as a greedy money-getter, with extraordinary intellectual capacities. But the moral and spiritual qualities of the previous Bacon would also have to find a field in which their energies could expand themselves. Devachan is such a field.

Hence – all the great plans of moral reform, of intellectual and spiritual research into abstract principles of nature, all the divine aspirations, would, in Devachan come to fruition, and the abstract entity previously known as the great Chancellor (Bacon) would occupy itself in this inner world of its own preparation, living, if not quite what one would call a conscious existence, at least a dream of such realistic vividness that none of the life-realities could ever match it. And this "dream" lasts until Karma is satisfied in that direction, the ripple of force reaches the edge of its cyclic basin, and the being moves into the next area of causes. This, it may find in the same world as before, or another, according to his or her stage of progression through the necessary rings and rounds of human development.
ML 25, pp. 191-92

(16) No, there are no clocks, no timepieces in Devachan, my esteemed chela, though the whole Cosmos is a gigantic chronometer in one sense. Nor do we mortals, – *ici bas meme* – take much, if any, cognizance of *time* during periods of happiness and bliss, and find them ever too short; a fact that does not in the

least prevent us from enjoying that happiness all the same – when it does come. Have you ever given a thought to this little possibility that, perhaps, it is because their cup of bliss is full to its brim, that the "devachanee" loses "all sense of the lapse of time" and that it is something that those who land in *Avitchi* do not, though as much as the *devachanee*, the *Avitchee* has no cognizance of *time* – i.e. of our earthly calculations of periods of time? *ML 25, pp. 193- 194*

(17) Yes, certainly there *is* "a change of occupation," a continual change in Devachan, just as much – and far more – as there is in the life of any man or woman, who happens to follow his or *her whole life,* one sole occupation whatever it may be; with that difference, that to *the Devachanee* his special occupation is always pleasant and fills his life with rapture. Change there must be, for that dream-life is but the fruition, the harvest-time of those psychic seed-germs dropped from the tree of physical existence in our moments of dreams and hopes, fancy glimpses of bliss and happiness stifled in an ungrateful social soil, blooming in the rosy dawn of Devachan and ripening under its ever fructifying sky. No failures *there*, no disappointments!

If man had but *one* single moment of ideal happiness and experience during his life – as you think – even then, if Devachan exists, it could not be as you erroneously suppose, the indefinite prolongation of that "single moment" but the infinite develop-ments, the various incidents and events, based upon, and outflowing from that one "single moment" or moments, as the case may be; all in short that would suggest itself to the "dreamer's" fancy. That one note, as I said, struck from the lyre of life, would form but the Key-note of the being's subjective state, and work out into numberless harmonic tones and semi-tones of psychic phantasmagoria. There – all unrealized hopes, aspirations, dreams, become fully realized, and the *dreams* of the objective become the *realities* of the subjective existence. And there, behind the curtain of Maya, its vapours and deceptive appearances are perceived by the adept, who has learnt the great secret: how to penetrate thus deeply into the Arcana of being. *ML 25, p. 197*

(18) ... there is no contradiction in saying that the ego, once reborn in the Devachan, "retains for a certain time, proportionate to its earth life, a *complete recollection* of his (Spiritual) life on earth." *ML 24B, p. 187*

(19) ... the sensations, perceptions and ideation of a *devachanee* in *Rupa-Loka*, will, of course, be of a less subjective nature than they would be in *Arupa*-Loka, in both of which the devachanic experiences will vary in their presentation to the subject-entity, not only as regards form, colour, and substance, but also in their formative potentialities. But not even the most exalted experience of a monad, in the highest devachanic state in *Arupa*-Loka (the last of the seven states) – is comparable to that perfectly subjective condition of pure spirituality from which the monad emerged to "descend into matter," and to which at the completion of the grand cycle it must return. Nor is Nirvana itself comparable to Para-Nirvana. *ML 25, p. 199*

(20) The stay in Devachan is proportioned to the unfinished psychic impulses originating in earth life: those persons whose attractions were preponderatingly material, will sooner be drawn back into rebirth by the force of *Tanha*. As our London opponent truly remarks, these subjects (metaphysical) are only partly for understanding. A higher faculty belonging to the higher life must see, and it is truly impossible to force it upon one's understanding – merely in words. One must see with his spiritual eye, hear with his Dharmakayic ear, feel with the sensations of his *Ashta-vijnana* (spiritual "I") before he can comprehend this doctrine fully; otherwise it may but increase

one's "discomfort" and add to his knowledge very little.
ML 25, p.200

(21) The Devachan State, I repeat, can be as little described or explained by giving a however minute and graphic description of the state of one ego taken at random, as all the human lives collectively could be described by the "Life of Napolean" or that of any other man. There are millions of various states of happiness and misery, emotional states having their source in the physical as well as the spiritual faculties and senses, and only the latter surviving. An honest labourer will feel differently from an honest millionaire. Miss. Nightingale's state will differ considerably from that of a young bride, who dies before the consummation of what she regards as happiness. The two former love their families; the philanthropist – humanity; the girl centres the whole world in her future husband; the *melomaniac* knows of no *higher* state of bliss and happiness than music – the most divine and *spiritual* of arts.

The Devachan merges from its highest into its lowest degree – by insensible gradations ... Remember every feeling is relative. There is neither good nor evil, happiness nor misery per se.
ML 24B, pp.187-188

Dhyan Chohans (Angels) and Devas

(1) Seven groups ... form the principle divisions of the Dwellers subjective world around us. It is in stock No. 1 (i.e. the *Rupa devas* – Dhyan Chohans, having form – Ed.) that are the *intelligent* Rulers of this world of Matter, and who, with all this intelligence are but the blindly obedient instruments of the ONE; the active agents of a Passive Principle. *ML 16, p. 107*

(2) Every such "world" within the Sphere of Effects has a Tathagata or "Dhyan Chohan" – to protect and watch over, not to interfere with it. *ML 16, p. 108*

(3) There are Dhyan Chohans and "Chohans of Darkness," not what they term *devils* but imperfect "Intelligences" who have never been born on this or any other earth or sphere, any more than the "Dhyan Chohans" have, and who will never belong to the "builders of the Universe," the pure Planetary Intelligences, who preside at every *Manvantara*, while the Dark Chohans preside at the *Pralayas* ....

As all in this universe is contrast (I cannot translate it better) so the light of the Dhyan Chohans and their pure intelligence is contrasted by the "*Ma-Mo* Chohans" – and their destructive intelligence. These are the gods the Hindus and Christians and Mahomedans and all others of bigoted religions and sects worship and so long as their influence is upon their devotees, we would no more think of associating with or counteracting them in their work than we do the Red-Caps on earth, whose evil results we try to palliate but whose work we have no right to meddle with, so long as they do not cross our path

... (No more can the Dhyan Chohans impede the work of the Mamo Chohans, for their Law is *darkness, ignorance, destruction* etc., as that of the former is Light, knowledge and creation. The

Dhyan Chohans answer to *Buddh*, Divine Wisdom and Life in blissful knowledge ....) *ML 34, pp. 462-463*

(4) And if at the end of all things – say in some millions of millions of years hence, Spirit will have to rest in its pure, *impersonal* non-existence, as the ONE or the Absolute, still there must be *"some* good" in the cyclic process, since every purified Ego has the chance in the long *interims*, between objective being upon the planets, to *exist* as a Dhyan Chohan – from the lowest "Devanchee" to the highest Planetary – enjoying the fruits of its collective lives."
ML 23B, p. 158

(5) ... *Adi-Buddhi*, the all pervading supreme and absolute intelligence with its periodically manifesting Divinity – "Avalokiteshvara" – the mystic name given by us to the hosts of the Dhyan Chohans (N.B. the solar Dhyan Chohans or the hosts of only our solar system) taken collectively, which host represents the mother source, the aggregate amount of all the intelligences that were, are, or ever will be, whether on our string of man bearing planets or on any part or portion of our solar system. And this will bring you, by analogy, to see that in its turn Adi-Buddhi (as its very name translated literally implies) is the aggregate intelligence of the universal intelligences, including that of the Dhyan Chohans, even of the highest order. That is all I dare now to tell you on this special subject, as I fear I have already transcended the limit. *ML 15, p. 90*

(6) The Dhyan Chohans, who have no hand in the guidance of the living human Ego, protect the helpless victim when it is violently thrust out of its element into a new one, before it is matured and made fit and ready for it. We tell you what we know, *for we are made to learn it through personal experience.*
ML 20C, p. 131

(7) As we have our Dhyan Chohans so have they (the vegetable and animal kingdoms) in their several kingdoms elemental guardians and are as well taken care of in the mass as is humanity in the mass. *ML 15, p. 97*

(8) Now there are – there *must* be "failures" in the ethereal races of the many classes of Dhyan Chohans or Devas, as well as among men. But still, as these failures are too far progressed and spiritualized to be thrown back forcibly from their Dhyan Chohanship, into the vortex of a new primordial evolution through the lower kingdoms – this then happens. When a new solar system is to be evolved these Dhyan Chohans are (remember the Hindu allegory of the *Fallen devas,* hurled by Siva into Antarala, who are allowed by Parabrahm to consider it as an intermediate state, where they may prepare themselves by a series of rebirths in that sphere for a higher state – a new regeneration) borne in by the influx "ahead" of the elementals and remain as a latent or inactive spiritual force in the aura of the nascent world of a new system, until the stage of human evolution is reached. Then Karma has reached them and they will have to accept to the last drop in the bitter cup of retribution. Then they become an active Force and commingle with the Elementals, or progressed entities of the pure animal kingdom, to develop little by little the full type of humanity. In this commingling they lose their high intelligence and spirituality of Devaship to regain them in the end of the seventh ring in the seventh round." *ML 14, p. 87*

(9) In esoteric teachings "Brahma," "Pitri," and "Deva" lokas are states of consciousness, belonging to the various ethereal hierarchies or classes of Dhyanis and Pitris (the "creators" and "ancestors" of Humanity) and of Devas – some far higher than man, (spiritually) some – among the Deva classes – far behind on the descending arc of evolution, and only destined to reach the

human stage in a future Manvantara. Exoterically these lokas represent Nirvana, Devachan and the Astral world. The meaning of the terms Devachan and Deva-loka, are identical; *"chan"* and *"loka"* equally signifying *place* or *abode*. "Deva" is a word too indiscriminately used in Eastern writings, and is at times merely a blind. *ML 69, p. 373*

(10) So you see, the insurmountable difficulties in the way of attaining not only *Absolute* but even primary knowledge in Occult Science for one situated as you are. How could you make yourself understood – command in fact, those semi-intelligent Forces whose means of communicating with us are not through spoken words but through sounds and colours, in correlations between the vibrations of the two? For sound, light, and colours are the main factors in forming these grades of Intelligences, these beings, of whose very existence you have no conception, nor *are you allowed* to believe in them – Atheists and Christians, materialists and Spiritualists, all bringing forward their respective arguments against such a belief – Science objecting stronger than either of these to such a "degrading superstition!" *ML 8, pp. 30-31*

(11) The last seventh Race will have its Buddha as every one of its predecessors had; but, its adepts will be far higher than any of the present race, for among them will abide the future Planetary, the Dhyan Chohan whose duty it will be to instruct or "refresh the memory" of the first race of the fifth Round men after this planet's future obscuration. *ML 23B, p. 157*

Diet

(1) When the "Seeress" (Anna Kingsford) is made to reveal that "immortality is by no means a matter of course for all" ... that "souls shrink away and expire," it being "the nature of them to *burn out* and expend themselves" ... etc., she is delivering herself of *actual* incontrovertible *facts*. And why? Because both Maitland and herself, as well as *their circle* – are *strict vegetarians*, while S.M. (Stainton Moses) is a flesh-eater and a wine and liquor drinker. Never will the Spiritualists find reliable, trustworthy mediums and Seers (not even to a degree) so long as the latter and "their circle" will saturate themselves with animal blood, and the millions of *infusoria* of the fermented fluids.

Since my return I found it *impossible* for me to breathe – even in the atmosphere of the *Headquarters*! M. had to interfere, and to force the whole household to give up meat; and they had, all of them, to be purified and thoroughly cleansed with disinfecting drugs before I could even help myself to my letters. And I am not, as you may imagine, half as sensitive to the loathsome emanations as a tolerably respectable disembodied shell would be – leaving out of question a real PRESENCE, though but a "projecting" one. In a year or so perchance earlier, I may find myself *hardened* again. At present I find it *impossible* – do what I may. *ML 48, p. 276*

(2) ... You use too much sugar in your food. Take fruit, bread, tea, coffee and milk and use them as freely as you would like to, but no chocolate, fat, pastry, and but very little sugar. The fermentation produced by it, especially in that climate of yours is very injurious. *ML 127, p. 455*

(3) I (K.H.) will try my best to make of him a vegetarian and a teetotaller. *Total* abstinence from flesh and liquor are very wisely

prescribed by Mr. Hume, if he would have good results. In good hands, E. (William Eglinton) will do an immense good to the T.S. in India, but for this he has to go through a training of purification. M. had to prepare him for six weeks before his departure; otherwise it would have been impossible for me to project into his atmosphere even the *reflection* of my "double." I told you already, my kind friend, that what he saw was *not me*. Nor will I be able to project that reflection for you – unless he is thoroughly purified. *ML 95, pp. 429-430*

(4) Concerning Eglinton I will beg you to wait for developments. In regard to your kind lady (A.O. Hume's wife) the question is more serious and I cannot undertake the responsibility of making her change her diet as ABRUPTLY as you suggest. Flesh and meat she can give up at any time as it can never hurt; as for liquor with which Mrs. H. has long been sustaining her system, You yourself know the fatal effects it may produce in an enfeebled constitution, were the latter to be suddenly deprived of its stimulant. Her physical life is not a real existence backed by a reserve of vital force, but a factitious one, fed upon the spirit of liquor, however small the quantity. While a strong constitution might rally after the first shock of such a change as proposed, the chances are that she would fall into a decline. So would she if opium or arsenic were her chief sustenance. *ML 6, pp. 64-65*

Discipline and the Spiritual Path

(1) Fasting, meditation, chastity of thought, word and deed; silence for certain periods of time, to enable nature herself to speak to him who comes to her for information; government of the animal passions and impulses; utter unselfishness of intention, the use of certain incense and fumigations for physiological purposes have been published as the means since the days of Plato and Iamblichus in the West and since the far earlier times of our Indian *Rishis*. How these must be complied with to suit each individual temperament is, of course, a matter for his own experiment and the watchful care of his tutor or *Guru*. Such is in fact part of his course of discipline, and his Guru or initiator can but assist him with his experience and will power but can do no more *until the last and Supreme initiation. **ML 49, p. 283***

(2) The truth is that, 'till the neophyte attains to the condition necessary for that degree of Illumination to which, and for which, he is entitled and fitted, most, *if not all* of the Secrets are *Incommunicable.* The receptivity must be equal to the desire to instruct. The illumination *must come from within.* 'Till then no hocus pocus of incantations, or mummery of appliances, no metaphysical lectures or discussions, no self-imposed penance can give it. All these are but means to an end, and all we can do is to direct the use of such means as have been found empirically by the experience of ages to conduce to the required object. And this was and has been no *secret* for thousands of years.
ML 49, p. 283

(3) You were told ... the path to Occult Sciences has to be trodden laboriously and crossed at the danger of life: that every new step in it leading to the final goal is surrounded by pitfalls and cruel thorns; that the pilgrim who ventures upon it is made first to

confront and conquer the thousand and one furies, who keep watch over its adamantine gates and entrance – furies called Doubt, Skepticism, Scorn, Ridicule, Envy and finally Temptation – especially the latter; and that he who would see beyond had to first destroy this living wall; that he must be possessed of a heart and soul clad in steel, and of an iron, never failing determination and yet be meek and gentle, humble and have shut out from his heart every human passion that leads to evil. Are you all this? Have you ever begun a course of training which would lead to it? No; you know it as I do. You are not born for it; nor are you in a position – a family man with wife and child to support, with work to do – fitted in any way for the life of an ascetic ... Then why should you complain that powers are not given to you, that even *proof of our own powers* begin to fail you, etc.? True, you have offered several times to give up meat and drink, and I have refused. Since you cannot become a regular *chela*, why should you? I thought you had understood all this long ago; that you had resigned yourself, satisfied to wait patiently for future developments and for my personal freedom. *ML 62, pp. 351-352*

(4) It is true that the married man cannot be an adept, yet without striving to become a *"Raja* Yogi" he can acquire certain powers and do as much good to mankind and often more, by remaining within the precincts of this world of his. Therefore, we shall not ask you to precipitately change fixed habits of life, before the full conviction of its necessity and advantage has possessed you. You are a man left to lead himself and may be so left with safety. Your resolution is taken to deserve much: time will effect the rest. There are more ways than one for acquiring occult knowledge. "Many are the grains of incense destined for one and the same altar; one falls sooner into the fire, the other later – the difference of time is nothing," remarked a great man when he was refused admission and supreme initiation into the mysteries. *ML 4, p. 17*

(5) I will not tell you to give up this or that, for, unless you exhibit *beyond any doubt* the presence in you of the necessary germs, it would be as useless as it would be cruel. But I say – TRY.

Ml 5, p. 20

(6) If you are a true Anglo-Saxon, no obstacle will daunt your zeal; and unless my Eye has been dimmed, this is your character – *au fond*. We have one word for all aspirants: TRY. **ML 35, p. 247**

(7) Look around you, my friend: see the "three poisons" raging within the heart of man – anger, greed, delusion, and the five obscurities envy, passion, vacillation, sloth, and unbelief – ever preventing them seeing truth. They will never get rid of the pollution of their vain, wicked hearts, nor perceive the spiritual portion of themselves. Will you not try – for the sake of short-ening the distance between us – to disentangle yourself from the net of life and death in which they are all caught, to cherish less – lust and desire. *ML 45, pp. 264-265*

(8) The pathway through earth life leads through many conflicts and trials, but he who does naught to conquer them can expect no triumph. Let then the anticipation of a fuller introduction into our mysteries, under more congenial circumstances, the creation of which depends *entirely upon yourself,* inspire you with patience to wait for, perseverance to press on to and full preparation to receive the blissful consummation of all your desires.

ML 42, p. 258

(9) … *you alone*, have to weave your destiny … Believe me: we may yet walk along the arduous path together. We may yet meet. But if at all, it has to be along and on – those "adamantine rocks with which our occult rules surround us" – never *outside* them, however bitterly we may complain. No, *never* can we pursue our

further journey – *if* hand in hand – along that high way, crowded thoroughfare, which encircles them, and on which Spiritualists and mystics, prophets and seers elbow each other now-day. Yea, verily, the motley crowd of candidates may shout for an eternity to come, for the *Sesame* to open. It never will, so long as they keep outside those rules. *ML 48, p. 273*

(10) Doubt not my friend: it is but from the very top of those "adamantine rocks" of ours, not at their foot, that one is ever enabled to perceive the whole Truth, by embracing the whole limitless horizon. And though they may seem to you to be standing in your way, it is simply because you have failed to discover, even so much as suspect, the reason and the operation of those laws; hence they appear so cold and merciless and selfish in your sight; although yourself have intuitively recognised in them the outcome of ages of wisdom. Nevertheless, were one but to obediently follow them out, they could be made to yield to one's desire and give to him all he asks of them.
ML 48, p. 274

(11) Remember: too anxious expectation is not only tedious, but dangerous too. Each warmer and quicker throb of the heart wears so much of life away. The passions, the affections are not to be indulged in him by him who seeks TO KNOW; for they "wear out the earthly body with their own secret power; and he who would gain his aim – *must be cold*." He must not even desire too earnestly or too passionately the object he would reach; else the very wish will prevent the possibility of its fulfilment ....
ML 48, p. 274

(12) He who would lift high the banner of mysticism and proclaim its reign near at hand, must give the example to others. He must be the first to change his modes of life; and regarding the study of occult mysteries as the upper step in the ladder of

Knowledge, must loudly proclaim it such, despite exact science and the opposition of society. "The Kingdom of Heaven is obtained by force" say the Christian mystics. It is but with armed hand, and ready to either conquer or perish, that the modern mystic can hope to achieve his object. *ML 2, pp. 6-7*

(13) If your efforts will teach the world but one single letter from the alphabet of Truth – that Truth which once pervaded the whole world – your reward will not miss you. *ML 31, p. 242*

(14) Is any of you so eager for knowledge and the beneficent powers it confers, as to be ready to leave your world and come into ours? Then let him come, but he must not think to return until the seal of the mysteries has locked his lips, even against the chances of his own weakness or indiscretion. Let him come by all means, as the pupil to the master, and without conditions; or let him wait, as so many others have, and be satisfied with such crumbs of knowledge as may fall in his way. *ML 2, p. 9*

(15) Does it seem to you a small thing that the past year has been spent only in your "family duties?" Nay, but what better cause for reward, what better discipline than the daily and hourly performance of duty? Believe me, my "pupil," the man or woman who is placed by Karma in the midst of small, plain duties and sacrifices and loving kindness, will through these faithfully fulfilled rise to the larger measure of Duty, Sacrifice and Charity to all humanity – what better path towards the enlightenment you are striving after than the daily conquest of Self, the perseverance in spite of want of visible psychic progress, the bearing of illfortune with that serene fortitude which turns it to spiritual advantage – since good and evil are not to be measured by events on the lower or physical plane.

Be not discouraged that your practice falls below your aspirations, yet be content with *admitting* this, since you clearly recognise that your tendency is too often towards mental and moral indolence, rather inclining to drift with the currents of life, than to steer a direct course of your own. Your spiritual progress is far greater than you know or can realize, and you do well to believe that such development is in itself more important than its realization by your physical plane consciousness. I will not now enter into other subjects, since this is but a line of sympathetic recognition of your efforts, and of earnest encouragement to hold a calm and brave spirit toward outward events in the present, and a hopeful spirit for the future on all planes .... *ML 68, p. 372*

Elementals and Elementaries

(1) I can assure you it is not worth your while now to study the true natures of the "Ernests" and "Joeys" and "other guides" as unless you become acquainted with the evolution of the *corruptions* of elemental dross, and those of the seven principles in man – you would ever find yourself at a loss to understand what they really are; there are no written statutes for them, and they can hardly be expected to pay their friends and admirers the compliment of truth, silence or forbearing. If some are related to them as some *soulless* physical mediums are – they shall meet. If not – better leave them alone. They gravitate but to their likes – the mediums; and their relation is not made but *forced* by foolish and sinful phenomena-mongers. They are both elementaries and elementals – at best a low, mischievous, degrading jangle. You want to embrace too much knowledge at once, my dear friend; you cannot attain at a bound all the mysteries.
ML 17, pp. 118- 119

(2) Your house, good friend, has a colony of Elementaries quartering in it, and to a sensitive like her (Laura C. Holloway) it was as dangerous an atmosphere to exist in as would be a fever cemetery to one subject to morbific physical influences. You should be more than ordinarily careful when you get back not to encourage sensitiveness in your household, not to admit more than can be helped the visits of known medium sensitives.

It would be well also to burn wood-fires in the rooms now and then, and carry about as fumigators open vessels (braziers?) with burning wood. You might also ask Damodar to send you some bundles of incense sticks for you to use for this purpose. These are helps, but the best means to drive out unwelcome guests of this sort is to live purely in deed and thought. The talismans you have had given you, will also powerfully aid you *if you keep your confidences in them and us unbroken.* **ML 55, p. 323**

(3) Now the causes producing the "new being" and determining the nature of *Karma* are, as already said – *Trishna* (or "Tanha") – thirst, desire for sentient existence and *Upadana* – which is the realization or consummation of *Trishna* or that desire. And both of these the medium helps to awaken and to develop … in an Elementary, be he a suicide or a victim. The rule is, that a person who dies a natural death will remain from "a few hours to several short years" within the earth's attraction, i.e. in the *Kama-Loka*. But exceptions are in the case of suicides and those who die a violent death in general. Hence one of such Egos, for instance, who was destined to live, say 80 or 90 years, but who either killed himself or was killed by some accident, let us suppose at the age of 20 – would have to pass in the *Kama-Loka* not "a few years," but in his case 60 or 70 years as an Elementary, or rather an "earth-walker," since he is not, unfortunately for him, even a *"shell."* Happy, thrice happy, in comparison, are those disembodied entities who sleep their long slumber and live in dream in the bosom of Space! **ML 16, p. 112**

(4) We see a vast difference between the qualities of two equal amounts of energy expended by two men, of whom one, let us suppose, is on his way to his daily quiet work, and another on the way to denounce a fellow creature at the police station, while the men of science see none. And we – not they – see a specific difference between the energy in the motion of the wind and that of a revolving wheel.

And why? Because every thought of man, upon being evolved, passes into the inner world and becomes an active entity by associating itself – coalescing, we might term it – with an elemental; that is to say with one of the semi-intelligent forces of the kingdoms. It survives as an active intelligence, a creature of the mind's begetting, for a longer or shorter period, proportionate with the original intensity of the cerebral action which generated it.

Thus a good thought is perpetuated as an active beneficent power; an evil one as a maleficent demon. And so man is continually peopling his current in space with a world of his own, crowded with the offspring of his fancies, desires, impulses and passions, a current which reacts upon any sensitive or and nervous organisation which comes in contact with it, in proportion to its dynamic intensity. The Buddhist calls this his "Skandha," the Hindu gives it the name of "Karma;" the adept evolves these shapes consciously, other men throw them off unconsciously.

First Letter of K.H. to A.O. Hume,
Combined Chronology by M. Conger, pp. 32-33

Healing and Mesmerism

(1) There is no reason why you should *not* "attempt mesmeric cures" by the help, not of your locket but the power of your own will. Without this latter in energetic function, no locket will do much good. The hair in it is in itself but an "accumulator" of the energy of him (K.H.) who grew it and can no more cure of itself than stored electricity can turn a wheel, until liberated and conducted to the objective point. Set your will in motion and you at once draw upon the person upon whose head it (the hair not the will) grew, through the psychic current which ever runs between himself and his severed tress.

To heal diseases it is not indispensable, however desirable, that the psychopathist should be absolutely pure; there are many in Europe and elsewhere who are not. If the healing be done under the impulse of perfect benevolence, unmixed with any latent selfishness, the philanthropist sets up a current, which runs like a fine thrill through the sixth condition of matter (buddhi) and is felt by him whom you summon to your help, if not at that moment engaged in some work which compels him to be repellent to all extraneous influences.

The possession of a lock of an adept's hair is of course a decided advantage, as a better tempered sword is to the soldier in battle; but the measure of its actual help to the psychopathist will be in ratio with the degree of will power he cites in himself, and the degree of psychic purity in his motive. The talisman and his *Buddhi* are in sympathy. *ML 59, p. 342*

(2) I am (Djual Khool) personally permitted ... to thank you very warmly for the genuine sympathy which you felt for me at the time when a slight accident, due to my forgetfulness, laid me on my bed of sickness.

Though you may have read in the modern works on

mesmerism, how that which we call "Will-Essence" – and you "fluid" – is transmitted from the operator to his objective point. You perhaps scarcely realize how everyone is practically, albeit unconsciously, demonstrating this law every day and every moment. Nor can you quite realize how the training for adeptship increases both one's capacity to emit and to feel this form of force. I assure you that I, (Djual Khool) though but a humble chela as yet, felt your good wishes flowing to me, as the convalescent in the cold mountains feels from the gentle breeze that blows upon him from the plains. *ML 35, p. 249*

(3) Two factors are needed to produce a perfect and instantaneous mental telegraphy – close concentration in the operation and complete receptive passivity in the "reader" subject. Given a disturbance of either condition, and the result is proportionately imperfect. The "reader" does not see the image as in the "telegrapher's" brain, but as arising in his own. When the latter's thought wanders, the psychic current becomes broken, the communication disjointed and incoherent.

In a case such as mine, the chela had, as it were, to pick up what he could from the current I was sending him and, as above remarked, patch the broken bits together as best he might. Do not you see the same thing in ordinary mesmerism – the *maya*, impressed upon the subject's imagination by the operator becoming now stronger, now feebler, as the latter keeps the intended illusive image more or less steadily before his own fancy? And how often the clairvoyants reproach the magnetiser for taking their thoughts off the subject under consideration.

And the mesmeric healer will always bear you witness that, if he permits himself to think of anything but the vital current he is pouring into his patient, he is at once compelled to either establish the current afresh or stop the treatment. *ML 93, p. 423*

(4) The greatest, as well as most promising of such schools in

Europe, the last attempt in this direction – failed most signally some 20 years ago in London. It was the secret school for the practical teaching of magick, founded under the name of a club, by a dozen of enthusiasts under the leadership of Lord Lytton's father. He had collected together for the purpose the most ardent and enterprising, as well as some of the most advanced scholars in mesmerism and "ceremonial magick," such as Eliphas Levi, Regazzoni, and the Copt, Zergvan Bey. And yet in the pestilent London atmosphere, the "Club" came to an untimely end. I (K.H.) visited it about half a dozen times and perceived from the first that there was and could be nothing in it. And this is also why the British T.S. does not progress one step practically. They are of the Universal Brotherhood *but in name* and gravitate at best towards *Quietism* – that utter paralysis of the Soul.

ML 28, pp. 209-210

Human Nature

(1) As for human nature in general, it is the same as it was a million years ago: Prejudice based upon selfishness; a general unwillingness to give up an established order of things for new modes of life and thought – and occult study requires all that and much more ... pride and stubborn resistance to Truth, if it but upset their previous notions of things – such are the character-istics of your age, and especially of the middle and lower classes. *ML 1, p. 3*

(2) In common with many, you blame us for our great secrecy. Yet we know something of human nature, for the experience of long centuries – aye, ages – has taught us. And we know, that so long as science has anything to learn, and a shadow of religious dogmatism lingers in the hearts of the multitudes, the world's prejudices have to be conquered step by step, not at a rush. As hoary antiquity had more than one Socrates, so the dim Future will give birth to more than one martyr. *ML 1, pp. 3-4*

(3) You (Hume) so love mankind, you say, that were not your generation to benefit by it, you would reject "Knowledge" itself. And yet, this philanthropic feeling does not even seem to inspire you with charity, towards those you regard as of an inferior intel-ligence. Why? Simply because the philanthropy you Western thinkers boast of, having no character of universality; i.e. never having been established on the firm footing of a moral, universal principle; never having risen higher than theoretical talk; and that chiefly among the ubiquitous Protestant preachers, it is but a mere accidental manifestation but no recognised LAW. The most superficial analysis will show that, no more than any other empirical phenomenon in human nature, can it be taken as an absolute standard of moral activity; i.e. productive of efficient

action. Since, in its empirical nature this kind of philanthropy is, like love, but something accidental, exceptional, and like that has its selfish preferences and affinities, it is necessarily unable to warm all mankind with its beneficent rays. This, I think, is the secret of the spiritual failure and unconscious egotism of this age. And you, otherwise a good and a wise man, being unconsciously to yourself the type of spirit unable to understand our ideas upon the Society as a *Universal Brotherhood*, and hence – turn away your face from it. *ML 28, p. 215*

(4) Human nature is unfathomable, and yours (Hume) is, perhaps, more intensely so than any other man I know of. Your last favour was certainly, if not quite a world of revelation, at least a very profitable addition to my store of observation of the Western character, especially that of the modern, highly intellectual Anglo-Saxon. *ML 28, 210*

(5) For it is "humanity" which is the great Orphan, the only disinherited one upon this Earth, my friend. And it is the duty of every man who is capable of an unselfish impulse to do something, however little, for its welfare. Poor, poor humanity! It reminds me of the old fable of the war between *the* Body and its members; here too, each limb of this huge "Orphan" – fatherless and motherless – selfishly cares but for itself. The body uncared for suffers eternally, whether the limbs are at war or at rest. Its suffering and agony never cease ... And who can blame it – as your materialistic philosophers do – if, in this everlasting isolation and neglect it has evolved gods unto whom "it ever cries for help but is not heard!" ... Thus –

"Since there is hope for man only in man
I would not let one cry whom I could save! ..."
ML 8, pp. 32-33

Immortality

(1) ... the word "immortality" has, for the initiates and occultists, quite a different meaning. We call "immortal" but the one *Life* in its universal collectivity and entire or Absolute Abstraction; that which has neither beginning nor end, nor any break in its continuity. Does the term apply to anything else? Certainly it does not. Therefore the earliest Chaldeans had several prefixes to the word "immortality," one of which is the Greek, rarely used term – *paneonic* immortality, i.e. beginning with the *manvantara* and ending with the *pralaya* of our Solar Universe. It lasts the eon, or "period" of our *pan* or "all nature."

Immortal then is he, in the *paneonic* immortality, whose distinct consciousness and perception of *Self under whatever form* – undergoes no disjunction at any time, not for one second, during the period of his *Egoship*. Those periods are several in number, each having its distinct name in the secret doctrines of the Chaldeans, Greeks, Egyptians and Aryans, and were they but amenable to translation – which they are not, at least so long as the idea involved remains inconceivable to the Western mind – I could give them to you.

Suffice it for you, for the present, to know that a man, an *Ego* like yours or mine, may be immortal from one to the other Round, i.e. having become a *full adept* (which unhappily I am not) I arrest the hand of Death at will and when finally obliged to submit to it, my knowledge of the secrets of nature puts me in a position to retain my consciousness and distinct perception of Self, as an object to my own reflective consciousness and cognition; and thus avoiding all such dismemberments of principles, that as a rule take place after the physical death of average humanity, I remain as Koot Hoomi in my *Ego*, throughout the whole series of births and lives across the seven worlds and *Arupa*-lokas, until finally I land again on this earth among the fifth race men of the full fifth Round beings. I would have been, in such a case – "immortal" for an inconceivable (to you) long period, embracing many milliards of years. And yet, am "I" *truly* immortal for all that?

Unless I make the same efforts as I do now, to secure for myself another such furlough from nature's Law, Koot Hoomi will vanish and may become a Mr. Smith or an innocent Babu, when his leave expires. There are men who become such mighty beings, there are men among us who may become immortal during the remainder of the Rounds and then take their appointed place among the highest Chohans, the Planetary *conscious* "Ego-Spirits." Of course the Monad "never perishes whatever happens" but Eliphas (Eliphas Levi) speaks of the personal not of the Spiritual Egos, and you have fallen into the same mistake (and very naturally too) as C.C.M., though I must confess the passage in *Isis* was very clumsily expressed, as I had already remarked to you about this same paragraph in one of my letters long ago. I had to "exercise my ingenuity" over it – as the Yankee express it, but succeeded in mending the hole, I believe, as I will have to many times more. I am afraid, before we are done with *Isis*, it really ought to be *re-written* for the sake of the family honour. *ML 20C, pp. 129-130*

(2) The mere acquisition of wonder-working powers can never secure immortality for the student of Occult Science, unless he has learnt the means of shifting gradually his sense of individuality from his corruptible material body, to the incorruptible and eternal *Non-Being* represented by his seventh principle.
ML 131, pp. 458-459

India

(I) I am (K.H.) first to thank you, (Hume) on behalf of the whole section of our fraternity that is especially interested in the welfare of India, for an offer of help whose importance and sincerity no one can doubt. Tracing our lineage through the vicissitudes of Indian civilization to a remote past, we have a love of our motherland so deep and passionate, that it has survived even the broadening and cosmoplitanizing (pardon me if this is not an English word) effect of our studies in the hidden laws of nature. And so I and every other Indian patriot feel the strongest gratitude for every kind word or deed that is given in her behalf. *First Letter of K.H. to A.O. Hume,*
Combined Chronology by M. Conger, p. 29

(2) Imagine then, that since we are convinced that the degradation of India is largely due to the suffocation of her ancient spirituality; and that whatever helps restore that higher standard of thought and morals must be a regenerating national force; every one of us would naturally and without urging be disposed to push forward a Society whose proposed foundation is under debate; especially if it really is meant to become a society untainted by selfish motive, and whose object is the revival of ancient science and tendency to rehabilitate our country in the world's estimation. Take this for granted without further asservations.

But you know, as any man who has read history, that patriots may burst their hearts in vain if circumstances are against them. Sometimes it has happened that no human power, not even the fury and force of the loftiest patriotism, has been able to blend an iron destiny aside from its fixed course, and nations have gone out like torches dropped into water in the engulfing blackness of ruin.

Thus we have the sense of our country's fall though not the power to lift her up at once, can not do as we would either as to general affairs or this particular one. And with the readiness but not the right to meet your advances more than halfway, we are forced to say that the idea entertained by Mr. Sinnett and yourself is impracticable in part. It is, in a word, impossible for myself or any Brother or even an advanced neophyte, to be specially assigned and set apart as the guiding Spirit or Chief of the Anglo-Indian Branch. We know it would be a good thing to have you and a few of our selected colleagues regularly instructed and shown the phenomena and their rationale. For though none but you few would be convinced, still it would be a decided gain to have even a *few* Englishmen of first class ability enlisted as students of Asiatic Psychology.

First Letter of K.H. to A.O. Hume,
Combined Chronology by M. Conger, pp. 29-30

(3) When the natives see that an interest is taken by the English and even by some high officials in India in their ancestral science and philosophies, they will themselves take openly to their study. And when they come to realise that the old "divine" phenomena were not *miracles,* but scientific effects, *superstition* will abate. Thus the greatest evil that now oppresses and retards the revival of Indian civilisation will, in time, disappear. The present tendency of education is to make them materialistic and root out spirituality. With a proper understanding of what their ancestors meant by their writings and teachings, education would become a blessing, whereas now it is often a curse.

At present (1880) the non-educated, as much as the learned natives, regard the English as too prejudiced, because of their Christian religion and modern science, to care to understand them or their traditions. They mutually hate and mistrust each other. This changed attitude toward the older philosophy would influence the native Princess and wealthy men to endow normal schools for the education of pundits; and old MSS hitherto buried out of the reach of the Europeans would again come to light, and with them the key to much of that which was hidden for ages from the popular understanding; for which your sceptical Sanscritists do not care, which your religious missionaries do not *dare* to understand. Science would gain much – humanity everything.

Under the stimulus of the Anglo-Indian Theosophical Society, we might, in time, see another golden age of Sanscrit literature. Such a movement would have the entire approbation of the Home Government as it would act as a preventive against discontent; and the sympathy of European Sanscritists, who, in their divisions of opinion need the help of native pundits now beyond their reach in the present state of mutual misunderstanding. They are even now bidding for such help. At this moment two educated Hindus of Bombay are assisting Max Muller; and a young pundit of Guzerat, a Fellow of the T.S. is aiding Prof. Monier Williams at Oxford and living in his house. The first two are materialists and do harm; the latter single-handed can do little, because the man whom he is serving is a prejudiced Christian.

First Letter of K.H. to A.O. Hume,
Combined Chronology by M. Conger, pp. 36-37

(4) The state of India is, just now, almost comparable to a great body of dry matter in which sparks are smouldering. Agitators of both races have been and are doing their best to stir up a great flame. *ML 67, p. 371*

(5) What have we, the disciples of the true *Arhats*, of esoteric Buddhism and of Sang-gyas to do with the *Shastras* and Orthodox Brahmanism? There are 100 of thousands of Fakirs, Sannyasis and Sadhus, leading the most pure lives and yet being as they are, on the path of *error*, never having had the oppor-

tunity to meet, see or even hear of us. Their forefathers have driven away the followers of the only true philosophy. *ML 134, p. 462*

(6) There was never a time when the help of a man like yourself (Sinnett) was more needed by India. We foresaw it, as you know and patriotically tried to make your way easy for a speedy return. But – alas! That it must be confessed – the word Patriotism has now scarcely any electric power over the Indian heart. The "Cradle Land of Arts and Creeds" swarms with unhappy beings, precariously provided for, and vexed by demagogues who have everything to gain by chicane and impudence. We know all this in the mass, but not one of us Aryans had sounded the depths of the Indian question as we have of late (1883.)

If it be permissible to symbolize things subjective by phenomena objective, I should say that to the psychic sight, India seems covered with a stifling grey fog – a mortal meteor (reference to meteoric dust – Ed.) – the odic emanation from her vicious social state. Here and there twinkles a point of light which marks a nature still somewhat spiritual, a person who aspires and struggles after the higher knowledge. If the beacon of Aryan occultism shall ever be kindled again, those scattered sparks must be combined to make its flame. And this is the task of the T.S., this is the pleasant part of its work, in which we would so gladly assist, were we not impeded and thrown back by the *would-be chelas* themselves. *ML 81, p. 384*

(7) No doubt life on the European continent and in England possesses charms lacked by poor, dull India. But the latter can, on the other hand, offer privileges and attractions undreamt of by the average mystic. I dare not say more; but, you are wrong friend, (Sinnett) *very* wrong in consenting to stay here (in India) ONLY for *my* sake. I at least do not feel myself selfish enough to accept the sacrifice .... *ML 79, p. 382*

(8) You pride yourself (Hume) upon not being a "patriot" – *I* (K.H.) *do not*; for in learning to love one's country, one but learns to love humanity the more. The lack of that you term *"low motives"* in 1857 caused my country men to be blown by yours from the mouths of their guns. Why then should I not fancy that a real philanthropist would regard the aspiration for a better understanding between the Govt. and people of India as a most commendable instead of an ignoble one? *ML 28, p. 212*

(9) Most of the peoples of India belong to the oldest or the earliest branchlet of the fifth human Race. *ML 17, p. 118*

(10) As said in my answer on your notes, most of the peoples of India – with the exception of the *Semitic* (?) Moguls – belong to the oldest branchlet of the present fifth Human race, which was evoluted in central Asia more than one million years ago. Western Science finding good reasons for the theory of human beings having inhabited Europe 400,000 years before your era – this cannot so shock you as to prevent your drinking wine tonight at your dinner. Yet Asia has, as well as Australia, Africa, America and the most northward regions, its remnants – of the fourth – even of the third race (cave men and Iberians.) At the same time, we have more of the seventh ring of the fourth race than Europe and more of the first ring of the fifth round, as, older than the European branchlets, our men have naturally come in earlier. Their being "less advanced" in civilization and refinement trouble their spirituality but very little. Karma being an animal which remains indifferent to pumps and white kid gloves.
ML 18, p. 121

Intellect, Intuition and Illumined Mind

(1) I am determined (K.H.) to make one more effort – (the last that I am permitted) – to open your inner intuition. If my voice, the voice of one who was ever friendly to you in the human principle of his being – fails to reach you (Sinnett) as it has often before, then our separation in the present and for all times to come becomes unavoidable. It pains me for you, whose heart I read so well – every protest and doubt of your purely intellectual nature, of your cold Western reason – notwithstanding.
ML 62, p. 351

(2) Unfortunately, however great your purely *human* intellect, your spiritual intuitions are dim and hazy, having been never developed. Hence, whenever you find yourself confronted by an apparent contradiction, by a difficulty, a kind of *inconsistency* of occult nature, one that is caused by our time honoured laws and regulations – (of which you know nothing, for your time has not yet come) – forthwith your doubts are aroused, your suspicions bud out – and one finds that they have made mock at your better nature, which is finally crushed down by all these deceptive appearances of outward things!

You have not the faith required to allow your Will to arouse itself in defiance and contempt against your purely worldly intellect and give you a better understanding of things hidden and laws unknown. You are unable, I see, to force your better aspirations – fed at the stream of real devotion to the Maya you have made yourself of me – (a feeling in you that has always profoundly touched me) – to lift up the head against cold, *spiritually blind* reason; to allow your heart to pronounce loudly and proclaim that which it has hitherto only been allowed to whisper: "Patience, patience. A great design has never been snatched at once." *ML 62, p. 351*

(3) If, throwing aside every preconceived idea, you (Sinnett) could TRY and impress yourself with this profound truth, that intellect is not all powerful by itself; that to become "a mover of mountains" it has first to receive life and light from its higher principle – Spirit, and then would fix your eyes upon everything occult, spiritually trying to develop the faculty according the rules, then you would soon read the mystery right.
ML 62, p. 356

(4) Asiatics are so poor as a rule and books are so inaccessible to them in these degenerate days (1880s) that you can see plainly how different a plan of intellectual culture – in preparation for practical experiments to unfold psychic power in themselves – must be thought. In the olden time, this want was supplied by the Guru, who guided the chela through the difficulties of childhood and youth and afforded him in oral teaching as much as, or more, than through books, the food for mental and psychic growth. The want of such a "guide, philosopher and friend" (and who so well deserves the tripartite title?) can never be supplied, try as you may. All we can do is to prepare the intellect: the impulse toward "soul culture" must be furnished by the individual. Thrice fortunate they who can break through the vicious circle of modern influence and come up above the vapours!
ML 35, pp. 246-247

(5) Knowledge for the mind, like food for the body, is intended to feed and help growth, but it requires to be well digested and the more thoroughly and slowly the process is carried out, the better both for body and mind. *ML 43, p. 262*

(6) Nature has linked all parts of her Empire together by subtle threads of magnetic sympathy, and there is a mutual correlation even between a star and a man; thought runs swifter than the

electric fluid, and your thought *will find me* if projected by a pure impulse, as mine will find, has found, and often impressed your mind. We may move in cycles of activity divided – not entirely separated from each other. Like the light in the sombre valley, seen by the mountaineer from his peaks, every bright thought in your mind, my brother (Sinnett) will sparkle and attract the attention of your distant friend and correspondent (K.H.) If thus we discover our allies in the *Shadow* world – your world and ours outside the precincts – and it is our law to approach every such a one, if even there be but the feeblest glimmer of the true "Tathagata" light within him – then how far easier for you to attract us. Understand this and the admission into the Society of persons often distasteful to you will no longer amaze you. "They that be whole need not the physician, but they that be sick" – is an axiom, whoever may have spoken it. **ML 45, pp. 267-268**

Karma and the Skandhas

(1) ... you can do nothing better than to study the two doctrines of *Karma* and Nirvana as profoundly as you can. Unless you are thoroughly well acquainted with the two tenets – the double key to the metaphysics of Abhidharma, you will always find yourself at sea in trying to comprehend the rest. We have several sorts of Karma and Nirvana in their various applications – to the Universe, the World, Devas, Buddhas, Bodhisattvas, men and animals – the second including its seven kingdoms. Karma and Nirvana are but two of the seven great MYSTERIES of Buddhist metaphysics; and but four of the seven are known to the best orientalists, and that very imperfectly. *ML 16, p. 110*

(2) If you ask a learned Buddhist priest, what is Karma? – he will tell you that Karma is what a Christian might call Providence (in a certain sense only) and a Mahomedan – *Kismet*, fate or destiny (again in one sense). That is that cardinal tenet which teaches that as soon as any conscious or sentient being, whether man, deva, or animal dies, a new being is produced and he or it reappears in another birth, on the same or another planet, under conditions of his own antecedent making. Or, in other words, that *Karma* is the guiding power, and *Trishna* (in Pali *Tanha*) the thirst or desire to sentiently live – the proximate force or energy, the resultant of human (or animal) action, which out of the old Skandhas, produces the new group that form the new being and control the nature of the birth itself. Or to make it still clearer, the new being is rewarded and punished from the meritorious acts and misdeeds of the old one; Karma representing an Entry Book, in which all the acts of man, good and bad, or indifferent are carefully recorded to his debt and credit – by himself, so to say, or rather by these very actions of his.

There, where Christian poetical fiction created and sees a

"Recording" Guardian Angel, stern and realistic Buddhist logic, perceiving that every cause should have its effect – shows its real presence. The opponents of Buddhism have laid great stress upon the alleged injustice that the doer should escape and an innocent be made to suffer – the doer and the sufferer are different beings. The fact is, that while in one sense they may be so considered, yet in another, *they are identical*. The "old being" is the sole parent – father and mother at once – of the "new being." It is the former who is the creator and fashioner of the latter in reality; and far more so in plain truth than any father in flesh. And once you have well mastered the meaning of *Skandhas* you will see what I mean. *ML 16, pp. 110-111*

(3) It is the group of Skandhas that form and constitute the physical and mental individuality we call man (or any being). This group consists (in the exoteric teaching) of five Skandhas namely: *Rupa* – the material properties or attributes; *Vedana* – sensations; *Sanna* – abstract ideas; *Samskara* – tendencies both physical and mental; and *Vinnana* – mental powers, an amplification of the fourth – meaning the mental, physical and moral predispositions. We add to them two more, the nature and names of which you may learn hereafter. Suffice for the present to let you know that they are connected with and productive of *Sakkayaditthi*, the "heresy or delusion of individuality" and of *Attavada* "the doctrine of Self," both of which (in the case of the fifth principle, the soul) lead to the maya of heresy and belief in the efficacy of vain rites and ceremonies, in prayers and intercession. *ML 16, p. 111*

(4) Now returning to the question of identity between the *old* man and the *new* "Ego." I may remind you that even your science has accepted the old, very old fact taught by our Lord, (Buddha) that a man of any given age, while sentiently the same, is yet physically not the same as he was a few years earlier (we say *seven*

years and are prepared to maintain and prove it.) Buddhistically speaking, his *Skandhas* have changed. At the same time they are ever and ceaselessly at work in preparing the abstract mould, the "privation" of the future new being. Well then, if it is just that a man of 40 should enjoy or suffer for the actions of a man of 20, so it is equally just that the being of the new birth, who is essentially identical with the previous being – since he is its outcome and creation – should feel the consequences of that begetting Self or personality

Your Western law, which punishes the innocent son of a guilty father by depriving him of his parent, rights and property; your civilised society which brands with infamy the guiltless daughter of an immoral, criminal mother; your Christian Church and Scriptures which teach that the "Lord God visits the sins of the fathers' upon the children unto the third and fourth gener-ation," are not all these far more unjust and cruel than anything done by Karma? Instead of punishing the innocent together with the culprit, *the Karma avenges and rewards the former,* which neither of your three western potentates, above mentioned, ever thought of doing. But perhaps, to our physiological remark the objectors may reply that it is only the body that changes, there is only a molecular transformation, which has nothing to do with the mental evolution; and that the *Skandhas* represent not only a material but also a set of mental and moral qualities. But is there, I ask, either a sensation, an abstract idea, a tendency of mind, or a mental power, that one could call an absolutely non-molecular phenomenon? Can even a sensation or the most abstract of thoughts, which is *something*, come out of *nothing*, be nothing?

Now, the causes producing the "new being" and determining the nature of *Karma* are, as already said – *Trishna* – thirst, desire for sentient existence and *Upadana* (form) which is the realization or consummation of *Trishna* or that desire. **ML 16, pp. 111-112**

(5) What the lives in *Devachan* and upon Earth shall be respec-

tively, in each instance is determined by Karma. *ML 25, p. 196*

(6) Occultism is certainly not necessary for a good, pure Ego to become an "Angel" or Spirit, in or out of the *Devachan*, since Angelhood *is* the result of Karma. *ML 54, p. 321*

(7) If our rule is to be chary of confidences, it is because we are taught from the first that each man is personally responsible, to the Law of Compensation for every word of his voluntary production. *ML 43, pp. 261-262*

(8) Place a long row of candles on your table. Light one and blow it out; then light the other and do the same; a third and fourth and so on. The same matter, the same gaseous particles – representing in our case the *Karma* of the personality – will be called forth by the conditions given them by your match to produce a new luminosity; but can we say that candle No.1 has not had its flame extinct for ever? *ML 23B, p. 172*

(9) Now every individuality will be followed on its ascending arc by the Law of retribution – Karma and death accordingly. The perfect man or the entity which reached full perfection (each of his seven principles being matured) will not be reborn here. His local terrestrial cycle is completed .... *ML 13, p. 77*

Life, the Absolute, and the One Reality

(1) Life, after all the greatest problem within the ken of human conception, is a mystery that the greatest of your men of science will never solve. In order to be correctly comprehended, it has to be studied in the entire series of its manifestations, otherwise it can never be, not only fathomed, but even comprehended in its easiest form – life, as a state of *being* on this earth. It can never be grasped so long as it is studied separately and apart from universal life. To solve the great problem one has to become an occultist; to analyze and experience it personally in all its phases, as life on earth, life beyond the limit of physical death, mineral, vegetable, animal and spiritual life; life in conjunction with concrete matter, as well as life present in the imponderable atom.

Let them try and examine or analyze life apart from organism, and what remains of it? Simply a mode of motion; which unless our doctrine of the all pervading, infinite, omnipresent Life is accepted – though it be accepted on no better terms than a hypothesis, only a little more reasonable than their *scientific* hypotheses which are all absurd – has to remain unsolved. Will they object? Well, we will answer them by using their own weapons. We will say that it is, and will remain for ever demonstrated, that since motion is all pervading and absolute rest inconceivable, that under whatever form or *mask* motion may appear, whether as light, heat, magnetism, chemical affinity or electricity – all these must be but phases of One and the same universal omnipotent Force, a Proteus they bow to as the Great "Unknown" (see Herbert Spencer) and we simply call the "One Life," the "One Law," and the "One Element."
ML 93B, pp. 158-159

(2) The greatest, the most scientific minds on earth, have been keenly pressing forward toward a solution of the mystery,

leaving no bye-path unexplored, no thread loose or weak in this darkest of labyrinths for them, and all had to come to the same conclusion – that of the Occultists when given only partially – namely, that life in its concrete manifestations, is the legitimate result and consequence of chemical affinity; as to life in its abstract sense, life pure and simple – well, they know no more of it today than they knew in the incipient stage of the Royal Society. *ML 23B, p. 159*

(3) If, as I hope, in a few years I am entirely my own master, I may have the pleasure of demonstrating to you, on your own writing table, that life, *as life,* is not only transformable into other aspects or phases of the all pervading Force, but that it can be actually infused into an artificial man. Frankenstein is a myth only so far as he is the hero of a mystic tale – he is a possibility; and the physicists and physicians of the last sub-race of the sixth Race, will inoculate life and revive corpses as they now inoculate smallpox, and often less comely diseases. Spirit, life and matter, are not natural principles existing independently of each other, but the effects of combinations produced by eternal motion in Space; and they better learn it. *ML 23B, p. 159*

(4) Far from "lacking philosophical breadth" then, our doctrines show but one principle in nature – spirit-matter or matter-spirit, the third, the ultimate Absolute or the quintessence of the two – if I may be allowed to use an erroneous term in the present application – losing itself beyond the view and spiritual perceptions of even the "Gods" or planetary Spirits. This third principle, say the Vedantic Philosophers – is the only reality, everything else being Maya, as none of the Protean manifestations of spirit-matter or Purusha and Prakriti have ever been regarded in any other light than that of temporary delusions of the senses. Even in the hardly outlined philosophy of *Isis* (*Isis Unveiled*) this idea is clearly carried out. *ML 22, p. 141*

(5) The ONE, can, when manifesting, become only 3. The unmanifested, when a simple duality, remains passive and concealed. The dual monad (the 7th and 6th principles) (Atma and Buddhi) has, in order to manifest itself as a *Logos*, the "Kwan-shai-yin," to first become a *triad* (7th, 6th and half of the 5th) (half of the 5th is higher mind – Ed.) Then, on the bosom of the "Great Deep," attracting within itself the *One Circle*, form out of it the perfect Square, thus "squaring the circle" – the greatest of all the mysteries, friend – and inscribing within the latter the WORD (the Ineffable Name) – otherwise the duality could never tarry as such and would have to be re-absorbed into the ONE. The "Deep" is *Space* – both male and female. "*Purush* (as Brahma) breathes in the Eternity; when 'he' in-breathes, Prakriti (as manifested Substance) disappears in his bosom; when 'he' *out-*breathes she re-appears as *Maya*," says the sloka. The One reality is *Mulaprakriti* (undifferentiated Substance) – the "Rootless root," the ... But we have to stop, lest there should remain but little to tell for your own intuitions. *ML 59, p. 347*

(6) Well may the Geometer of the R.S. (The Royal Society) not know that the apparent absurdity of attempting to square the circle covers a mystery ineffable. ... to many such metaphysical minds it would be worse than useless to divulge the fact, that the Unmanifested Circle – *the Father* or *Absolute* Life – is non-existent outside the Triangle and Perfect Square and is only manifested in the *Son*; and that it is when reversing the action and returning to its absolute state of Unity, and the square expands once more into the Circle, that "the Son returns to the bosom of the Father." There it remains until called back by his Mother, the "Great Deep," to remanifest as a *triad* – the *Son* partaking at once of the Essence of the Father and of that of the Mother – the active Substance, *Prakriti* in its differentiated condition. "My Mother – (Sophia, the manifested Wisdom) – took me," says Jesus in a Gnostic treatise; and he asks his disciples to tarry *till he comes* ....

The true "Word" may only be found by tracing the mystery of the passage inward and outward of the Eternal Life, through the states typified in these three geometric figures. *ML 59, pp. 347*

(7) You will easily understand what is meant by the "one and only" element or principle in the universe and that *androgynous*; the seven-headed serpent *Ananta* of Vishnu, the *Nag* around Buddha – the great dragon eternity biting with its *active* head its *passive* tail, from the emanations of which spring worlds, beings and things. You will comprehend the reason why the first philosopher proclaimed ALL – Maya – but that one principle which rests during the *maha*-pralayas only – the "nights of Brahm." *ML 13, p. 73*

(8) The God of the Theologians is simply an imaginary power, *un loup garou* as d'Holbach expressed it – a power which has never yet manifested itself. Our chief aim is to deliver humanity of this nightmare, to teach man virtue for its own sake, and to walk in life relying on himself, instead of leaning on a theological crutch that for countless ages was the direct cause of nearly all human misery.

Pantheistic we may be called – agnostic – NEVER. If people are willing to accept and to regard as God our ONE LIFE, immutable and unconscious in its eternity, they may do so and thus keep to one more gigantic misnomer. But then they will have to say with Spinoza that there is not and that we cannot conceive any other substance than God; ... who but a Theologian nursed on mystery, and the most absurd supernaturalism, can imagine a self-existent being, of necessity infinite and omnipresent *outside* the manifested *boundless* universe. The word infinite is but a negative which excludes the idea of bounds. It is evident that a being independent and omnipresent cannot be limited by anything which is outside of himself; that there can be nothing exterior to himself – not even vacuum, then where is there room for matter? for that manifested universe, even though the latter (be) limited?

If we ask the theist is your God vacuum, space or matter, they will reply no. And yet they hold that God penetrates matter, though he is not himself matter. When we speak of the One Life we also say that it penetrates, nay is the essence of every atom of matter; and that therefore it not only has correspondence with matter but has all its properties likewise, etc. – hence material, is *matter itself. ML 10, p. 53*

(9) Your all pervading supreme power exists, but it is exactly matter, whose life is motion, will, and nerve power, electricity. Purush (Spirit) can think but through Prakriti (Matter).
Cosmological Notes, LBS – First Edition, p. 381

(10) … We are not Adwaitees (followers of the Hindu Advaita philosophy – Ed.) but our teaching, respecting the one life, is identical with that of the Adwaitees with regard to Parabrahm. And no true philosophically trained Adwaitee will ever call himself an agnostic, for he knows that he is Parabrahm and identical in every respect with the universal life and soul – the macrocosm is the microcosm and he knows that there is no God apart from himself, no creator as no being. Having found Gnosis we cannot turn our backs on it and become agnostics.
ML 10, pp. 53-54

Mahatmas Koot-Hoomi and Morya

(1) It was Mr. Sinnett, who of his own motion, addressed to a "Brother" two long letters, even before Mad. B. had obtained either permission or promise from any of us to answer him, or knew to whom of us to deliver his letter. Her own chief (M.) having refused point blank to correspond, it was to me that she applied. Moved by regard for her, I consented, even telling her she might give you all my Thibetan mystic name and – I answered our friend's letter. Then came yours (Hume's) – as unexpectedly. You did not even know my name! But your first letter was so sincere, its spirit so promising, the possibilities it opened for doing general good seemed so great, that if I did not shout *Eureka* after reading it, and throw my Diogenes' lantern into the bushes at once, it was only because I knew too well human and – you must excuse me – Western nature. Unable, nevertheless, to undervalue the importance of this letter, I carried it to our venerable Chief. All I could obtain from Him, though, was the permission to temporarily correspond, and let you speak your whole mind, before giving any definite promise. (K.H.) *ML 28, p. 210*

(2) It is from the depths of an unknown valley, amid the steep crags and glaciers of Terich-Mir – a vale never trodden by European foot since the day its parent mount was itself breathed out from within our Mother Earth's bosom – that your friend sends these lines. For it is there K.H. received your "Affectionate homages," and there he intends passing his "summer vacations."

A letter "from the abodes of eternal snow and purity" sent to and received – "At the abodes of vice!" ... Queer *n'est-ce-pas*? Would, or rather could I be with you at those "abodes?" No; but I was at several different times, elsewhere, though neither in "astral" nor in any other tangible form, but simply in thought.
(K.H.) *ML 31, p. 240*

(3) I have laboured for more than a quarter of a century, night and day, to keep my place within the ranks of that invisible, but as ever, busy army which labours and prepares for a task which can bring no reward but the consciousness that we are doing our duty to humanity. (K.H.) *ML 31, p. 242*

(4) A few days before leaving us, Koot Hoomi speaking of you said to me (M.) as follows: "I feel tired and weary of these never ending disputations. The more I try to explain to both of them the circumstances that control us and that interpose between us so many obstacles to free intercourse, the less they understand me! Under the most favourable aspects this correspondence must always be unsatisfactory, even exasperatingly so at times; for nothing short of personal interviews, at which there could be discussion and the instant solution of intellectual difficulties as they arise, would satisfy them fully. It is as though we were hallooing to each other across an impassable ravine and only one of us seeing his interlocutor. In point of fact, there is nowhere in physical nature a mountain abyss so hopelessly impassable and obstructive to the traveller as that spiritual one, which keeps them back from me." *ML 29, p. 219*

(5) Two days later, when his "retreat" was decided upon, in parting he asked me: "Will you watch over my work, will you see it falls not into ruins?" I promised. What is there I would not have promised him at that hour! At a certain spot not to be mentioned to outsiders, there is a chasm spanned by a frail

bridge of woven grasses and with a raging torrent beneath. The bravest of your Alpine clubs would scarcely dare to venture the passage, for it hangs like a spider's web and seems to be rotten and impassable. Yet it is not; and he who dares the trial and succeeds – as he will if it is right that he should be permitted – comes into a gorge of surpassing beauty of scenery – to one *of our* places and to some of *our* people, of which and whom there is no note or minute among European geographers. At a stone's throw from the old lamasery stands the old tower, within whose bosom have gestated generations of Bodhisattvas. It was there, where now rests your lifeless friend (K.H.) – my brother, the light of my soul, to whom I made a faithful promise to watch during his absence over *his* work. (M.) *ML 29, p. 219*

(6) Since Master (K.H.) will not be able to write to you himself for a month or two longer (though you will always hear of him) – He begs you to proceed for his sake with your metaphysical studies and not to be giving up the task in despair whenever you meet with incomprehensible ideas in M. Sahib's notes, the more so, as M. Sahib's only hatred in his life is for writing. (Djual Khool) *ML 37, p. 250*

(7) My Brother – I have been on a long journey after supreme knowledge, I took a long time to rest. Then, upon coming back, I had to give all my time to duty, and all my thoughts to the Great Problem. It is all over now; the New Year's festivities are at an end and I am "Self" once more. But what is *Self*? Only a passing guest, whose concerns are all like a mirage of the great desert .... (K.H.) *ML 45, p. 264*

(8) Alas! By no means are we all "gods" especially when you remember that since the palmy days of "impressions" and "precipitations" – "K.H." has been born into a *new* and *higher* light. And even that one, in no wise the most dazzling to be

acquired on this earth. Verily the *Light of Omniscience* and infallible Prevision on this earth – that shines only for the highest CHOHAN alone – is yet far away from me. (K.H.)
ML 93, pp. 424-425

(9) The chief object of our struggles and *initiations* is to achieve this union (blending the fourth, fifth and seventh principles of man into the sixth – Ed.) while yet on this earth. Those who will be successful have nothing to fear during the fifth, sixth, and seventh rounds. But this is a mystery. Our beloved K.H. is on his way to the goal – the highest of all beyond as on this sphere. (M.)
ML 13, p. 78

(10) Ever since I undertook the extraordinary task of teaching two grown up pupils, with brains in which the methods of western science had crystallized for years; one of whom is willing enough to make room for the new iconoclastic teaching, but who, nevertheless, requires a careful handling, while the other will receive nothing but on condition of grouping the subjects as *he wants them to group*, not in their natural order – I have been regarded by all our Chohans as a lunatic. I am seriously asked whether my early association with Western "Pelings" has not made of me a half-Peling and turned me also into a "dzing-dzing" visionary. All this had been expected. I do not complain .... (K.H.) *ML 24B, p. 186*

(11) Quotations from Tennyson? Really cannot say. Some stray lines picked up in the astral light or in somebody's brain and remembered. I never forget what I once see or read. A bad habit. So much so, that often and unconsciously to myself, I string together sentences of stray words and phrases before my eyes, and which may have been used a hundred years ago or will hundred years hence, in relation to quite a different subject. Laziness and real lack of time. The "Old Lady" called me a

"brain pirate" and a plagiarist the other day, for using a whole sentence of five lines which, she is firmly convinced, I must have pilfered from Dr. Wilder's brain, as three months later he reproduced it in an essay of his own prophetic intuition. Never had a look into the old philosopher's brain cells. Got it somewhere in a northern current – don't know. Write this for your information as something new for you, I suppose. (K.H.) *ML 49, p. 286*

(12) I cannot close without telling you of an incident which, however ludicrous, has led to something that makes me thank my stars for it, and will please you also. Your letter, enclosing that of C.C.M.(Charles Massey) was received by me on the morning following the date you had handed it over to the "little man" (Dharbagiri Nath – a chela of K.H.). I was then in the neighbourhood of Pari-Jong, at the gom-pa of a friend, and was very busy with important affairs. When I received intimation of its arrival, I was just crossing the larger inner courtyard of the monastery. Bent upon listening to the voice of Lama Tondhub Gyatcho, I had no time to read the contents. So, after mechanically opening the thick packet, I merely glanced at it and put it, as I thought, into the travelling bag I wear across the shoulder. In reality, though, it had dropped on the ground; and since I had broken the envelope and emptied it of its contents, the latter were scattered in their fall.

There was no one near me at the time, and my attention being wholly absorbed with the conversation, I had already reached the staircase leading to the library door when I heard the voice of a

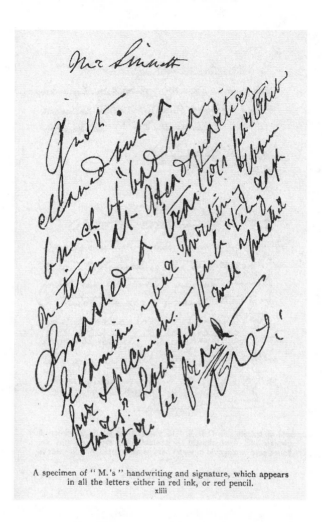

A specimen of " M.'s " handwriting and signature, which appears
in all the letters either in red ink, or red pencil.
xliii

young *gyloong* calling out from a window and expostulating with
someone at a distance. Turning round I understood the situation
at a glance; otherwise your letter would never have been read by
me, for I a saw a venerable old goat in the act of making a
morning meal of it.

The creature had already devoured part of C.C.M.'s letter and
was thoughtfully preparing to have a bite at yours, more delicate
and easy for chewing with his old teeth than the tough envelope
and paper of your correspondent's epistle. To rescue what

remained of it took but one short instant, disgust and opposition of the animal notwithstanding – but there remained mighty little of it!

The envelope with your crest on had nearly disappeared, the contents of the letters made illegible – in short I was perplexed at the disaster. Now you know *why* I felt embarrassed: I had no right to restore it, the letters *coming* from the "Eclectic" (the Simla Eclectic Theosophical Society) and connected directly with the hapless "Pelings" on all sides. What could I do to restore the missing parts! I had already resolved to humbly crave permission from the Chohan to be allowed an exceptional privilege in this dire necessity, when I saw his holy face before me, with his eye twinkling in quite an unusual manner, and heard his voice: "Why break the rule? I will do it myself." These simple words *Kam mi ts'har* – "I'll do it," contain a world of hope for me. He had restored the missing parts and done it quite neatly too, as you see, and even transformed a crumpled broken envelope, very much damaged, into a new one – crest and all. Now I know what great power had to be used for such a restoration, and this leads me to hope for a relaxation of severity one of these days. Hence, I thanked the goat heartily and since he does not belong to the ostracised Peling race, to show my gratitude, I strengthened what remained of teeth in his mouth and set the dilapidated remains firmly in their sockets, so that he may chew food harder than English letters for several years to come. (K.H.) *ML 54, pp. 320-321*

(13) ... I was coming down the defiles of Kouenlun – Karakorum you call them – and saw an avalanche tumble. I had gone personally to our chief (the Mahachohan – Ed.) to submit Mr. Hume's important offer, and was crossing over to Ladakh on my way home ... But just as I was taking advantage of the awful stillness which usually follows such cataclysm ... I was rudely recalled to my senses. A familiar voice, as shrill as the one

attributed to Saraswati's peacock – which if we may credit tradition, frightened off the King of the Nagas – shouted along the currents "Olcott has raised the very devil again! ... The Englishmen are going crazy ... Koot Hoomi, *come quicker* and help me!" – and in her excitement forgot she was speaking English. I must say that the "Old Lady's" telegrams (H.P.B's – Ed.) do strike one like stones from a catapult!

What could I do but come? Argument through space with one who was in cold despair and in a state of moral chaos was useless. So I determined to emerge from the seclusion of many years and spend some time with her, to comfort her as well as I could. But our friend is not one to cause her mind to reflect the philosophical resignation of Marcus Aurelius. The fates never wrote that she could say: "It is a royal thing, when one is doing good, to hear evil spoken of himself."

... I had come for a few days, but now find that I myself cannot endure for any length of time the stifling magnetism, even of my own countrymen. I have seen some of our proud old Sikhs drunk and staggering over the marble pavement of their sacred Temple. I have heard an English speaking Vakil declaim against *Yog Vidya* and Theosophy, as a delusion and a lie, declaring that English Science had emancipated them from such "degrading superstitions," and saying that it was an insult to India, to maintain that the dirty Yogees and Sannyasis knew anything about the mysteries of nature; or that any living man can or ever could perform any phenomena! I turn my face homeward tomorrow. (K.H.) *ML 4, p. 12*

(14) You may misunderstand us, are more than likely to do so, for our language must always be, more or less, that of parable and suggestion when treading upon forbidden ground; we have our own peculiar modes of expression and what lies behind the fence of words is even more important than what you read. But still – TRY. (K.H.) **ML 59, p. 348**

(15) ... you ... will hardly, if ever, be able to appreciate such characters as Morya's: a man as stern for himself, as severe for his own shortcomings, as he is indulgent for the defects of other people, not *in words* but in the innermost feelings of his heart; for, while ever ready to tell you to your face anything he may think of you, he yet was ever a stauncher friend to you than myself, who may often hesitate to hurt anyone's feelings, even in speaking the strictest truth. (K.H.) *ML 30, p. 233*

(16) I am commanded by my beloved Master, known in India and the Western lands as Koot Hoomi Lal Singh, to make in his name the following declaration, in answer to a certain statement made by M. W. Oxley and sent by him for publication in the Theosophist. It is claimed by the said gentleman that my Master, Koot Hoomi (a) has thrice visited him "by the astral form" and (b) that he had a conversation with Mr. Oxley ... Therefore my Master declares that –

(Section) 1. Whomever Mr. Oxley may have seen and conversed with at the time described, it was not with Koot Hoomi, the writer of the letters published in the *Occult World*.

(Section) 2. Notwithstanding that my Master knows the gentleman in question, who once honoured him with an autograph letter, thereby giving him the means of making his (Mr. Oxley's) acquaintance and of sincerely admiring his intuitional powers and western learning – yet he has never approached him, whether astrally or otherwise: Nor has he ever had any conversation with Mr. Oxley, least of all one of that nature, in which both the subject and predicate, the premises and conclusions are all wrong.

(Section) 3. In consequence of the said claims, the repetition of which is calculated to lead many of our theosophists into error, my Master has determined to issue the following resolution.

Henceforth, any medium or seer who will feel disposed to claim either to have been visited by, or to have held conversation with, or to have seen my Master – will have to substantiate the claim, by prefixing his or her statement with THREE SECRET WORDS, which he, my Teacher, will divulge to and leave in the safe keeping of Mr. A. O. Hume and Mr. A. P. Sinnett, the respective President and Vice President of "The Eclectic Theosophical Society" of Simla. As long as they do not find these three *words* correctly repeated by a medium or heading a statement to that effect, whether verbal or printed, emanating from him or her, or on his or her behalf, the claim shall be regarded as a gratuitous assumption and no notice will be taken of it. To his regret, my Master is forced to adopt this step, as unfortunately, of late, such self-deceptions have become quite frequent and would demand a speedy check. (Djual Khool) *ML 125, pp. 453-454*

(17) You know both of us (K.H. and M.) love our country and our race; that we regard the Theos. Society as a great potentiality for their good in proper hands; that he (K.H.) has joyfully welcomed Mr. Hume's identification with the cause and that I have placed a high – but only a proper – value upon it. And so you ought to realize that whatever we could do to bind you and him closer to us, we would do with all our heart. But still, if the choice lies between our disobeying the lightest injunction of our Chohan, as to when we may see either of you, or what we may write, or how, or where, and the loss of good opinion, even the feelings of animosity and the disruption of the Society, we should not

hesitate a single instant. (M.) *ML 24, p. 226*

(18) (Question) Have you (K.H.) the power of looking back to the former lives of persons now living, and identifying them?

(Answer) Unfortunately, some of us have. I, for one do not like to exercise it. *ML 23A, p. 145*

(19) Before another line passes between us, we must come to an agreement, my impulsive friend (Sinnett). You will have first to promise me faithfully, never to judge either of us, nor of the situation, nor of anything else bearing any relation to the "mythical brothers" – tall or short – thick or thin – by your worldly experience or you will never come at the truth. By doing so until now, you have only disturbed the solemn quiet of my evening meals several nights running and made my snake-like signature, what with your writing it and thinking about it, to haunt me even in my sleep – as by sympathy I felt it being pulled by the tail at the other side of the hills. Why will you be so impatient? You have a lifetime before you for our correspondence …. (M.) *ML 43, p. 258*

(20) And now it is time to put a stop to my abominable penmanship and so relieve you from the task. Yes – your "cosmogony!" Well, good friend, your cosmology is – between the leaves of *my Khuddaka Patha* – (my family Bible) – and making a supreme effort, I will try to answer it as soon as I am relieved, for just now I am on duty. It is a lifelong task you have chosen, and somehow, instead of generalizing, you manage always to rest upon those details that prove the most difficult to a beginner. Take warning, my good Sahib. The task is difficult, and K.H. in remembrance of old times, when he loved to quote poetry, asks me to close my letter with the following to your address:

"Does the road wind up-hill all the way?"

"Yes to the very end."

"Will the day's journey take the whole long day?"

"From morn to night, my friend."

(M.) *ML 43, p. 262*

(21) Morya ... wanted me to acquaint you with the totality of the subtle bodies and their collective aggregate, as well as with the disturbance aggregate or the *sheaths*. I believe it is premature. Before the world can be made to understand the difference between the "Sutratma" (thread soul) and "Taijasa" (the brilliant or the luminous) they have to be taught the nature of the grosser elements. What I blame him for, is that he allowed you to begin from the wrong end – the most difficult, unless one has thoroughly mastered the preparatory ground. (K.H.)

ML 48, p. 279

(22) What H.P.B. repeated to you is correct: "the natives do not see Bennett's coarseness and K.H. is also a native." What did I (M.) mean? Why simply that our Buddha-like friend (K.H.) *can see thro' the varnish* the grain of the wood beneath, and inside the slimy, stinking oyster – the "priceless pearl within!" B – is an honest man and of a sincere heart, besides being one of tremendous moral courage and a martyr to boot. Such our K.H. loves – whereas he would have only scorn for a Chesterfield and a Grandison. I suppose that the stooping of the finished "gentleman" K.H., to the coarse-fibred infidel, Bennett, is no more surprising than the alleged stooping of the "gentleman" Jesus to the prostitute Magdalene. There's a moral smell as well as a physical one, good friend. See how well K.H. read your character, when he would not send the Lahore youth to talk with you without a change of dress. The sweet pulp of the orange is *inside* the skin – Sahib: try to look inside boxes for jewels and do not trust to those lying in the lid. I say again: the man is an honest man and a very earnest one; not exactly an angel – they

must be hunted for in fashionable churches, parties at aristocratic mansions, theatres and clubs and such other *sanctums* – but as angels are outside our cosmogony, we are glad of the help of even honest and plucky tho' dirty men. (M.) ***ML 43, p. 261***

(23) … I confess that I, individually, am not yet exempt from some of the terrestrial attachments. I am still attracted towards *some* men more than toward others, and philanthropy as preached by our Great Patron – "the Saviour of the World – the Teacher of Nirvana and the Law," has never killed in me either individual preferences of friendship, love for my next of kin, or the ardent feeling of patriotism for the country in which I was last materially individualized. (K.H.) ***ML 8, p. 33***

(24) For you know – or think you know, of *one* K.H. – and can know but of one, whereas there are two distinct personages answering to that name *in him* you know. The riddle is only apparent and easy to solve, were you only to know what a real Mahatma is. You have seen by the Kiddle incident – perchance allowed to develop to its bitter end for a purpose – that even an "adept" when acting in his body is not beyond mistakes due to carelessness. You now understand that he is as likely as not to make himself look absurd, in the eyes of those who have no right understanding of the phenomena of thought-transference and astral precipitations – and all this, thro' lack of simple caution. There is always that danger if one has neglected to ascertain whether the words and sentences rushing into the mind have come all from within or whether some may have been impressed from without.

I feel sorry to have brought you into such a false position before your many enemies and even your friends. That was one of the reasons why I had hesitated to give my consent to print my private letters and specifically excluded a few of the series from the prohibition. I had no time to verify their contents – nor have

I now.

I have a habit of often quoting, minus quotation marks – from the maze of what I get in the countless folios of our Akashic libraries, so to say – with eyes shut. Sometimes I may give out thoughts that will see light years later; at other times what an orator, a Cicero, may have pronounced ages earlier, and at others, what was not only pronounced by modern lips but already either written or printed – as in the Kiddle case. All this I do (not being a trained writer for the Press) without the smallest concern as to where the sentences and strings of words may have come from, so long as they serve to express and fit in with my thoughts.

I have received a lesson now on the European plane on the danger of corresponding with western literati! But my "inspirer" Mr. Kiddle is none the less ungrateful, since to me alone he owes the distinguished honour of having become known by name and having his utterances repeated even by the grave lips of Cambridge "Dons." If fame is sweet to him, why will he not be consoled with the thought that the case of the "Kiddle – K.H. *parallel* passages" has now become as much a *cause celebre* in the department of "who is who," and "which plagiarized from the other?" as the Bacon-Shakespeare mystery; that in intensity of scientific research if not of value, our case is on a par with that of our two great predecessors. (K.H.) *ML 55, p. 324*

(25) ... I am determined to do that, for once, which hitherto I have never done; namely, to *personate myself* under *another form,* and perhaps – character. Therefore, you need not grudge Eglinton the pleasure of seeing me personally, to talk with me, and – be "dumbfounded" by me, and with the results of my visit to him on board "The Vega." This will be done between the 21st and 22nd of this month and, when you read this letter, will be "a vision of the past" ....

"All things being are in mystery; we expound mysteries by mysteries" – you may perhaps say. Well, well; to you as to one forewarned it will not be one; since, for several reasons – one more plausible than the other – I take you into my confidence. One of them is – to save you a feeling of involuntary envy (the word is queer isn't it?) when you hear of it. As he will see somebody quite different from the real K.H., though it *will still be* K.H., you need not feel like one wronged by your trans-Himalayan friend. Another reason is, to save the poor fellow from the suspicion of boasting; the third and *chiefest,* though neither least nor last, is that theosophy and its adherents have to be vindicated at last. Eglinton is going home; and were he upon his return to know nothing of the Brothers, there would be a sore day of trial for poor old H.P.B. and H.S.O. Mr. Hume twitted us for not appearing to Eglinton. He chuckled and defied us to do it before Fern and others. For reasons which he may or may not be able to appreciate – but that *you will* – we could not or rather would not do so, as long as E. was in India. No less had we very good reasons to forbid H.P.B. to either correspond with him, or take too much notice of him in the *Theosophist.* But now that he is gone and will be on the 22nd, hundreds of miles away at sea; and that no suspicion of fraud can be brought against either of them, the time for the experiment has come. He thinks of putting *her* to test – he will be tested himself ....

Now for Mr. Hume. He *has* worked for us, and is certainly entitled to our consideration – so far. I would fain have written to him myself, but that the sight of my familiar characters may produce a diversion in his feelings – for the worse – before he goes to the trouble of reading what I have to say. Will you kindly undertake the delicate task of notifying him of what I now write to you? Tell him that there are persons – *enemies* – who are anxious to catch the "old lady" at CHEATING, to entrap her, so to say, and that for that very reason I am determined to settle the question and have it once forever at rest. Say to him that profiting by his suggestion and advice I, – K.H., will appear to Eglinton in *propria persona* as *in actu,* at sea, between the 21 and 22 of this month; and that, if successful on bringing the rebel who denies the "Brothers" to his senses, Mrs. Gordon and consort will be notified of the fact *immediately.* That's all. We have waited on purpose to produce our experiment until his departure and now – WE MEAN TO ACT. (K.H.) *ML 89, p. 411-412*

(26) You, my good friend, (Sinnett) whom I had once or twice the pleasure of hearing playing on your piano, in the quiet intervals between dress-coating and a beef-and-claret dinner – tell me, could you favour me as readily as with one of your easy *waltzes* – with one of Beethoven's Grand Sonatas? (K.H.) *ML 16, p. 115*

Man

(1) Only the progress one makes in his study of Arcane Knowledge from its rudimental elements, brings him gradually to understand our meaning. Only thus and not otherwise, does it, strengthening and refining those mysterious links of sympathy between intelligent men – the temporarily isolated fragments of the universal Soul and the cosmic Soul itself – bring them into full rapport. Once this is established, then only will these awakened sympathies serve indeed to connect MAN with – what for the want of a European scientific word more competent to express the idea, I am again compelled to describe as that energetic chain, which brings together the material and Immaterial Kosmos, Past, Present, and Future, and quicken his perceptions so as to clearly grasp, not merely all things of matter, but of Spirit also. *ML 8, p. 29*

(2) The only object to be striven for is the amelioration of the condition of MAN, by the spread of truth suited to the various stages of his development and that of the country he inhabits and belongs to. TRUTH has no ear-mark and does not suffer from the name under which it is promulgated – if the said object is attained. *ML 85, p. 399*

(3) As man is a creature born with a free will and endowed with reason, whence spring all his notions of right and wrong, he does not per se represent any definite moral ideal. The conception of morality in general relates first of all to the object or motive, and only then to the means or modes of action. Hence, if we do not and would never call a moral man him who, following the rule of a famous religious schemer, uses bad means for a good object, how much less would we call him moral, who uses seemingly good and noble means to achieve a decidedly wicked or

contemptible object? *ML 28, p. 211*

(4) Indulge not in apprehensions of what evil might happen if things should not go as your worldly wisdom thinks they ought; doubt not, for this complexion of doubt unnerves and pushes back one's progress. To have cheerful confidence and hope is quite another thing from giving way to the fool's blind optimism: the wise man never fights misfortune in advance. *ML 45, p. 268*

(5) He (Fiske) is both right and wrong. Right about the race having been "dumb," for long ages of silence were required for the evolution and mutual comprehension of speech, from the moans and mutterings of the first remove of man above the highest anthropoid (a race now extinct since "nature shuts the door behind her" as she advances, in more than one sense) – up to the first monosyllable uttering man. *ML 12, p. 69*

(6) Man (physically) is a compound of all the kingdoms, and spiritually – his individuality is no worse for being shut up within the casing of an ant than it is for being a king. It is not the *outward* or physical shape that dishonours and pollutes the five principles – but the *mental* perversity. Then it is but at his fourth round, when arrived at the full possession of his *Kama*-energy and completely matured, that man becomes *fully responsible*, at the sixth, he may become a *Buddha* and at the seventh before the pralaya – a "Dhyan Chohan." *ML 13, p. 75*

(7) I will not enter here on the details of mineral and vegetable evolution, but I will notice only man – or – *animal-man*. He starts downward as a simply spiritual entity – an unconscious seventh principle (a *Parabrahm* in contradistinction to *Para-parabrahm*) – with the germs of the other six principles lying latent and dormant in him. Gathering solidity at every sphere – his six principles. When passing through the worlds of effects, and his

outward form in the world of causes (for these worlds or stages on the descending side we have other names) when he touches our planet he is but a glorious bunch of light upon a sphere, itself yet pure and undefiled (for mankind and every living thing on it increase in their materiality with the planet.) *ML 13, pp. 75-76*

(8) The present mankind is at its fourth round (mankind as a genus or a kind, not a RACE *nota bene*) of the post-pralayan cycle of evolution; and as its various races, so the individual entities in them are unconsciously, to themselves, performing their local sevenfold cycles – hence the vast difference in the degrees of their intelligence, energy and the Law of retribution – Karma and death accordingly. The perfect man or the entity which reached full perfection, (each of his seven principles being matured) will not be reborn here. His local terrestrial cycle is completed .... (The incomplete entities have to be reborn or reincarnated.) On their fifth round, after a partial Nirvana, when the zenith of the grand cycle is reached, they will be held responsible henceforth in their descents from sphere to sphere, as they will have to appear on this earth as a still more perfect and intellectual race ... The above is the rule. The Buddhas and Avatars form the exception, as verily we have yet some Avatars left to us on earth. *ML 13, p. 77*

(9) Man has two distinct physical brains; the cerebrum with its two hemispheres at the frontal part of the head – the source of the voluntary nerves; and the cerebellum, situated at the back portion of the skull – the fountain of the involuntary nerves, which are the agents of the unconscious or mechanical powers of the mind to act through. And weak and uncertain as may be the control of man over his involuntary functions, such as the blood circulation, the throbbing of the heart and respiration, especially during sleep – yet how far more powerful, how much more potential appears man as master and ruler over the blind

molecular motion – the *laws* which govern his body (a proof of this being afforded by the phenomenal powers of the Adept and even of the common Yogi) than that which you *will* call God shows over the immutable laws of Nature. *ML 22, p. 137*

Nirvana

(1) The highest state of Nirvana is the highest state of non-being. There comes a time when the whole infinitude sleeps or rests, when All is reimmersed in the one eternal and uncreated sum of all. The sum of the latent unconscious potentiality.
Cosmological Notes, LBS – First Edition, p. 386

(2) When the solar pralaya comes, the whole purified humanity merges into Nirvana and from that inter-solar Nirvana will be reborn in higher systems. The string of worlds is destroyed and vanishes like a shadow from the wall in the extinguishment of light. We have every indication that at this very moment such a solar pralaya is taking place, while there are two minor ones ending somewhere. *ML 15, p. 98*

(3) When the Spirit-man reaches the last bead of the chain and passes into *final* Nirvana, this last world also disappears or passes into subjectivity. There are among the stellar galaxies, births and deaths of worlds ever following each in the orderly procession of natural Law. And – as said already – the last bead is strung upon the thread of "Mahayuga." *ML 12, p. 67*

(4) To sum up: the misuse of knowledge by the pupil always reacts upon the initiator; nor do I believe you know yet, that in sharing his secrets with another, the Adept, by an immutable Law, is delaying his own progress to the Eternal Rest.
ML49, p. 284

(5) And thus also you shall hear from me *direct* at the earliest, practicable opportunity, "for we are not ungrateful and even Nirvana cannot obliterate GOOD." *ML 37, p. 249*

(6) ... existence in the seventh state of matter is *Nirvana* and not *Devachanic* conditions. **ML 86, p. 404**

(7) ... these sublime words of our Lord and Master: "O ye Bhikkhus and Arhats – be friendly to the race of men – our brothers! Know ye all, that he, who sacrifices not his *one* life to save the life of his fellow-being; and he who hesitates to give up more than life – his *fair name and honour* to save the fair name and honour of the many, is unworthy of the sin-destroying, immortal, transcendent Nirvana." **ML 82, p. 387**

(8) The Chaldean "resurrection in life eternal," borrowed by the Xtians, means resurrection in Nirvana.
Appendix 1, LBS – First Edition, p. 25

(9) But the *complete* recollection of all the lives – (earthly and devachanic) *omniscience* – in short – comes but at the great end of the full seven Rounds (unless one had become in the interim a Bodhisattva, an Arhat) – the "threshold" of Nirvana meaning an indefinite period. Naturally a man, a *Seventh-rounder* (who completes his earthly migrations at the beginning of the last race and ring) will have to wait longer at that threshold than one of the very last of those Rounds. That *Life* of the Elect between the minor Pralaya and Nirvana – or rather *before* the Pralaya – is the *Great Reward*, the grandest, in fact, since it makes of the Ego (though he may never have been an adept, but simply a worthy, virtuous man in most of his existences) – virtually a God, an omniscient, conscious being, a candidate – for eternities of eons – for a Dhyan Chohan ... Enough – I am betraying the mysteries of initiation. **ML 25, p. 198**

(10) But what has Nirvana to do with the recollections of objective existences? That is a state still higher and in which all things objective are forgotten. It is a State of absolute Rest and

assimilation with Parabrahm – it is Parabrahm itself. Oh for the sad ignorance of our philosophical truths in the West, and for the inability of your greatest intellects to seize the true spirit of those teachings. What shall we – what can we do! *ML 25, p. 198*

(11) The vegetable and animal kingdoms, which at the end of the minor manwantra had reached only a partial development, are not destroyed. Their life or vital entities, call some of them *nati* if you will – find also their corresponding night and rest – they also have a Nirvana of their own. And why should they not, these foetal and infant entities? They are all like ourselves, begotten of the one element .... *ML 15, p. 97*

(12) Once unfettered (and) delivered from their dead weight of dogmatic interpretations, personal names, anthropomorphic conceptions and salaried priests, the fundamental doctrines of all religions will be proved identical in their esoteric meaning. Osiris, Chrishna, Buddha, Christ, will be shown as different means for one and (the) same royal highway to final bliss, *Nirvana*. Mystical Christianity, that is to say that Christianity which teaches *self*-redemption through one's own *seventh principle* – the liberated Para-atma, (Augoeides) called by the one, Christ, by others, Buddha and equivalent to regeneration or rebirth in spirit – will be found just the same truth as the Nirvana of mystical Buddhism. *K.H.'s View of the Chohan Letter, Combined Chronology by M. Conger, pp. 44-45*

(13) Oh, for the final rest! For that Nirvana where – "to be one with Life, yet – to live not." Alas, alas! Having personally realized that: "... the soul of Things is sweet, the Heart of Being is celestial Rest," one does long for – eternal REST! (K.H.)
ML 16, p. 116

The Occult Brotherhood and Its Mission

(1) The Egyptian Hierophant, the Chaldean Mage, the Arhat, and the Rishi, were bound in days of yore on the same voyage of discovery and ultimately arrived at the same goal, though by different tracks. There are even at the present moment, three centres of the Occult Brotherhood in existence, widely separated geographically, and as widely *exoterically* – the true esoteric doctrine being identical in substance, though differing in terms; all aiming at the same grand object, but no two agreeing *seemingly* in the details of procedure. It is an every day occurrence to find students belonging to different schools of occult thought sitting side by side at the feet of the same Guru. *Upasika* (Madame B.) and Subba Row, though pupils of the same Master, have not followed the same Philosophy – the one is Buddhist and other an Adwaitee. *ML 85, p. 399*

(2) We have offered to exhume the primeval strata of man's being, his basic nature, and lay bare the wonderful complications of his inner Self – something never to be achieved by physiology or even psychology in its ultimate expression – and demonstrate it scientifically. It matters not to them if the excavations be so deep, the rocks so rough and sharp, that diving into that, to them, fathomless ocean, most of us perish in the dangerous exploration; for it is we who were the divers and the pioneers, and the men of science have but to reap where we have sown. It is our mission to plunge and bring the pearls of Truth to the surface; theirs – to clean and set them into scientific jewels. And, if they refuse to touch the ill-shapen oyster-shell, insisting that there is not, nor *cannot* be any precious pearl inside it, then shall we once more wash our hands of any responsibility before humankind. For countless generations hath the adept built a fane of imperishable rocks, a giant's Tower of INFINITE

THOUGHT, wherein the Titan dwelt, and will yet, if need be, dwell alone, emerging from it but at the end of every cycle, to invite the elect of mankind to co-operate with him and help in his turn enlighten superstitious man. And we will go on in that periodical work of ours; we will not allow ourselves to be baffled in our philanthropic attempts, until the day when the foundations of a new continent of thought are so firmly built that no amount of opposition and ignorant malice, guided by the Brethren of the Shadow will be found to prevail. *ML 9, p. 51*

(3) But above all, good and faithful friend, do not allow yourself to misconceive the real position of our Great Brotherhood. Dark and tortuous as may seem, to your Western mind, the paths trodden and the ways by which our candidates are brought to the great Light – you will be the first to approve of them when you know *all*. Do not judge on appearances – for you may thereby do a great wrong and lose your own personal chances to learn more. Only be vigilant and – watch. *ML 53, p. 301*

(4) Every Western Theosophist should learn and remember, especially those of them who would be our followers – that in our Brotherhood all personalities sink into one idea – abstract right and absolute practical justice for all. And that, though we may not say with the Christians, "return good for evil" – we repeat with Confucius, "return good for good; for evil – JUSTICE." *ML 85, p. 401*

(5) … but remember that my Brother and I are the only among the Brotherhood who have at heart the dissemination (to a certain limit) of our doctrines, and H.P.B. was hitherto our sole machinery, our most docile agent. *ML 66, pp. 367-368*

(6) We are held and described by some persons as no better than refined or "cultured tantrikas." Well, we ought to feel grateful for

the prefixed adjective, since it would have been as easy for our would-be biographers to call us *unrefined* tantrikas. Moreover, the easy way with which you notify us of the comparison made, makes me feel confident of the fact that you know little, if anything, about the professors of that sect; otherwise you would have hardly, as a gentleman, given room to such a simile in your letter. One more word will suffice. The "tantrikas" – at least the modern sect, for over 400 years – observe rites and ceremonies, the fitting description of which will never be attempted by the pen of one of our Brotherhood. In the light of the Europeans, "character" for adepts and ascetics seems as indispensable as to servant-maids. We are sorry we are unable to satisfy, at present, the curiosity of our well-wishers as to our real worth.

Letter to A.O. Hume - The Theosophist, June 1907, pp. 702-706

(7) In view of the ever increasing triumph and at the same time misuse of free-thought and *liberty*, (the Universal reign of Satan, Eliphas Levi would have called it) how is the combative *natural* instinct of man to be restrained from inflicting hitherto unheard of cruelties and enormities, tyranny, injustice, etc., if not through the soothing influence of a brotherhood and of the practical application of Buddha's exoteric doctrines.

K.H.'s View of the Chohan Letter,
Combined Chronology by M. Conger, p. 44

(8) Of your several questions we will first discuss, if you please, the one relating to the presumed failure of the "Fraternity" to "leave any mark upon the history of the world." They ought, you think, to have been able with their extraordinary advantages to have "gathered into their schools a considerable portion of the more enlightened minds of every race."

How do you know they have made no such mark? Are you acquainted with their efforts, successes, and failures? Have you any dock upon which to arraign them? How could your world collect proofs of the doings of men who have sedulously kept closed every possible door of approach by which the inquisitive could spy upon them.

The prime condition of their success was that they should never be supervised or obstructed. What they have done, they know; all those outside their circle could perceive was results, the causes of which were masked from view. To account for these results, men have in different ages, invented theories of the inter-position of "Gods," Special providences, fates, and the benign or hostile influences of the stars. There never was a time within or before the so-called historical period, when our predecessors were not moulding events and "making history," the facts of which were subsequently and invariably distorted by "histo-rians" to suit contemporary prejudices. Are you quite sure that the visible heroic figures in the successive dramas were not often but their puppets?

We never pretended to be able to draw nations in the mass to this or that crisis, in spite of the general drift of the world's cosmic relations. The cycles must run their rounds. Periods of mental and moral light and darkness succeed each other, as day does night. The major and minor yugas must be accomplished according to the established order of things. And we, borne along the mighty tide, can only modify and direct some of its minor currents.

If we had the power of the imaginary Personal God, and the universal and immutable laws were but toys to play with, then indeed might we have created conditions that would have turned this earth into an Arcadia for lofty souls. But having to deal with an immutable Law, being ourselves its creatures, we have had to do what we could and rest thankful. There have been times when "a considerable portion of enlightened minds" were taught in our schools. Such times there were in India, Persia, Egypt, Greece and Rome. But as I remarked in a letter to Mr. Sinnett, the adept is the efflorescence of his age, and comparatively few ever appear in a single century. Earth is the battleground of moral no less than of physical forces; and the boisterousness of animal passions, under the stimulus of the rude energies of the lower group of etheric agents, always tends to quench spirituality. *First Letter of K.H. to A.O. Hume,*

   Combined Chronology by M. Conger, pp. 34-35

Occult Science

(1) The Occult Science is *not* one in which secrets can be communicated of a sudden by a written or even verbal communication. If so, all the "Brothers" would have to do, would be to publish a *Hand-book* of the art which might be taught in schools as grammar is. It is the common mistake of people that we willingly wrap ourselves and our powers in mystery – that we wish to keep our knowledge to ourselves, and of our own will refuse – "wantonly and deliberately" to communicate it.
ML 49, pp. 282-283

(2) We will be at cross purposes in our correspondence until it has been made entirely plain that occult science has its own methods of research, as fixed and arbitrary as the methods of its antithesis, physical science, are in their way. If the latter has its dicta so also has the former; and he who would cross the boundary of the unseen world can no more prescribe how he will proceed than the traveller who tries to penetrate to the inner, subterranean recesses of L'Hassa (Lhasa) – the blessed, could show the way to his guide. The mysteries never were, never can be, put within the reach of the general public, not, at least, until that longed for day when our religious philosophy becomes universal. At no time have more than a scarcely appreciable minority of men possessed nature's secret, though multitudes have witnessed the practical evidence of the possibility of their possession. *ML 2, p. 6*

(3) The world – meaning that of individual existences – is full of those latent meanings and deep purposes which underlie all the phenomena of the Universe and Occult Sciences – i.e. *reason* elevated to super sensuous Wisdom – can alone furnish the key wherewith to unlock them to the intellect. *ML 31, p. 241*

(4) The time has gone by to argue, and the hour when it will be

proved to the world that Occult Science instead of being, in the words of Dr. R. Chambers – "superstition itself," as they may be disposed to think it, will be found the explanation and the extinguisher of all superstitions. *ML 89, p. 410-411*

(5) Occult Science is a jealous mistress and allows not a shadow of self indulgence; and it is "fatal" not only to the ordinary course of married life but even to flesh and *wine drinking*. *ML 18, p. 122*

(6) Our philosophy falls under the definition of Hobbes. It is preeminently the science of effects by their causes and of causes by their effects, and since it is also the science of things deduced from first principle, as Bacon defines it, before we admit any such principle, we must know it and have no right to admit even its possibility. *ML 10, p. 52*

(7) Everything in the occult universe, which embraces all the primal causes, is based upon two principles – Kosmic energy (Fohat or breath of wisdom) and Kosmic ideation. Thyan Kam – the knowledge of bringing about – giving the impulse to Kosmic energy in the right direction.
Cosmological Notes, LBS – First Edition, p. 376

(8) The truths and mysteries of occultism constitute, indeed, a body of the highest spiritual importance, at once profound and practical for the world at large. Yet it is not as a mere addition to the tangled mass of theory and speculation in the world of science that they are being given to you, but for their practical bearing on the interests of mankind. *ML 6, p. 23*

(9) And to show you how exact a science is occultism, let me tell you that the means we avail ourselves of are all laid down for us in a code, as old as humanity to the minutest detail, but every

one of us has to begin from the beginning, not from the end. Our laws are as immutable as those of Nature, and they were known to man an eternity before this strutting game-cock, modern science, was hatched. If I have not given you the *modus operandi* or begun by the wrong end, I have at least shown you that we build our philosophy upon experiment and deduction – unless you choose to question and dispute this fact equally with all others. Learn first our laws and educate your perceptions, dear Brother. *ML 22, p. 144*

(10) Only while the Western sciences make confusion still more confused, our science explains all the seeming discrepancies and reconciles the wildest theories. *ML 32, p. 244*

(11) If you believe in my friendship for you, if you value the word *of honour* of one who never – *never* during his whole life polluted his lips with an untruth, then do not forget the words I once wrote to you (see my last letter) *of those who engage themselves in the occult sciences;* he who does it "must either reach the goal or perish. Once fairly started on the way to the great Knowledge, to doubt is to risk insanity; to come to a dead stop is to fall; to recede is to tumble backward, headlong into an abyss." Fear not – if you are sincere, and that you are – now. Are you as sure of yourself as to the *future? ML 8, p. 31*

(12) If you would learn and acquire Occult Knowledge, you have, my friend, to remember that such tuition opens in the stream of chelaship many an unforeseen channel, to whose current even a "lay" chela must perforce yield, or else strand upon the shoals; and knowing this to abstain forever judging on mere appearances. *ML 64, p. 361*

(13) To give more knowledge to a man than he is yet fitted to receive is a dangerous experiment … The sudden communication

of facts, so transcending the ordinary, is in many instances fatal, not only to the neophyte but to those directly about him. It is like delivering an infernal machine or a cocked and loaded revolver into the hands of one who had never seen such a thing. Our case is extremely analogous. We feel that the time is approaching, and that we are bound to choose between the triumph of Truth or the Reign of Error and – terror. We have to let a few chosen ones into the great secret, or allow the infamous *Shammars* (followers of the left-hand path – Ed.) to lead Europe's best minds into the most insane and fatal of superstitions – Spiritualism; and we *do* feel as if we were delivering a whole cargo of dynamite into the hands of those we are anxious to see defending themselves against the Red capped Brothers of the Shadow. *ML 49, p. 284*

(14) The world of force is the world of Occultism and the only one whither the highest initiate goes to probe the secrets of being. Hence, no one but such an initiate can know anything of these secrets. *ML 22, pp. 143-144*

(15) My dear friend, I strongly advise you not to undertake, at present, a task beyond your strength and means; *for once pledged* were you to break your promise it would cut you off for years ... Occultism is not to be trifled with. It demands all or nothing. *ML 132, p. 460*

(16) Well may you admire and more should you wonder at the marvellous lucidity of that remarkable seeress, (Anna Kingsford) who ignorant of Sanskrit or Pali, and thus shut out from their metaphysical treasures, has yet seen a great light shining from behind the dark hills of exoteric religions. How think you did the writers of "the Perfect Way" (Anna Kingsford and Edward Maitland) come to know that Adonai was the Son and not the Father; or that the third Person of the Christian Trinity is – female? Verily, in that work they lay their hands several times

upon the keystone of Occultism. Only does the lady – who persists using without any explanation the misleading term "God" in her writings – know how nearly she comes up to our doctrine when saying – "Having for Father Spirit which is Life (the endless Circle or Parabrahm) and Mother, the Great deep, which is Substance (Prakriti in its undifferentiated condition) – Adonai possesses the potency of both and wields the dual powers of all things." We would say *triple*, but in the sense as given, this will do. **ML 59, pp. 346-347**

(17) You ask us to teach you true Science, the occult aspect of the known side of nature; and this you think can be as easily done as asked. You do not seem to realize the tremendous difficulties in the way of imparting even the rudiments of our Science to those who have been trained in the familiar methods of *yours*. You do not see that the more you have of the one, the less capable you are of intuitively comprehending the other, for a man can only think in his worn grooves and unless he has the courage to lift up these and make new ones for himself, he must perforce travel on the old lines.

First Letter of K.H. to A.O. Hume,
Combined Chronology by M. Conger, pp. 30-31

Phenomena and Siddhis

(1) ... try to break thro' that great *maya* against which occult students the world over have always been warned by their teachers – the hankering after phenomena. Like the thirst for drink and opium, it grows with gratification. The Spiritualists are drunken with it ... If you cannot be happy without phenomena, you will never learn our philosophy. If you want healthy, philosophic thought and can be satisfied with such – let us correspond. *ML 43, p. 262*

(2) Badly as the phenomena may have been shown, there have still been – as yourself admits – certain ones that are unimpeachable. The "raps on the table when no one touches it," and the "bell sounds in the air" have, you say "always been regarded as satisfactory," etc. etc. From this, you reason that good "test phenomena" may easily be multiplied *ad infinitum*. So they can – in any place where our magnetic and other conditions are constantly offered; and where we do not have to act through an enfeebled female body in which, as we might say, a vital cyclone is raging much of the time. *ML 2, p. 9*

(3) My good friend – it is very easy for us to give phenomenal proofs when we have necessary conditions. For instance – Olcott's magnetism, after 6 years of purification, is intensely sympathetic with ours – physically and morally is constantly becoming more and more so. Damodar and Bhavani Rao, being congenitally sympathetic, their auras help – instead of repelling and impeding phenomenal experiments. After a time you may become so – it depends on yourself. To force phenomena in the presence of difficulties, magnetic and other, is forbidden, as strictly as for a bank cashier to disburse money which is only entrusted to him. Mr. Hume cannot comprehend this and

therefore is "indignant" that the various tests he has secretly prepared for us have all failed. They demanded a tenfold expenditure of power, since he surrounded them with an aura not of the purest – that of mistrust, anger, and anticipated mockery. *ML 88, p. 410*

(4) The alternate breakings out and subsidences of mystical phenomena, as well as their shifting from one centre to another of population, show the conflicting play of the opposing forces of spirituality and animalism. And lastly, it will appear that the present tidal wave of phenomena, with its varied effects upon human thought and feeling, made the revival of Theosophical enquiry an indispensable necessity. *ML 8, p. 35*

(5) What then would be the results of the most astounding phenomena, supposing we consented to have them produced? However successful, danger would be growing proportionately with success. No choice would soon remain but to go on, ever *crescendo*, or to fall in this endless struggle with prejudice and ignorance, killed by our own weapons. Test after test would be required and would have to be furnished; every subsequent phenomenon expected to be more marvellous than the preceding one. Your daily remark is that one cannot be expected to believe unless he becomes an eye witness. Would the lifetime of a man suffice to satisfy the whole world of sceptics? It may be an easy matter to increase the original number of believers at Simla to hundreds and thousands. But what of the hundreds of millions of those who could not be made eye-witnesses? The ignorant – unable to grapple with the invisible operators – might some day vent their rage on the visible agents at work; the higher and educated classes would go on disbelieving as ever, tearing you to shreds as before. *ML 1, p. 3*

(6) It is not *physical* phenomena that will ever bring conviction to

the hearts of the unbelievers in the "Brotherhood" but rather phenomena of *intellectuality, philosophy* and logic, if I may so express it. *ML 35, p. 246*

(7) The terms "unscientific," "impossible," "hallucination," "imposter," have hitherto been used in a very loose, careless way, as implying in the occult phenomena something either mysterious and abnormal, or a premeditated imposture. And this is why our chiefs have determined to shed upon a few recipient minds, more light upon the subject and to prove to them that such manifestations are as reducible to law as the simplest phenomenon of the physical universe.

The wiseacres say: "The age of miracles is past," but we answer, "it never existed!" While not unparalleled or without their counterpart in universal history, these phenomena must and WILL come with an overpowering influence upon the world of sceptics and bigots. They *have* to prove both destructive and constructive – *destructive* in the pernicious errors of the past, in the old creeds and superstitions which suffocate in their poisonous embrace like the Mexican weed nigh all mankind; but *constructive* of new institutions of a genuine, practical Brotherhood of Humanity, where all will become coworkers of nature, will work for the good of mankind *with* and *through* the higher *planetary Spirits* – the only "Spirits" we believe in. Phenomenal elements, previously unthought of – undreamt of – will soon begin manifesting themselves day by day, with constantly augmented force, and disclose at last the secrets of their mysterious workings. *ML 6, p. 23*

(8) Believe me, good friend, learn what you can under the circumstances ... the *philosophy* of the phenomena and our doctrines on Cosmogony, inner man etc. This Subba Row will help you to learn, though his terms – he being an initiated Brahmin and holding to the *Brahmanical* esoteric teaching – will

be different from those of the "Arhat Buddhist" terminology. But essentially both are the same – *identical* in fact. *ML 76, p. 376*

(9) Only where you are and will be ever wrong, my dear sir, it is in entertaining the idea that phenomena can ever become "a powerful engine" to shake the foundations of erroneous beliefs in the Western mind. None but those who see for themselves will ever believe, do what you may. "Satisfy us and then we will satisfy the world," you once said. You were satisfied and what are the results? *ML 29, p. 227*

(10) Such phenomena as you crave, have ever been reserved as a reward for those who have devoted their lives to serve the goddess Saraswati – our Aryan *Isis* (goddess of wisdom.) Were they given to the profane what would remain for our faithful ones? *ML 1, p. 4*

(11) The original policy of the T.S. must be vindicated if you would not see it fall into ruin and bury your reputations under it. I have told you long ago. For years to come the Soc. will be unable to stand when based upon "Tibetan Brothers" and phenomena alone. *ML 55, p. 323*

(12) I said it was easy to produce phenomena, when the necessary conditions were given, but not that even the presence of Olcott and Mallapura at your house brought such an accession of force as would suffice for the tests you propose.
ML 35, p. 246

(13) ... my good friend, abandon all notion that this "Professor" can bodily appear and instruct you for years to come. *I* may come to you personally – unless you drive me off, as Mr. Hume did – I cannot come to ALL. You may get phenomena and proofs but even were you to fall into the old error and attribute them to

"Spirits" we could but show you your mistake by philosophical and logical explanations; no adept would be allowed to attend your meetings. *ML 5, p. 21*

(14) ... I must tell you (Sinnet) now, that for opening "direct communication" the only possible means would be: (1) For each of us to meet in our own *physical* bodies. I being where I am, and you in your own quarters, there is a material impediment *for me*. (2) For both to meet in our astral form – which would necessitate your "getting out" of yours, as well as my leaving my body. The spiritual impediment to this is on your part. (3) To make you hear my voice either within you or near you as "the old lady" does.

This would be feasible in either of two ways: (a) My chiefs would have but to give permission to set up the condition – and this for the present they refuse; or (b) for you to hear my voice, i.e., my *natural voice* without any psycho-physiological *tamasha* (entertainment – Ed.) being employed by me (again as we often do among ourselves). But then, to do this, not only have one's spiritual senses to be abnormally opened, but one must himself have mastered the great secret – yet undiscovered by science – of, so to say, abolishing all the impediments of space; of neutralizing, for the time being, the natural obstacle of intermediary particles of air and forcing the waves to strike your ear in reflected sounds or echo. Of the latter you know as yet only enough to regard this as an unscientific absurdity. *ML 8, p. 28*

(15) Such a development of your psychical powers of hearing, as you name – the Siddhi of hearing occult sounds – would not be at all the easy matter you imagine. It was never done to any one of us, for the iron rule is that what powers one gets, *he must himself acquire.* And when acquired and ready for use, the powers lie dumb and dormant in their potentiality, like the wheels and clockwork inside a musical box; and only then does it become

easy to wind up the key and set them in motion. Of course you have *now* more chances before you than my zoophagous friend, Mr. Sinnett, who were he even to give up feeding on animals, would still feel a craving for such a food, a craving over which he would have no control and – the impediment would be the same in that case. Yet every earnestly disposed man *may* acquire such powers practically. That is the finality of it; there are no more distinctions of persons in this than there are as to whom the sun shall shine upon or the air give vitality to. There are the powers of all nature before you; *take what you can*. **ML 11, p. 65**

(16) Just now, I am able to give you a bit of information which bears upon the so often discussed question of our allowing phenomena. The Egyptian operations of your blessed countrymen involve such local consequences to the body of Occultists still remaining there and to what they are guarding, that two of our adepts are already there, having joined some Druze brethren, and three more on their way. I was offered the agreeable privilege of becoming an eye witness to the human butchery, but – declined with thanks. For such great emergency is our Force stored up, and hence – we dare not waste it on fashionable tamasha. **ML 16, p. 116**

(17) Well. Well, well; there's one thing at any rate we can never be accused of inventing; and that is *Mr. Hume himself*. To invent his like transcends the highest *Siddhi* powers we know of.
ML 24B, p. 185

Planetary Spirits

(1) I will first say that there can be no Planetary Spirit that was not once material or what you call human ... Many are those who "break through the eggshell," few who once out are able to exercise their *Nirara namastake* fully when completely out of the body. *Conscious* life in Spirit is as difficult for some natures as swimming is for some bodies. Though the human frame is lighter in its bulk than water, and though every person is born with the faculty, so few develop in themselves the art of treading water, that death by drowning is the most frequent of accidents. The planetary Spirit of that kind (the Buddha like) can pass at will into other bodies – of more or less etherealised matter, inhabiting other regions of the Universe. There are many other grades and orders, but there is no *separate* and eternally constituted order of Planetary Spirits. *ML 9, pp. 43-44*

(2) The bodies of the Planetary Spirits are formed of that, which Priestley and others called *Phlogiston* and for which we have another name – this essence in its highest, seventh state, forming that matter of which the organisms of the highest and purest Dhyans are composed, and in its lowest or densest form (so impalpable yet that science calls it energy and force) serving as a cover to the Planetaries of the 1st or lowest degree. *ML 10, p. 56*

(3) ... so far as the highest Planetary Spirits have ascertained (who, remember well have the same relations with the transcosmical world, penetrating behind the veil of this, our gross physical world) the infinite mind displays to them, as to us, no more than the regular, unconscious throbbings of the eternal and universal pulse of nature, throughout the myriads of worlds within as without the primitive veil of our solar system.
So far – WE KNOW. *Within* and to the utmost limit, to the very

edge of the cosmic veil we know the fact to be correct – owing to personal experience, for the information gathered as to what takes place beyond, we are indebted to the Planetary Spirits, to our blessed Lord Buddha. This of course may be regarded as secondhand information. *ML 22, p. 138*

(4) What lies beyond and outside the worlds of form and being, in worlds and spheres in their most spiritualized state – is useless for anyone to search after, since even the Planetary Spirits have no knowledge or perception of it. *ML 22, p. 139*

(5) Nath is right about the phonetic pronunciation of the word "Kiu-te." people usually pronounce it as Kiu-to, but it is *not* correct; and he is wrong in his view about Planetary Spirits. He does not know the word, and thought you meant the "devas" – the servants of the Dhyan Chohans. It is the latter who are the "Planetary" and of course it is *illogical* to say that adepts are greater than they, since we all strive to become Dhyan-Chohans in *the end*. Still, there have been adepts "greater" than the *lower* degrees of the Planetary. *ML 54, p. 321*

(6) At the beginning of each Round, when humanity reappears under quite different conditions than those afforded for the birth of each new race and its sub-races, a "Planetary" has to mix with these primitive men and to refresh their memories, and reveal to them the truths they knew during the preceding Round. *Hence the confused traditions about Jehovahs, Ormazds, Osirises, Brahms, and the tutti quanti.* But that happens only for the benefit of the *first* Race. It is the duty of the latter to choose the fit recipients among its sons, who are "set apart" – to use a Biblical phrase – as the vessels to contain the *whole stock of knowledge,* to be divided among the future races and generations, until the close of that Round ... Why should I say more since you *must* understand my whole meaning; and that I *dare* not reveal it in full. Every Race

had its adepts; and with every new race we are allowed to give them out as much of our knowledge as the men of that race deserve. The last seventh Race will have its Buddha as every one of its predecessors had; but, its adepts will be far higher than any of the present race, for among them will abide the future Planetary, the Dhyan Chohan whose duty it will be to instruct or "refresh the memory" of the first race of the fifth Round men, after this planet's future obscuration. *ML 23B, p. 157*

(7) ... these (Planetary Spirits) appear on Earth but at the origin of every new human kind; at the juncture of and close of the two ends of the great cycle. And, they remain with man no longer than the time required for the eternal truths they teach to impress themselves so forcibly upon the plastic minds of the new races as to warrant them from being lost or entirely forgotten in ages hereafter by the forthcoming generations. The mission of the planetary Spirit is but to strike the KEY NOTE OF TRUTH. Once he has directed the vibration of the latter to run its course uninterruptedly along the catenation of that race and to the end of the cycle – the denizen of the highest inhabited sphere disappears from the surface of our planet – 'till the following "resurrection of flesh." The vibrations of the Primitive Truth are what your philosophers name "innate ideas." *ML 9, p. 41*

(8) The notions of hells and purgatory, of paradises and resurrections are all caricatured, distorted echoes of the primeval one Truth, taught humanity in the infancy of its races by every First messenger – the Planetary Spirit ... and whose remembrance lingered in the memory of man as Elu of the Chaldees, Osiris the Egyptian, Vishnu, the first Buddha and so on. *ML 9, p. 48*

The Planets

(1) No planets but one hath hitherto (1882) been discovered outside of the solar system, with all their photometers, while we know, with the sole help of our spiritual, naked eye, a number of them; every *completely matured* Sun-star having, like in our own system, several companion planets in fact ... (Neither) the Chaldees nor yet our old Rishis had either your telescopes or photometers; and yet their astronomical predictions were faultless, the mistakes, very slight ones in truth – fathered upon them by their modern rivals – proceeding from the mistakes of the latter. *ML 23B, p. 165*

(2) Not all of the Intra-Mercurial planets, nor yet those in the orbit of Neptune are yet discovered, though they are strongly suspected. We know that such exist and where they exist; and that there are innumerable planets "burnt out" they say – *in obscuration*, we say – planets in formation and not yet luminous, etc. But then "we know" is of little use in science, when the Spiritualists will not admit our knowledge. Edison's tasimeter, adjusted to its utmost degree of sensitiveness and attached to a large telescope, may be of great use when perfected. When so attached, the *"tasimeter"* will afford the possibility, not only to measure the heat of the remotest of visible stars, but to detect by their invisible radiations stars that are unseen and otherwise undetectable, hence planets also.

The discoverer, an F.T.S., a good deal protected by M., thinks that if at any point in a blank space of heavens – a space that appears blank even through a telescope of highest power – the *tasimeter* indicates an accession of temperature and does so invariably, this will be a regular proof that the instrument is in range, with the stellar body either non-luminous or so distant as to be beyond the reach of telescopic vision. His *tasimeter*, he says, "is affected by a wider range of etheric undulations than the eye can take cognizance of." Science will *hear* sounds from certain planets before she *sees* them. This is a *prophecy*. Unfortunately I am not a Planet –- not even a "planetary." Otherwise I would advise you to get a *tasimeter* from him and thus avoid me the trouble of writing to you. I would manage then to find myself "in range" with you. *ML 23B, pp. 169-170*

(3) ... every planet and mineral that exists in space or inside the earth is known and recorded in our books thousands of years ago; many a true hypothesis was timidly brought forward by their own scientific men and as constantly rejected by the majority, with whose preconceptions it interfered. ... Whenever discovered that "it is verily so," the discovery will be attributed to him who corroborated the evidence – as in the case of Copernicus and Galileo, the latter having availed himself but of the Pythagorean MSS. *ML 23B, p. 153*

(4) There are other and innumerable manvantaric chains of globes bearing intelligent beings – both in and out of our solar system – the crowning apexes of evolutionary being in their respective chains, some – physically and intellectually – lower, others immeasurably higher than the man of our chain. But beyond mentioning them we will not speak of these at present. *ML18, p. 119*

(5) The whole of our system is imperceptibly shifting its position in space. The relative distance between planets remaining ever the same and being in no wise affected by the displacement of the whole system; and the distance between the latter and the stars and other suns being so incommensurable as to produce but little if any perceptible change for centuries and millennium to come, no astronomer will perceive it *telescopically*, until Jupiter

and some other planets, whose little luminous points hide now from sight millions upon millions of stars (all but some 5000 or 6000) – will suddenly let us have a peep at a few of the *Raja-Suns* they are now hiding.

There is such a king-star right behind Jupiter, that no mortal physical eye has ever seen during this, our Round. Could it be so perceived it would appear, through the best telescope with a power of multiplying its diameter ten thousand times, still a small dimensionless point, thrown into the shadow by the brightness of any planet; nevertheless – this world is thousands of times larger than Jupiter. The violent disturbance of its atmosphere, and even its red spot that so intrigues science lately, are due – (1) to that shifting and (2) to the influence of that Raja-Star.

In its present position in space, imperceptibly small though it be, the metallic substances of which it is mainly composed are expanding and gradually transforming themselves into aeriform fluids – the state of our own earth and its six sister globes before the first Round – and becoming part of its atmosphere. Draw your inferences and deductions from this, my dear "lay" chela (Sinnett), but beware, lest in doing so you sacrifice your humble instructor and the occult doctrine itself on the altar of your wrathful Goddess – *modern* science. **ML 23B, p. 167**

(6) If our greatest adepts and Bodhisattvas have never penetrated themselves beyond our solar system ... they still know of the existence of other such solar systems, with as mathematical a certainty as any western astronomer knows of the existence of invisible stars, which he can never approach to explore. But of that which lies within the worlds and systems, not in the transinfinite – (a queer expression to use) – but in the cis-infinitude rather, in the state of the purest and inconceivable immateriality, no one ever knew or will ever tell, hence it is something non-existent for the universe. **ML 22, p. 139**

Pralayas and Manvantaras

(1) There are three kinds of pralayas and manvantara:–

(Section) 1. The Universal or Maha pralaya and manvantara;
(Section) 2. The solar pralaya and manvantara;
(Section) 3. The minor pralaya and manvantara.

When the pralaya No.1 is finished, the universal manvantara begins. Then the whole universe must be re-evoluted *de novo*. When the pralaya of a solar system comes, it affects that solar system only. A solar pralaya = 7 minor pralayas. The minor pralayas of No.3 concern but our little string of globes, whether man bearing or not. To such a string our Earth belongs.

Besides this, within a minor pralaya, there is a condition of planetary *rest* or as the astronomers say "death," like that of our present moon – in which the rocky body of the planet survives but the life impulse has passed out. For example, let us imagine that our earth is one of a group of seven planets or man bearing worlds, more or less elliptically arranged. Our earth being at the exact lower central point of the orbit of evolution, viz. halfway round – we will call the first globe A, the last Z. After each solar pralaya there is a *complete* destruction of our system and after each solar pralaya, begins the absolute objective reformation of our system and each time everything is more perfect than before. *ML 15, p. 93-94*

(2) The periods with pralaya and manvantara are called by Dikshita (initiates) "Surya manvantaras and pralayas." Thought is baffled in speculating how many of our solar pralayas must come before the great Cosmic night – but that will come. *ML 15, p. 97*

(3) ... In the minor pralayas there is no starting *de novo* – only resumption of arrested activity. *ML 15, p. 97*

(4) When strikes the hour of the solar pralaya – though the process of man's advance on his last seventh round is precisely the same, each planet, instead of merely passing out of the visible into the invisible as he quits it, in turn is annihilated. With the beginning of the seventh Round of the seventh minor manvantara, every kingdom having now reached its last cycle, there remains on each planet after the exit of man but the maya of once living and existing forms. With every step he takes on the descending and ascending arcs, as he moves on from Globe to Globe, the planet left behind becomes an empty chrysaloidal case. At his departure, there is an outflow from every kingdom of its entities. Waiting to pass into higher forms in due time, they are nevertheless liberated: for to the day of that evolution they will rest in their lethargic sleep in space, until again energized into life in the new solar manvantara. The old elementals will rest until they are called to become, in their turn, the bodies of mineral, vegetable and animal entities (on another and a higher string of globes) on their way to become human entities, (see *Isis*) while the germinal entities of the lowest forms – and in that time of general perfection there will remain but few of such – will hang in space like drops of water suddenly turned to icicles. They will thaw at the first hot breath of a solar manvantara and form the soul of the future globes .... *ML 15, pp. 97-98*

(5) For, as planetary evolution is as progressive as human or race evolution, the hour of the pralaya's coming catches the series of worlds at successive stages of evolution i.e. each has attained to some one of the periods of evolutionary progress – each stops there, until the outward impulse of the next *manvantara* sets it going from that very point – like a stopped timepiece rewound. *ML 12, p. 67*

(6) At the coming of the Pralaya, no human, animal, or even vegetable entity will be alive to see it, but there will be the earth or globes with their mineral kingdoms; and all these planets will be physically disintegrated in the pralaya, yet not destroyed; for they have their places in the sequence of evolution, and their "privations" coming again out of the subjective, they will find the exact point from which they have to move on around the chain of "manifested forms." This, as we know, is repeated endlessly throughout ETERNITY. Each man of us has gone this ceaseless round and will repeat it for ever and ever. The deviation of each one's course, and his rate of progress from Nirvana to Nirvana, is governed by causes which he himself creates, out of the exigencies in which he finds himself entangled.

ML 12, pp. 67-68

(7) You have among the learned members of your society one Theosophist who, without familiarity with our occult doctrine, has yet intuitively grasped from scientific data the idea of a solar pralaya and its manvantara in their beginnings. I mean the celebrated French astronomer Flammarion – "La Resurrection et la Fin des Mondes"... He speaks like a true seer. The facts are as he surmises, with slight modifications. In consequence of the secular refrigeration, (old age rather and loss of vital power) solidification and desiccation of the globes, the earth arrives at a point when it begins to be a relaxed conglomerate. The period of child-bearing is gone by. The progeny are all nurtured, its term of life is finished. Hence, "its constituent masses cease to obey those laws of cohesion and aggregation which held them together." And becoming like a cadaver which, abandoned to the work of destruction, would leave each molecule composing it free to separate itself from the body forever to obey in future the sway of new influences, the attraction of the moon (would that he could know the full extent of its pernicious influence) would

itself undertake the task of demolition, by producing a tidal wave of earth particles instead of an aqueous tide. *ML 15, pp. 98-99*

(8) There comes a time when polarity ceases to exist *or act,* as everything else. In the night of mind, all is equilibrised in the boundless cosmos, in a state of non-action or non-being. *Cosmological Notes, LBS – First Edition, p. 379*

Precipitation – "The Writing Process"

(1) Of course *I have to read* every word you write: otherwise I would make a fine mess of it. And whether it be through my physical or spiritual eyes, the time required for it is practically the same. As much may be said of my replies. For whether I "precipitate" or dictate them or write my answers myself, the difference in time saved is very minute. I have to *think* it over, to photograph every word and sentence carefully in my brain before it can be repeated by "precipitation."

As the fixing on chemically prepared surfaces of the images formed by the camera requires a previous arrangement within the focus of the object to be represented, for otherwise – as often found in bad photographs – the legs of the sitter might appear out of all proportion with the head, and so on, so we have to first arrange our sentences and impress every letter to appear on paper in our minds before it becomes fit to read.

For the present, it is all I can tell you. When science will have learned more about the mystery of the lithophyl (or lithobiblion) and how the impress of leaves comes originally to take place on stones, then I will be able to make you better understand the process. But you must know and remember one thing: we but follow and *servilely copy nature* in her works. ***ML 6, pp. 22***

(2) And before I proceed any further, I must give you some explanations of this mode of *precipitation*. The recent experiments of the Psychic Research Society will help you greatly to comprehend the rationale of this "mental telegraphy." You observed in the Journal of that body, how thought transference is cumulatively effected. The image of the geometrical or other figure, which the active brain has had impressed upon it, is gradually imprinted upon the recipient brain of the passive subject – as the series of reproductions illustrated in the cuts

show.

Two factors are needed to produce a perfect and instantaneous mental telegraphy – close concentration in the operator, and complete receptive passivity in the "reader" subject. Given a disturbance of either condition and the result is proportionately imperfect. The reader does not see the image as in the "telegrapher's" brain but as arising in his own. When the latter's thought wanders, the psychic current becomes broken, the communications disjointed and incoherent. In a case such as mine, the chela had, as it were, to pick up what he could from the current I was sending him and as above remarked, patch the broken bits together as best he might. *ML 93, p. 422-423*

(3) Put into a mesmeric subject's hand a sheet of blank paper, tell him it contains a certain chapter of some book that you have read, concentrate your thoughts upon the words, and see how – *provided that he has himself not read the chapter,* but only takes it from your memory – his reading will reflect your own more or less vivid successive recollections of your author's language.

The same as to the precipitation by the chela of the transferred thought upon (or rather, into) paper; if the mental picture received be feeble, his visible reproduction of it must correspond. And the more so in proportion to the closeness of attention he gives. He might – were he but merely a person of the true mediumistic temperament – be employed by his "Master" as a sort of *psychic printing machine* producing lithographed or psychographed impressions of what the operator had in mind; his nerve-system, the machine, his nerve-aura the printing fluid, the colours drawn from that exhaustless storehouse of pigments (as of everything else) the Akasa. But the medium and the chela are diametrically dissimilar and the latter acts consciously, except under exceptional circumstances during development, not necessary to dwell upon here. *ML 93, pp. 423-424*

The Problem of Evil

(1) Evil has no existence *per se* and is but the absence of good and exists but for him who is made its victim. It proceeds from two causes, and no more than good is it an independent cause in nature. Nature is destitute of goodness or malice; she follows only immutable laws when she either gives life and joy, or sends suffering and death, and destroys what she has created. Nature has an antidote for every poison and her laws a reward for every suffering. The butterfly devoured by a bird becomes that bird, and the little bird killed by an animal goes into a higher form. It is the blind law of necessity and the eternal fitness of things and hence cannot be called Evil in Nature. *ML 10, pp. 56-57*

(2) The real evil proceeds from human intelligence and its origin rests entirely with reasoning man, who dissociates himself from Nature. Humanity, then, alone is the true source of evil. Evil is the exaggeration of good, the progeny of human selfishness and greediness. Think profoundly and you will find that save death – which is no evil but a necessary law, and accidents which will always find their reward in a future life – the origin of every evil whether small or great is in human action, in man whose intelligence makes him the one free agent in Nature ... Food, sexual relations, drink are all natural necessities of life; yet excess in them brings on disease, misery, suffering, mental and physical and the latter are transmitted as the greatest evils to future generations, the progeny of the culprits. *ML 10, p. 57*

(3) Ambition, the desire of securing happiness and comfort for those we love by obtaining honours and riches, are praiseworthy natural feelings, but when they transform man into an ambitious cruel tyrant, a miser, a selfish egotist they bring untold misery on those around him; on nations as well as on individuals. All this

then – food, wealth, ambition, and a thousand other things we have to leave unmentioned, becomes the source and cause of evil whether in its abundance or through its absence. Lack all this and you starve, you are despised as a nobody, and the majority of the herd, your fellow men, make of you a sufferer your whole life. Therefore, it is neither nature nor an imaginary Deity that has to be blamed, but human nature made vile by *selfishness*. Think well over these few words; work out every cause of evil you can think of and trace it to its origin and you will have solved *one-third* of the problem of evil. *ML 10, pp. 57-58*

(4) And now, after making due allowance for evils that are natural and cannot be avoided – and so few are they that I challenge the whole host of Western metaphysicians to call them evils or to trace them directly to an independent cause – I will point out the greatest, the chief cause of nearly two-thirds of the evils that pursue humanity ever since that cause became a power. It is religion under whatever form and in whatsoever nation. It is the sacerdotal caste, the priesthood and the churches; it is in those illusions that man looks upon as sacred that he has to search out the source of that multitude of evils which is the great curse of humanity and that almost overwhelms mankind. Ignorance created Gods and cunning took advantage of the opportunity. Look at India and look at Christendom and Islam, at Judaism and Fetichism. It is priestly imposture that rendered these Gods so terrible to man; it is religion that makes of him the selfish bigot, the fanatic that hates all mankind out of his own sect, without rendering him any better or more moral for it. *ML 10, pp 57-58*

(5) It is belief in God and Gods, that makes two-thirds of humanity the slaves of a handful of those who deceive them under the false pretence of saving them. Is not man ever ready to commit any kind of evil if told that his God or Gods demand the

crime – voluntary victim of an illusionary God, the abject slave of his crafty ministers? The Irish, Italian and Slavonian peasant will starve himself and see his family starving and naked to feed and clothe his padre and pope. For two thousand years, India groaned under the weight of caste, Brahmins alone feeding on the fat of the land, and today the followers of Christ and those of Mahomet are cutting each other's throats in the names of and for the greater glory of their respective myths. Remember the sum of human misery will never be diminished unto that day when the better portion of humanity destroys, in the name of Truth, morality, and universal charity, the altars of their false gods. *ML 10, p. 58*

(6) If it is objected that we too have temples, we too have priests and that our lamas also live on charity ... let them know that the objects above named have in common with their Western equivalents but the name. Thus in our temples there is neither a god nor gods worshipped, only the thrice sacred memory of the greatest, as the holiest man that ever lived. If our lamas to honour the fraternity of the *Bhikkhus*, established by our blessed master himself, go out to be fed by the laity, the latter, often to the number of 5 to 25,000 is fed and taken care by the *Samgha*, (the fraternity of lamaic monks) the lamasery providing for the wants of the poor, the sick, the afflicted. Our lamas accept food, never money, and it is in those temples that the origin of evil is preached and impressed upon the people. There they are taught the four noble truths – *ariya* sacca, and the chain of the causation (the 12 nidanas) gives them a solution of the problem of the origin and the destruction of suffering. *ML 10, p. 58*

(7) And now to your extraordinary hypothesis that Evil, with its attendant train of sin and suffering, is not the result of matter, but may be perchance the wise scheme of the moral Governor of the Universe. Conceivable as the idea may seem to you, trained

in the pernicious fallacy of the Christian – "the ways of the Lord are inscrutable" – it is utterly inconceivable for me. Must I repeat again that the best Adepts have searched the Universe during millennium and found nowhere the slightest trace of such a Machiavellian schemer – but throughout, the same immutable, inexorable law. *ML 22, pp. 142-143*

Reincarnation

(1) A.P. Sinnett is *not* "an absolutely *new* invention." He is the child and creation of his antecedent personal self; the *karmic* progeny, for all he knows of Nonius Asprenas, Council of the Emperor Domitian – (94 A.D.) together with Arricinius Clemens (should be Clemens Arretinus – Ed.) and friend of the *Flamen Dialis* of that day (the high priest of Jupiter and chief of the *flamenes*) or of that *Flamen himself* – which would account for A.P. Sinnett's suddenly developed love for mysticism. A.P.S., the friend and brother of K.H. will go to *Devachan*; and A.P.S., the Editor and the lawn-tennis man, the Don Juan, in a mild way, in the palmy days of "Saints, Sinners and Sceneries," ... will, perhaps, be abusing the Babus through a medium of some old friend in California or London.

The Spiritual Ego will not think of the A.P.S. the shell, any more than it will think of the last suit of clothes it wore; nor will it be conscious that the individuality is gone, since the only *individuality* and *Spiritual personality* it will then behold (will be) in itself alone. *ML 23B, p. 175*

(2) ... he (man) has to perform seven rings through seven races and seven multiplied by seven offshoots ... one life in each of the seven root races; seven lives in each of 49 sub-races – or 7x7x7 = 343 and add 7 more. And then a series of lives in offshoot and branchlet races; making the total incarnations of man in each station or planet 777. Not much to divide over some millions of years that man passes on one planet. Let us take but one million years – suspected and now accepted by your science – to represent man's entire term upon our earth in this Round (i.e. 5th Root Race – Ed.) and allowing an average of a century for each life, we find that whereas he has passed in all his lives upon our planet (in this round) but 77,700 years, he has been in the

177

subjective spheres 922,300 years. Not much encouragement for the extreme modern reincarnationists, who remember their several previous existences!

Should you indulge in any calculations, do not forget that we have computed above only full average lives of consciousness and responsibility. Nothing has been said of the failures of nature in abortions, death of children in their first septenary cycles, nor of the exceptions of which I cannot speak. No less have you to remember that average human life varies greatly according to the Rounds. Though I am obliged to withhold information about many points, yet if you should work out any of the problems by yourself it will be my duty to tell you so. Try to solve the problem of the 777 incarnations.
ML 14, pp. 82-83

(3) Each of the seven races send seven ramifying branchlets from the Parent Branch: and through each of these in turn, man *has* to evolute before he passes on to the next higher race; and that – seven times. Well may you open wide your eyes, good friend, and feel puzzled – it is so. *ML 18, p. 119*

(4) Through every race, then, man has to pass, making seven successive entrances and exits and developing intellect to degrees from the lowest to the highest in succession. In short, this earth-cycle with its rings and *sub*-rings is the exact counterpart of the Great Cycle – only in miniature. Bear in mind again, that the intervals even between these special "race re-incarnations" are enormous, as even the dullest of the African Bushmen has to reap the reward of his Karma, equally with his brother Bushman, who may be six-times more intelligent.
ML 18, p. 120

(5) Yes, the "full" remembrance of our lives (*collective* lives) will return back at the end of *all the seven Rounds*, at the threshold of

the long, long Nirvana that awaits us after we leave Globe Z (i.e. the 7th globe of our earth chain – Ed.). At the end of isolated Rounds, we remember but the sum total of our last impressions, those we had selected, or that have rather *forced* themselves upon us and followed us in *Devachan*. Those are all "probationary" lives, with large indulgences and new trials afforded us with every new life. But at the close of the minor cycle, after the completion of all the seven Rounds, there awaits *us no other* mercy but the cup of good deeds, of *merit*, outweighing that of *evil* deeds and *demerit* in the scales of Retributive Justice.
ML 23B, p. 171

(6) ... the monad, having no *Karmic* body to guide its rebirth, falls into *non-being* for a certain period and then reincarnates – certainly not earlier than a thousand or two thousand years ... Save a few exceptional cases in the case of the initiated, such as our Teshu-Lamas and the Bodhisatwas and a few others, no monad ever gets reincarnated before its appointed time.
ML 23B p. 176

(7) All of us ... bring some characteristics from our previous incarnations. It is *unavoidable. ML 23A, p. 145*

(8) "Man know thyself," said the Delphian oracle. There is nothing "improper" – certainly in such a curiosity (regarding the inquiry of particulars of one's previous life/lives –Ed.) Only would it not be still more proper to study our own, present, personality before attempting to learn anything of its *creator*, predecessor and fashioner – the man *that was? ML 23A p. 145*

(9) The "astral monad" is the "personal Ego" and therefore it *never* reincarnates, as the French Spiritists will have it, but under "exceptional circumstances" in which case, reincarnating, *it does not become a shell*, but if successful in its second reincarnation will

become one, and then gradually lose its personality, after being, so to say, *emptied* of its best and highest spiritual attributes by the immortal or the *"Spiritual Ego,"* during the last and supreme struggle. **ML 24B, p. 183**

(10) And this weary round of birth upon birth must be ever and ever run through, until the being reaches the end of the seventh round or – attains in the interim the wisdom of an Arhat, then that of a Buddha and thus gets relieved for a round or two – having learned how to burst through the vicious circles – and to pass periodically into the Paranirvana. **ML 25, p. 196**

(11) You cannot persuade him (Stainton Moses) that + (Imperator) is a living brother, for that was tried and – failed; unless, indeed, you convert him to popular *exoteric* Lamaism, which regards our "Byang-chubs" and "Tchang-chubs" – the Brothers who pass from the body of one great Lama to that of another – as *Lhas* or *disembodied* Spirits … The *Tchang-chub* (an adept who has, by the power of his knowledge and soul enlightenment, become exempt from the curse of UNCONSCIOUS transmigration) – may at his will and desire, and instead of reincarnating himself only after bodily death, do so, and repeatedly – during his life if he chooses. He holds the power of choosing for himself new bodies – whether on this or any other planet – while in possession of his old form, that he generally preserves for purposes of his own. Read the book of Kiu-te and you will find in it these laws. She (H.P.B.) might translate for you some paras, as she knows them by rote. **ML 49, p. 285**

(12) Not even in the case of the "failures of nature," of the *immediate* reincarnation of children … can we call them the *identical* ex-personalities; *though the whole of the same life-principle and identically the same* Manas (fifth principle) *re-enters a new body* and may be truly called a "reincarnation of the *personality*" –

whereas, in the rebirth of the Egos from devachans and avitchis into karmic life, it is only the spiritual attributes of the Monad and its Buddhi that are reborn. All we can say of the reincarnated "failures" is, that they are the reincarnated Manas, the fifth principle of Mr. Smith or Miss. Grey, but certainly not that these are the reincarnations of Mr. S. and Miss. G. *ML 23B, p. 172*

(13) Thus far, Mrs. Kingsford's ideas that the human Ego is being reincarnated in several successive human bodies is the true one. As to its being reborn in animal forms after *human* incarnation, it is the result of her loose way of expressing things and ideas. Another WOMAN – all over again. Why, she confounds "Soul and Spirit," refuses to discriminate between the animal and spiritual Egos ... two things as different as body and mind, and – *mind* and *thought* are! *ML9, p. 46*

(14) What has the number of incarnations to do with the shrewdness and cleverness, or the stupidity of an individual? A strong craving for physical life may lead an entity through a number of incarnations and yet these may not develop its higher capacities. The Law of Affinity acts through the inherent *Karmic* impulse of the Ego, and governs its future existence. Comprehending Darwin's Law of Heredity for the body, it is not difficult to perceive how the birth seeking Ego may be attracted at the time of rebirth to a new body, born in a family which has the same propensities as those of the reincarnating Entity. *ML 86, p, 404*

(15) I have no right to look into your past life. Whenever I may have caught glimpses of it, I have inevitably turned my eyes away, for I have to deal with the present A.P. Sinnett – (also and by far more "a new invention" than the ex-A.P.S.) – not with the ancient man. *ML 24B, p. 188*

(16) "Nature spews the lukewarm out of her mouth" means only that she annihilates their *personal* Egos (not the shells, nor yet the sixth principle) in the Kama Loka and the Deva-chan. This does not prevent them from being immediately reborn – and, if their lives were not very, very bad – there is no reason why the eternal Monad should not find the page of that life intact in the Book of Life. *ML 20C, p. 134*

Rounds, Globes and Chains

(1) As the new round begins it catches the new influx of life, reawakens to vitality and begets all its kingdoms of a superior order to the last. After this has been repeated seven times, comes a minor pralaya; the chain of globes are not destroyed by disintegration and dispersion of their particles but pass in abscondito. From this they will re-emerge in their turn, during the next septenary period. Within one solar period (of a p. and m.) occur seven such minor periods, in an ascending scale of progressive development. To recapitulate, there are in the round seven planetary or earth rings for each kingdom and one obscuration of each planet. The minor manvantara is composed of seven rounds, 49 rings and 7 obscurations, the solar period of 49 rounds etc.
ML 15, p. 97

(2) The first race (or stock) of the first round ... would then be a god-man race of an almost impalpable shape, and so it is; but then comes the difficulty to the student to reconcile this fact with the evolution of man from the animal – however high his form among the anthropoids. And yet, it is reconcilable, for whomsoever will hold religiously to a strict analogy between the works of the two worlds, the visible and the invisible – one world, in fact, as one is working within itself so to say.
ML 14 pp. 86-87

(3) Thus we have:

1st Round. – An ethereal being – *non-intelligent*, but super-spiritual. In each of the subsequent races and sub-races and minor races of evolution he grows more and more into an encased or incarnate being, but still preponderatingly ethereal.

And like the animal and vegetable he develops monstrous bodies correspondential with his coarse surroundings.

2nd Round. – He is still gigantic and ethereal, but growing firmer and more condensed in body – a more physical man, yet still less intelligent than spiritual; for mind is a slower and more difficult evolution than the physical frame, and the mind would not develop as rapidly as the body.

3rd Round. – He has now a perfectly concrete or compacted body; at first the form of a giant ape, and more intelligent (or rather cunning) than spiritual. For in the downward arc he has now reached the point where his primordial spirituality is eclipsed or overshadowed by nascent mentality. In the last half of this third round his gigantic stature decreases, his body improves in texture … and he becomes a more rational being – though still more an ape than a Deva man.

4th Round. – Intellect has an enormous development in this round. The dumb races will acquire our human speech on our globe, on which from the 4th race language is perfected and knowledge in physical things increases. At this half way point of the fourth round, humanity passes the *axial point of the minor manvantaric circle* … At this point then the world teems with the results of intellectual activity and *spiritual decrease*. In the first half of the fourth race, sciences, arts, literature and philosophy were born, eclipsed in one nation, reborn in another, civilization and intellectual development whirling in septenary cycles as the rest; while it is but in the latter half that the spiritual Ego will begin its real struggle with body and mind to manifest its transcendental powers. Who will help in the forthcoming gigantic struggle? Who? Happy the man who helps a helping hand.

5th Round. – The same relative development and the same

struggle continues.

6th Round.

7th Round.

Of these we need not speak. **ML 14, pp. 87-88**

(4) At each Round there are less and less animals – the latter themselves evoluting into higher forms. During the first Round it is *they* that were the "kings of *creation*." During the seventh men will have become *Gods*, and animals – intelligent beings. Draw your inferences. Beginning with the second Round, already evolution proceeds on quite a different plan. Everything is evolved and has but to proceed on quite a different plan on its cyclic journey and get perfected ... The method changes entirely for the second Round; but – I have learned prudence with you; and will say nothing before the time for saying it has come. And now you have had a volume; when will you digest it?
ML 23B, pp. 177-178

(5) Drawn by its "chemical affinity" ... to coalesce with other like atoms, the aggregate sum of such united atoms will in time become a man-bearing globe after the stages of the cloud, spiral and sphere of fire-mist and of the condensation, consolidation, shrinkage and cooling of the planet have been successively passed through. But mind, not every globe becomes a "man bearer." I simply state the fact without dwelling further upon it in this connection.

The great difficulty in grasping the idea in the above process lies in the liability to form more or less incomplete mental conceptions of the working of the *one* element, of its inevitable presence in every imponderable atom, and its subsequent ceaseless and almost illimitable multiplication of new centres of

activity, without affecting in the least its own original quality.
ML 15, p. 89

(6) Our earth being at the exact lower central point of the orbit of evolution viz., half way round – we will call the first globe A, the last Z. After each solar pralaya there is a *complete* destruction of our system and after each solar p. begins the absolute objective reformation of our system and each time everything is more perfect than before.

Now the life impulse reaches "A" or rather that which is destined to become "A" and which so far is but cosmic dust. A centre is formed in the nebulous matter of the condensation of the solar dust disseminated through space and a series of three evolutions invisible to the eye of flesh occur in succession, viz. three kingdoms of elementals or nature forces are evoluted: in other words the animal soul of the future globe is formed; or as a Kabalist will express it, the gnomes, salamanders, and the undines are created ....

The three evolutions completed, palpable globes begin to form. The mineral kingdom, fourth in the whole series but first in this stage, leads the way. Its deposits are at first vaporous, soft and plastic, only becoming hard and concrete in the seventh ring. When this ring is completed it projects its essence to globe B – which is already passing through the preliminary stages of formation and mineral evolution begins on that globe. At this juncture the evolution of the vegetable kingdom commences on globe A. When the latter has made its seventh ring its essence passes on to globe B. At that time the mineral essence moves to globe C and the germs of the animal kingdom enter A. When the latter has made its seventh ring its essence passes on to globe B. At that time the mineral essence moves to globe C and the germs of the animal kingdom enter A. When the animal has seven rings there, its life principle goes to globe B and the essences of vegetable and mineral move on. Then comes man on A, an ethereal foreshadowing of the compact being he is destined to become on our earth. Evolving seven parent races with many offshoots of sub-races, he, like the preceding kingdoms, completes his seven rings and is then transferred successively to each of the globes, onward to Z (the last of the seven globes of the earth chain – Ed.). *ML 15, p. 94-95*

(7) From the first, man has all the seven principles included in him in germ but none are developed. If we compare him to a baby, we will be right; no one has ever, in the thousands of ghost stories current, seen the ghost of an infant, though the imagination of a loving mother may have suggested to her the picture of her lost babe in dreams. In each of the rounds he makes, one of the principles develop fully. In the first round his consciousness on our earth is dull and but feeble and shadowy, something like that of an infant. When he reaches our earth in the second round, he has become responsible in a degree, in the third he becomes so entirely. At every stage and every round his development keeps pace with the globe on which he is.

The descending arc from A to our earth is called the shadowy, the ascending to Z, the "luminous"... We men of the fourth round are already reaching the latter half of the fifth race of our fourth round humanity, while the men (the few earlier comers) of the fifth round, though only in their first race (or rather class), are yet immeasurably higher than we are – spiritually if not intellectually; since with the completion or full development of this fifth principle, (intellectual soul) they have come nearer than we have, are closer in contact with their sixth principle, Buddhi. Of course many are the differentiated individuals even in the fourth round, as germs of principles are not equally developed in all, but such is the rule. *ML 15, p. 95*

(8) When all kingdoms have reached globe Z, they will not move forward to re-enter A in precedence of man but under a law of

retardation operative from the central point – or earth ... they will have just finished their respective evolution of genera and species when man reaches his highest development on globe Z – in this or any round. The reason for it is found in the enormously greater time required by them to develop their infinite varieties, as compared with man; the relative speed of development *in the rings* therefore naturally increases as we go up the scale from the mineral. But these different rates are so adjusted by man stopping longer in the inter-planetary spheres of rest, for weal or woe – all kingdoms finish their work simultaneously on the planet Z. For example, on our globe we see the equilibrating law manifesting.

From the first appearance of man, whether speechless or not, to his present one as a fourth and the coming fifth round being, the structural intention of his organization has not radically changed, ethnological characteristics, however varied, affecting in no way man as a *human being*. The fossil of man or his skeleton, whether of the period of that mammalian branch of which he forms the crown, whether cyclop or dwarf, can be still recognized at a glance as a relic of man. Plants and animals meanwhile, have become more and more unlike what they were ... The scheme with its septenary details would be incomprehensible to man, had he not the power, as the higher Adepts have proved, of prematurely developing his 6th and 7th senses – those which will be the natural endowment of all in the corresponding rounds ....

When man is perfected in a given round on Globe A, he disappears thence (as had certain vegetables and animals). By degrees this Globe loses its vitality and finally reaches the moon stage, i.e. death, and so remains while man is making his seven rings on Z and passing the inter-cyclic period before starting on his next round. So with each Globe in turn. *ML 15, pp. 95-96*

(9) And now, as man, when completing his seventh ring upon A has but begun his first on Z and as A dies when he leaves it for B

etc. and as he must also remain in the inter-cyclic sphere after Z, as he has between every two planets, until the impulse again thrills the chain, clearly no one can be more than one round ahead of his kind. And Buddha only forms an exception by virtue of the *mystery*.

We have fifth round men among us because we are in the latter half of our septenary earth ring. In the first half this could not have happened. The countless myriads of our fourth round humanity, who have outrun us and completed their seven rings on Z, have had time to pass their inter-cyclic period (and) begin their new round and work onto globe D (ours). But how can there be men of the 1st, 2nd, 3rd, 6th and 7th rounds? We represent the first three, and the sixth can only come at rare intervals and prematurely, like Buddha (only under prepared conditions) and the last named, the seventh, are not yet evolved! We have traced man out of a round, into the Nirvanic state, between Z and A. A was left in the last round dead. *ML 15, pp. 96-97*

Science

(1) You (Hume) say there are few branches of science with which you do not possess more or less acquaintance and that you believe you are doing a certain amount of good, having acquired the position to do this by long years of study. But will you permit me to sketch for you still clearly the difference between the modes of – physical called exact – often out of mere politeness – and metaphysical sciences? The latter, as you know, being incapable of verification before mixed audiences, is classed by Mr. Tyndall with the fictions of poetry. Now for us poor and unknown philanthropists, no fact of either of these sciences is interesting, except in the degree of its potentiality of moral results and in the ratio of its usefulness to mankind. And what, in its proud isolation, can be more utterly indifferent to every one and everything, or more bound to nothing but the selfish requisites for its advancement, than this materialistic and realistic science of fact?

May I not ask then, without being taxed with a vain "display of science," what have the laws of Faraday, Tyndall, or others to do with philanthropy in their abstract relations with humanity, viewed as an integral whole? What care they for MAN as an isolated atom of this great and harmonious Whole, even though they may sometimes be of practical use to him? Cosmic energy is something eternal and incessant, matter is indestructible, and there stand the scientific *facts*. Doubt them and you are an ignoramus; deny them, a dangerous lunatic; a bigot; pretend to improve upon the theories – an impertinent charlatan.

And yet, even these scientific facts never suggested any proof in the world of experimenters that nature consciously prefers that matter should be indestructible under organic rather than under inorganic forms; and that she works slowly but incessantly towards the realisation of this object – the evolution of conscious life out of inert material. Hence their ignorance about the scattering of concretion of cosmic energy in its metaphysical aspects; their division about Darwin's theories; their uncertainty about the degree of conscious life in separate elements; and as a necessity, the scornful rejection of every phenomena outside their own stated conditions and the very idea of worlds of semi-intelligent, if not intellectual, forces at work in hidden corners of nature.

First Letter of K.H. to A.O. Hume,
Combined Chronology by M. Conger, pp. 31-32

(2) Exact experimental science has nothing to do with morality, virtue, philanthropy, therefore can make no claim upon our help until it blends itself with metaphysics. Being but a cold classification of facts outside man, and existing before and after him, her domain of usefulness ceases for us at the outer boundary of these facts; and whatever the inferences and results for humanity from the materials acquired by her methods, she little cares. Therefore as our sphere lies entirely outside hers – as far as the path of *Uranus* – we distinctly refuse to be broken on any wheel of her construction.

Heat is but a mode of motion to her, and motion develops heat; but why the mechanical motion of the revolving wheel should be metaphysically of a higher value than the heat which is gradually transformed – she has yet to discover. The philosophical but transcendental (hence absurd?) notion of the medieval theosophists, that the final progress of human labour aided by the incessant discoveries of man, must one day culminate in a process, which in imitation of the sun's energy – in its capacity of a direct motor – shall result in the evolution of nutritious food out of inorganic matter – is unthinkable for men of science.

Were the sun, the great nourishing father of our planetary System, to hatch granite chickens out of a boulder "under test conditions" tomorrow, (the men of science) would accept it as a scientific fact, without wasting a regret that the fowls were not alive so as to feed the hungry and the starving.

But let a Shaberon cross the Himalayas in a time of famine and multiply sacks of rice for the perishing multitudes – as he could – and your magistrates and collectors would probably lodge him in jail, then make him confess what granary he had robbed. This is exact science and your realistic world. And though, as you say, you are impressed by the vast extent of the world's ignorance on every subject, which you pertinently designate as: "a few palpable facts collected and roughly generalized and a technical jargon invented to hide man's ignorance of all that lies behind these facts" and though you speak of your faith in the infinite possibilities of nature – yet you are content to spend your life in a work which aids only that same exact science ....

First Letter of K.H. to A.O. Hume,
Combined Chronology by M. Conger, pp. 33-34

(3) The adept, to be successful and preserve his power, must dwell in solitude and more or less within his own soul. Still less does exact science perceive that while the building ant, the busy bee, the nidifacient bird accumulate, each in their own humble way, as much cosmic energy in its potential form as a Hayden, a Plato, or a ploughman turning his furrow, in theirs; the hunter who kills game for his pleasure or profit, or the positivist who applies his intellect to proving that + X + = −, are wasting and scattering energy no less than the tiger which springs upon its prey. They all rob nature instead of enriching her and will all, in the degree of their intelligence, find themselves accountable.

K.H.'s First Letter to A.O. Hume,
Combined Chronology by M. Conger, p. 33

(4) What does modern science know of force proper or say the forces, the cause or causes of motion? How can there be such a

thing as *potential energy,* i.e. an energy having latent *inactive power,* since it is energy *only while it is moving matter,* and that *if it ever ceased to move matter, it would cease to be* and with it, matter itself would disappear? Is force any happier term?

Some thirty-five years back, a Dr. Mayer offered the hypothesis now accepted as an axiom, that force, in the sense given it by modern science, like matter, is *indestructible;* namely, when it ceases to be manifest in one form it still exists and has only *passed into some other form.* And yet your men of science have not found a single instance where one *force* is transformed into another and Mr. Tyndall tells his opponents that "in no case is the force producing the motion annihilated or changed into anything else." *ML 11, pp. 60-61*

(5) Science may go on speculating for ever yet, so long as she does not renounce two or three of her cardinal errors, she will find herself groping forever in the dark. Some of her greatest misconceptions, are found in her limited notions on the law of gravitation; her denial that matter may be imponderable; her newly invented term "force" and the absurd and tacitly accepted idea that force is capable of existing *per se,* or of acting any more than life, *outside,* independent of, or in any other wise than *through* matter; in other words, that *force is anything but matter* in one of her highest *states,* the last three of the ascending scale being denied because only science knows nothing of them; and her utter ignorance of the universal Proteus, its functions and importance in the economy of nature – magnetism and electricity.
ML 23B, p. 164

(6) There are – even among English men of Science – those who are already prepared to find our teachings in harmony with the results and progress of their own researches, and who are not indifferent to their application to the spiritual needs of humanity

at large. Amongst these it may be your task to throw the seeds of Truth and point out the path. Yet as my brother reminded you, not one of those who have only tried to help on the work of the Society, however imperfect and faulty their ways and means, will have done so in vain. *ML 33, p. 244*

(7) So the great Mr. Crookes has placed one foot across the threshold for the sake of reading the (Royal) Society's papers? Well and wisely done, and really brave of him. Heretofore he was bold enough to take a similar step and loyal enough to truth to disappoint his colleagues by making his facts public ... If Mr. Crookes would penetrate Arcana beyond the corridors the tools of modern science have already excavated, let him – Try. He tried and found the Radiometer; tried again and found Radiant matter; may try again and find the "Kama-rupa" of matter – its *fifth state*. But to find its *Manas*, he would have to pledge himself stronger to secrecy than he seems inclined to. You know our motto and that its practical application has erased the word "impossible" from the occultist's vocabulary. If he wearies not of trying, he may discover the most noble of all facts, his true SELF. But he will have to penetrate many strata before he comes to *It*.
ML 59, p. 341

(8) ... Lord Crawford and Balacarres, an excellent man – imprisoned by the world. His is a sincere and noble, though may be a little too repressed, nature. He asks what hope he may have? I say – *every hope*. For he has within himself that so very few

possess, an exhaustless source of magnetic fluid which, if he only had the time, he could call out in torrents and need no other master than himself. His own powers would do the work and his own great experience be a sure guide for him ... Were he a poor man, he might have become an English Dupotet, (Francis Baron de Potet – an early investigator of mesmerism – Ed.) with the addition of great scientific achievements in exact science. But alas! What the peerage has gained, psychology has lost ... And yet it is not too late. But see, even after mastering magnetic science and giving his powerful mind to the study of the noblest branches of exact science, how even he has failed to lift more than a small corner of the veil of mystery. Ah! That whirling, showy, glittering world, full of insatiable ambition, where family and the State parcel out between them a man's nobler nature, as two tigers a carcass and leave him without hope or light! How many recruits could we not have from it, if no sacrifice were exacted! *ML 8, pp. 26-27*

(9) Rain can be brought on in a small area of space – artificially and without any claim to miracle or superhuman powers, though its secret is no property of mine that I should divulge it. I am now trying to obtain permission to do so.

We know of no phenomenon in nature entirely unconnected with either magnetism or electricity – since where there are motion, heat, friction, light, there magnetism and its alter ego (according to our humble opinion) electricity will always appear, as either cause or effect – or rather both if we but fathom the manifestation to its origin. All the phenomena of earth currents, terrestrial magnetism and atmospheric electricity are due to the fact that the earth is an electrified conductor, whose potential is ever changing owing to its rotation and its annual orbital motion, the successive cooling and heating of the air, the formation of clouds and rain, storms and winds, etc.

This you may perhaps find in some text book. But then

Science would be unwilling to admit all these changes are due to akasic magnetism, incessantly generating electric currents which tend to restore the disturbed equilibrium. By directing the most powerful of electric batteries, the human frame, electrified by a certain process, you can stop rain on some given point by making "a hole in the rain cloud," as the occultists term it. By using other strongly magnetized implements within, so to say, an insulated area, rain can be produced artificially. I regret my inability to explain to you the process more clearly. You know the effects produced by trees and plants on rain clouds and how their strong magnetic nature attracts and even feeds those clouds over the tops of the trees. Science explains it otherwise, maybe. Well, I cannot help it, for such is our knowledge and fruits of millennium of observations and experience. *ML 23B, p. 160*

(10) Let some physicists calculate the amount of heat required to vaporize a certain quantity of water. Then let them compute the quantity of rain needed to cover an area – say of one square mile – to a depth of *one* inch. For this amount of vaporization they will require, of course, an amount of heat that would be equal to at least five thousand tons of coal.

Now, the amount of energy of which this consumption of heat would be the equivalent corresponds (as any mathematician could tell you) – to that which would be required to raise a weight of upwards of ten million tons, one mile high. How can *one man* generate such amount of heat and energy? Preposterous, absurd! – we are all lunatics, and you who will listen to us will be placed in the same category if you ever venture to repeat this proposition. Yet I say that *one man* alone can do it, and very easily if he is but acquainted with a certain "physico-*spiritual*" lever in himself, far more powerful than that of Archimedes. Even simple muscular contraction is always accompanied with electric and magnetic phenomena and there is the strongest connection between the magnetism of the earth, the changes of weather and man, who is the best barometer living, if he but knew (how) to decipher properly .... *ML 23B, pp. 160-161*

(11) Tell Science that even in those days of the decline of the Roman Empire, when the tattooed Britisher used to offer to the Emperor Claudius his *nazzur* (tributary offering) of "electron" in the shape of a string of amber beads – that even then there were yet men remaining aloof from the immoral masses who knew more of electricity and magnetism than they, the men of science, do now, and science will laugh at you as bitterly as she now does over your kind dedication to me. *ML 23B, p. 164*

(12) But with us, it is an established fact that it is the earth's magnetism that produces wind, storms, and rain. What science seems to know of it is but secondary symptoms, always induced by that magnetism and she may very soon find out her present errors. Earth's magnetic attraction of meteoric dust and the direct influence of the latter upon the sudden changes of temperature, especially in the matter of heat and cold, is not a settled question to the present day, I believe. *ML 23B, p. 161*

(13) It was doubted whether the fact of our earth passing through a region of space, in which there are more or less of meteoric masses, has any bearing upon the height of our atmosphere being increased or decreased, or even upon the state of the weather. But we think we could easily prove it; and since they (scientists) accept the fact that the relative distribution and proportion of land and water on our globe *may be due* to the great accumulation upon it of meteoric dust; snow – especially in our northern regions – being full of meteoric iron and magnetic particles and deposits of the latter being found even at the bottom of seas and oceans.

I wonder how Science has not hitherto understood that, every atmospheric change and disturbance was due to the combined magnetism of the two great masses between which our atmosphere is compressed! I call this meteoric dust a "mass" for it is really one. High above our earth's surface, the air is impregnated and space *filled* with magnetic, or meteoric dust, which does not even belong to our solar system. Science having luckily discovered that, as our earth, with all the other planets, is carried along through space, it receives a greater proportion of that dust matter on its northern than on its southern hemisphere, knows that to this are due the preponderating number of the continents in the former hemisphere, and the greater abundance of snow and moisture. Millions of such meteors and even of the finest particles, reach us yearly and daily and all our temple knives are made of this "heavenly" iron, which reaches us without having undergone any change – the magnetism of the earth keeping them in cohesion. Gaseous matter is continually added to our atmosphere, from the never ceasing fall of meteoric, strongly magnetic matter, and yet it seems with them still an open question, whether magnetic conditions have anything to do with the precipitation of rain or not! *ML 23B, P. 161-162*

(14) ... we believe in MATTER alone, in matter as visible nature and matter in its invisibility as the invisible omnipresent, omnipotent Proteus, with its unceasing motion which is its life and which nature draws from herself, since she is the great whole outside of which nothing can exist. For as Bellinger truly asserts, "motion is a manner of existence that flows necessarily out of the essence of matter; that matter moves by its own peculiar energies; that its motion is due to the force which is inherent in itself; that the variety of motion and the phenomena that result proceed from the diversity of the properties of the qualities and of the combinations which are originally found in the primitive matter" of which nature is the assemblage and of which your science knows less than one of our Tibetan Yak-drivers of Kant's metaphysics. *ML 10, p. 56*

(15) Heat they (scientists) say, generates and produces electricity yet they find *no decrease* in the heat in the process. Electricity produces heat we are told? Electometers show that the electrical current passes through some poor conductor, a platinum wire say, and heats the latter. Precisely the same quantity of electricity, there being no loss of electricity, *no decrease*. What then has been converted into heat? Again electricity is said to produce magnetism. I have on the table before me primitive electrometers, in whose vicinity chelas come the whole day to recuperate their nascent powers. I do not find the slightest decrease in the electricity stored. The chelas are magnetized, but their magnetism or rather that of *their rods* is not *that* of electricity under a new mask. No more than the flame of a thousand tapers, lit at the flame of the *Fo* lamp, is the flame of the latter. Therefore, if, by the uncertain twilight of modern science, it is an axiomatic truth "that during vital processes, the *conversion* only and never the *creation* of matter or force occurs" ... it is for us but half a truth. It is neither *conversion* nor *creation*, but something for which science has yet no name. *ML 11, pp. 62-63*

(16) Perhaps now you will be prepared to better understand the difficulty with which we have to contend. Modern science is our best ally. Yet it is generally the same science which is made the weapon to break our heads with. *ML 11, p. 63*

(17) However, you will have to bear in mind (a) that we recognise but *one* element in Nature (whether spiritual or physical) outside which there can be no Nature, since it is *Nature* itself, and which as the *Akasa* pervades our solar system, every atom being part of itself, pervades throughout *space* and is space in fact, which pulsates as in profound sleep during the pralayas .... *ML 11, p. 63*

(18) The vril of the "Coming Race" was the common property of

races now extinct. And as the existence of those gigantic ancestors of ours is now questioned – though in the *Himavats*, on the very territory belonging to you, we have a cave full of the skeletons of these giants and their huge frames when found are invariably regarded as isolated freaks of nature, so the vril of *Akas* – as we call it – is looked upon as an impossibility, a myth. And without a thorough knowledge of *Akas*, its combination and properties, how can science hope to account for such phenomena? *ML 1, p. 2*

(19) As hoary antiquity had more than one Socrates, so the dim Future will give birth to more than one martyr. Enfranchised science contemptuously turned away her face from the Copernican opinion, renewing the theories of Aristarchus Samius, who "affirmeth that the earth moveth circularly about her own centre" years before the Church sought to sacrifice Galileo as a holocaust to the Bible. The ablest mathematician at the Court of Edward V1 – Robert Recorde – was left to starve in jail by his colleagues, who laughed at his *Castle of Knowledge*, declaring his discoveries "vain phantasies." Wm. Colchester – Queen Elizabeth's physician – died poisoned, only because this real founder of experimental science in England has had the audacity of anticipating Galileo; of pointing out Copernicus' fallacy as to the "third movement," which was gravely alleged to account for the parallelism of the earth's axis of rotation!

The enormous learning of the Paracelsi, of the Agrippas and the Dee's was ever doubted. It was science which laid her sacrilegious hand upon the great work "De Magnete" ("Concerning the Magnet and the *Magnetism of Bodies and the Great Magnet, the Earth*" by Dr. William Gilbert – 16th century – Ed.), "The Heavenly Virgin" (*Akas*) and others. And it was the illustrious "Chancellor of England and of Nature" – Lord Verulam-Bacon – who having won the name of the Father of Inductive Philosophy, permitted himself to speak of such men as the above-named as the "Alchemicians of the Fantastic philosophy." *ML 1, p. 4*

(20) And suppose, for one instant, I were to describe to you the hues of those colour rays that lie *beyond* the so-called "visible spectrum" – rays invisible to all but a very few even among us; to explain, how we can fix in space any one of the so-called subjective or *accidental* colours – the *complement*, (to speak mathematically*) moreover, of any other given colour of a dichromatic body,* (which alone sounds like an absurdity) could you comprehend, do you think, their optical effect or even my meaning?

And since you see them not, such rays, nor can know them, nor have you any names for them as yet in Science, if I were to tell you – "My good friend Sinnett, if you please, without moving from your writing desk, try, search for, and produce before your eyes the whole solar spectrum, decomposed into fourteen prismatic colours (seven being complementary) as it is but with the help of that occult light that you can see me from a distance as I see you" ....

What think you, would be your answer? What would you have to reply? Would you not be likely enough to retort by telling me in your own quiet, polite way, that as there never were but seven (now three) primary colours, which, moreover, have never yet by any known physical process been seen decomposed further than the seven prismatic hues – my invitation was as "unscientific" as it was "absurd?" Adding that my offer to search for an imaginary solar "complement" being no compliment to your knowledge of physical science – I had better, perhaps, go and search for my mythical "dichromatic" and solar "pairs" in Tibet, for modern science has hitherto been unable to bring under any theory, even so simple a phenomenon as the colours of all such dichromatic bodies. And yet – truth knows – *these* colours are objective enough! *ML 8, p. 30*

The Septenary Principle

(1) Whenever any question of evolution or development in any Kingdom presents itself to you, bear constantly in mind that everything comes under the Septenary rule of series in their correspondences and mutual relation throughout nature.
ML 14, p. 86

(2) At the beginning of the solar manvantara the hitherto subjective elements of the material world, now scattered in cosmic dust – receiving their impulse from the new Dhyan Chohans of the new solar system (the highest of the old one having gone higher) will form into primordial ripples of life and separating into differentiating centres of activity, combine in a graduated scale of seven stages of evolution.

Like every other orb of space our Earth has, before obtaining its ultimate materiality – and nothing now in this world can give you an idea of what this state of matter is – to pass through a gamut of seven stages of density. I say gamut advisedly, since the diatonic scale best affords an illustration of the perpetual rhythmic motion of the descending and ascending cycle of Swabhavat – graduated as it is by tones and semi-tones.
ML 15, p. 98

(3) The correspondence between a mother-globe and her child-man may be thus worked out. Both have their seven principles. In the Globe, the elementals (of which there are in all seven species) form (a) a gross body, (b) her fluidic double (*linga* sariram), (c) her life principle (jiva), (d) her fourth principle, kama rupa, is formed by her creative principle working from centre to circumference, (e) her fifth principle (animal soul or *Manas*, physical intelligence) is embodied in the vegetable (in germ) and animal kingdoms, (f) her sixth principle (or spiritual soul, Buddhi) is

man (g) and her seventh principle (Atma) is in a film of spiritualised akasa that surrounds her. *ML 15, p. 94*

(4) All is one Law. Man has his seven principles, the germs of which he brings with him at his birth. So has a planet or a world. From first to last, every sphere has its world of effects, the passing through which will afford a place of final rest to each of the human principles – the seventh principle excepted.
ML 13, p. 73

(5) As man is a seven-fold being so is the universe – the septenary microcosm being to the septenary macrocosm but as the drop of rainwater is to the cloud from whence it dropped and whither in the course of time it will return. *ML 15, p. 91*

(6) Seventh principle (is) always there as a latent force in every one of the principles – even body. As the macrocosmic *Whole* it is present even in the *lower* sphere, but there is nothing there to assimilate it to itself. *ML 13*, p. 75

(7) The worlds of effects are not lokas or localities. They are the shadow of the world of causes, their *souls* – worlds having like men their seven principles, which develop and grow simultaneously with the body. Thus the *body of man* is wedded to and remains for ever within the body of his planet; his individual *jivatma* life principle, that which is called in physiology *animal spirits* returns after death to its source – *Fohat*; his *linga shariram* will be drawn into *Akasa*; his *Kamarupa* will commingle with the Universal *Sakti* – the Will-Force, or universal energy; his "animal soul" borrowed from the breath of *Universal Mind* will return to the Dhyan Chohans; his sixth principle – whether drawn into or ejected from the matrix of the Great Passive Principle, must remain in its own sphere – either as part of the crude material or an individualized entity to be re-born in a higher world of

causes. The seventh will carry it from the *Devachan* and follow the new *Ego* to its place of re-birth .... *ML 13, pp. 71-72*

(8) (Question) We understand that the man bearing cycle of necessity of our solar system consists of thirteen objective globes, of which ours is the lowest, six above it in the ascending, and six in the descending cycle, with a fourteenth world lower still than ours. Is this correct?

(Answer) There are seven objective and seven subjective globes, (I have been just permitted for the first time to give you the right figure) the worlds of causes and of effects. The former have our earth occupying the lower turning point, where spirit-matter equilibrates. But do not trouble yourself to go into calculations, even on this correct basis, for it will only puzzle you, since the infinite ramifications of the number seven (which is one of our greatest mysteries) being so closely allied and interdependent with the seven principles of Nature and man – this figure is the only one I am permitted (so far) to give you ....
ML 14, p. 78

(9) (Question) We understand that below man you reckon not three kingdoms as we do (mineral, vegetable and animal) but seven. Please enumerate and explain these.

(Answer) Below man there are three (Kingdoms) in the objective and three in the subjective, with man a septenary. Two of the three former none but an initiate could conceive of; the third is the Inner kingdom – below the crust of the earth – which we could name but would feel embarrassed to describe. Below man there are three (kingdoms) in the objective and three in the subjective. These seven kingdoms are preceded by other and numerous septenary stages and combinations. *ML 14, pp. 78-79*

(10) Yes, *Love* and *Hatred* are the only immortal feelings; but the gradations of tones along the seven by seven scales of the whole

keyboard of life are numberless. And, since it is those two feelings – (or, to be correct, shall I risk being misunderstood again and say those two poles of man's "Soul" which is a unity?) – that mould the future state of man, whether for *Devachan* or *Avitchi*, then the variety of such states must also be inexhaustible.
ML 24B, p.188

Solomon's Seal

(1) Does your B.T.S. (British Theosophical Society) know the meaning of the white and black interlaced triangles of the Parent Society's seal that it has also adopted? Shall I explain? The double triangle, viewed by the Jewish Kabalists as Solomon's Seal is, as many of you doubtless know the *Sri-yantra* of the archaic Aryan Temple, the "mystery of Mysteries," a geometrical synthesis of the whole occult doctrine. The two interlaced triangles are the *Buddhangams* of Creation. They contain the "squaring of the circle," the "philosophers' stone," the great problems of Life and Death, and – the Mystery of Evil. The *chela* who can explain this sign from every one of its aspects – *is virtually an adept.*

How is it then, that the only one among you who has come so near to unravelling the mystery, is also the only one who got none of her ideas from books? Unconsciously she gives out – to him who has the key – the first syllable of the *Ineffable name!* Of course you know that the double triangle – the *Satkiri Chakram of Vishnu* – or the six-pointed star, is the perfect seven. In all the old Sanskrit works – *Vedic* and *Tantrik* – you find the number 6 mentioned more often than the 7 – this last figure, the central point, being implied, for it is the germ of the six and their matrix. It is then thus ... (at this point in the original, there is a rough drawing of the interlaced triangles inscribed in a circle – Ed.) – the central point standing for seventh, and the circle, the *Mahakasha* – endless space – for the seventh *Universal* Principle.

In one sense, both are viewed as *Avalokitesvara*, for they are respectively the Macrocosm and the microcosm. The interlaced triangles – the upper pointing one Wisdom concealed, and the downward pointing one Wisdom *revealed* (in the phenomenal world). The circle indicates the bounding, circumscribing quality of the *All*, the Universal principle, which from any given point expands so as to embrace all things, while embodying the potentiality of every action in the Cosmos. At this point, then, is the centre round which the circle is traced, they are identical and one, though from the standpoint of *Maya* and *Avidya* – (illusion and ignorance) – one is separated from the other by the manifested triangle, the 3 sides of which represent the three *gunas* – finite attributes. In symbology the central point is *Jivatma* (the 7th principle) and hence *Avalokitesvara*, the *Kwan-Shai-yin*, the manifested "Voice," (or *Logos*) the germ point of manifested activity; hence, in the phraseology of the Christian Kabalists, "The Son of the Father and Mother," and agreeable to ours – "the Self manifested in Self ... Yih-sin, the "one form of existence," the child of *Dharmakaya*, (the universally diffused Essence) both male and female. Parabrahm or "Adi-Buddha," while acting through that germ point outwardly as an active force, reacts from the circumference inwardly as the Supreme but latent Potency.

The double triangles symbolize the Great Passive and the Great Active; the male and female; Purusha and Prakriti. Each triangle is a Trinity because presenting a triple aspect. The white represents in its straight lines: *Gnanam* – (Knowledge); *Gnata* – (the Knower); and *Gnayam* – (that which is known). The black – form, colour, and substance, also the *creative*, *preservative*, and *destructive* forces, and these are mutually correlating.

ML 59, pp. 345-346

The Soul

(1) In *reality*, there is no contradiction between that passage in *Isis* (Isis Unveiled) and our later teaching; to anyone who never heard of the *seven* principles constantly referred to in *Isis* as a trinity, without any more explanation – there certainly appeared to be as good a contradiction as could be. "You will write so and so, give *so far*, and no more" – she was constantly told by us when writing her book. It was at the very beginning of a new cycle, in days when neither Christians nor Spiritualists ever thought of, let alone mentioned more than two principles in man – *body* and *Soul*, which they called Spirit.

If you had time to refer to the spiritualistic literature of that day, you would find that with the phenomenalists, as with the Christians, *Soul* and *Spirit* were synonymous. It was H.P.B. who, acting under the order of Atrya (one whom you do not know) was the first to explain in the *Spiritualist* the difference there was between *psyche* and *nous*, *nefesh* and *Ruach* – Soul and Spirit. She had to bring the whole arsenal of proofs with her, quotations from Paul and Plato, from Plutarch and *James*, etc. before the Spiritualists admitted that the theosophists were right. It was then that she was ordered to write *Isis* – just a year after the Society had been founded.

And as there happened such a war over it, endless polemics and objections to the effect that *there could not be in man two souls* – we thought it premature to give the public more than they could possibly assimilate and before they had digested the "two souls" – and thus the further sub-division of the trinity into 7th principles was left unmentioned in Isis. And is it because she obeyed our orders, and wrote purposely *veiling* some of her facts – that now, when we think the time has arrived to give most of, if not the whole truth – that she has to be left in the lurch?
ML 52, pp. 289-290

(2) I may answer you, what I said to G. H. Fechner (Professor Fechner of Leipzig, Germany – Ed.) one day, when he wanted to know the Hindu view on what he had written – "You are right ... 'every diamond, every crystal, every plant and star has its own individual soul, besides man and animal ...' and 'there is a hierarchy of souls from the lowest forms of matter up to the World Soul,' but you are mistaken when adding to the above assurance that 'the spirits of the departed hold *direct* psychic communication with Souls that are still connected with a human body' – for they do not." *ML 9, pp. 44-45*

(3) By the bye, you ought to come to some agreement as to the terms used when discussing cyclic evolutions. Our terms are untranslatable and without a good knowledge of our complete system (which cannot be given but to regular initiates) would suggest nothing definite to your perceptions but only a source of confusion as in the case of the terms "Soul" and "Spirit" with all your metaphysical writers – especially the Spiritualists.
ML 12, p. 70

(4) And once that we are discussing "individuality" and "personality," it is curious that H.P.B., when subjecting poor Mr. Hume's brain to torture with her muddled explanations, never thought – until receiving the explanation from himself of the difference that exists between individuality and personality – that it was the very same doctrine she had been taught: that of *Pacceka-Yana*, and of *Amata-Yana*. The two terms as above given by him are the correct and literal translation of the Pali, Sanskrit, and even of the Chino-Tibetan technical names for the many personal entities blended in one *Individuality* – the long string of lives emanating from the same Immortal MONAD. You will have to remember them: –

(Section) 1. The *Pacceka-Yana* – (in Sanskrit *"Pratyeka"*) means literally the "personal vehicle" or personal *Ego*, a combination of the five lower principles. While –

(Section) 2. The *Amata-Yana* – (in sanskrit "Amrita") is translated "the immortal vehicle," or the *Individuality*, the Spiritual Soul, or the Immortal *monad* – a combination of the fifth, sixth and seventh (principles). ***ML 16, p. 114***

Spirit, Matter and Atma

(1) Spirit or LIFE is indivisible. And when we speak of the seventh principle it is neither quality nor quantity, nor yet form that are meant, but rather the space occupied in that ocean of spirit by the results or effects – (beneficent as are all those of a co-worker with nature) – impressed thereon. *ML 13, p. 74*

(2) Bereaved of Prakriti (Matter), Purusha (Spirit) is unable to manifest itself, hence ceases to exist – becomes *nihil*. Without spirit or Force, even that which Science styles as "not living" matter, the so-called mineral ingredients which feed plants, could never have been called into form. There is a moment in the existence of every molecule and atom of matter when for one cause or another, the last spark of spirit or motion or life (call it by whatever name) is withdrawn, and in the same instant, with the swiftness which surpasses that of the lightning glance of thought, the atom or molecule, an aggregation of molecules is annihilated to return to its pristine purity of intracosmic matter. It is drawn to the mother fount with the velocity of a globule of quicksilver to the central mass. Matter, force and motion are the trinity of physical objective nature, as the Trinitarian unity of spirit-matter is that of the spiritual or subjective nature. Motion is eternal because spirit is eternal. But no modes of motion can ever be conceived unless they be in connection with matter. *ML 22, p. 142*

(3) But what is "Spirit" pure and impersonal *per se*? Is it possible that you should not have realized yet our meaning? Why, such a *Spirit* is a non-entity, a pure abstraction, an absolute blank to our senses – even to the most spiritual. It becomes *something* only in union with matter – hence it is always *something*, since matter is infinite and indestructible and *non-existent* without Spirit, which,

in matter, is *Life*. Separated from matter it becomes the absolute negation of *life* and *being*, whereas matter is inseparable from it. **ML 23B, p. 158**

(4) In the book of Kiu-te, Spirit is called the ultimate sublimation of matter, and matter the crystallization of spirit. And no better illustration could be afforded than in the very simple phenomenon of ice, water, vapour and the final dispersion of the latter, the phenomenon being reversed in its consecutive manifestation and called the Spirit falling into generation or matter. This trinity resolving itself into unity – a doctrine as old as the world of thought – was seized upon by some early Christians, who had it in the schools of Alexandria, and made (it) up into the Father, or generative spirit; the Son or matter – man; and into the Holy Ghost, the immaterial essence, or the apex of the equilateral triangle, an idea found to this day in the pyramids of Egypt. *ML 22, p. 142*

(5) The conception of matter and spirit as entirely distinct, and both eternal, could certainly never have entered my head, however little I may know of them, for it is one of the elementary and fundamental doctrines of Occultism that the two are one and are distinct but in their respective manifestations, and only in the limited perceptions of the world of senses. *ML 22, p. 141*

(6) ... neither Atma nor Buddhi ever were *within* man – a little metaphysical axiom that you can study with advantage in Plutarch and Anaxogoras. The letter made the spirit self-potent, the *nous* that alone recognised *noumena*, while the former taught on the authority of Plato and Pythagoras that ... this nous (atma-buddhi) always remained without the body; that it floated and overshadowed, so to say, the extreme part of man's head, it is only the vulgar who think it is within them.

Says the Buddha, "you have to get rid entirely of all the

subjects of impermanence composing the body, that your body should become permanent. The permanent never merges with the impermanent although the two are one. But it is only when all outward appearances are gone, that there is left that one principle of life which exists independently of all external phenomena. It is the fire that burns in the eternal light, when the fuel is expended and the flame is extinguished; for that fire is neither in the flame nor in the fuel, nor yet inside either of the two but above, beneath and everywhere." (Parinirvana Sutra Kuan XXX1X)
ML 127, p. 455

(7) It (Avalokitesvara) is, when correctly interpreted, in one sense "the *divine Self* perceived or seen by *Self,*" the *Atman* or seventh principle ridded of its mayavic distinction from its Universal Source – which becomes the object of perception for and by the *individuality* centred in *Buddhi,* the sixth principle, something that happens only in the highest state of *Samadhi.*

This is applying it to the microcosm. In the other sense Avalokitesvara implies the seventh *Universal* Principle, as the object perceived by the Universal *Buddhi,* "Mind" or Intelligence which is the synthetic aggregation of all the Dhyan Chohans, as of all other intelligences whether great or small, that ever were, are or will be. Nor is it the "Spirit of Buddhas present in the church," but the Omnipresent Universal Spirit in the temple of nature – in one case and the seventh principle – the *Atman* in the temple – man in the other. *ML 59, pp. 343-344*

Spiritualism and Mediumship

(1) ... it is not against *true* Spiritualism that we set ourselves, but only against indiscriminate mediumship and physical manifestations – materializations and trance *possessions* especially. Could the Spiritualists be only made to understand the difference between *individuality* and *personality*, between *individual* and *personal* immortality and some other truths, they would be more easily persuaded that Occultists may be fully convinced of the *monad's* immortality, and yet deny that of the soul – the vehicle of the *personal Ego*; that they can firmly believe in and themselves practice spiritual communications with the *disembodied* Egos of the *Rupa-Loka*, and yet laugh at the insane idea of "shaking hands" with a "Spirit!"; that finally, as the matter stands, it is the Occultists and the Theosophists who are true Spiritualists, while the modern sect of that name is composed simply of *materialistic* phenomenalists. *ML 16, pp. 113-114*

(2) ... *what the Spiritualists fail to perceive, I see, and their "Spirits"* *to explain (the latter knowing no more than what they can find in the* *brains of the former) ... They, as well as ourselves,* have all a duty *to* *perform, a task* set before us; that of sweeping away as much as possible the dross left to us by our pious forefathers. New ideas have to be planted on clean places, for these ideas touch the most momentous subjects. It is not physical phenomena or *the agency* *called Spiritualism* but these universal ideas *that we have precisely to* study; the *noumenon not the phenomenon*, for to comprehend the LATTER we have first to understand the FORMER. They *do* touch man's true position in the Universe, to be sure, *but only* in relation to his future not previous births. *It is not physical phenomena,* *however wonderful, that can ever explain to man* his origin, *let alone* his ultimate destiny, *or as one of them expresses it* – the relation of the mortal to the immortal, of the temporary to the eternal, of the

finite to the infinite. *ML 93, pp. 425-426*

(3) Many of the *subjective* spiritual communications – most of them when the sensitives are pure-minded – are real; but it is most difficult for the *uninitiated* medium to fix in his mind the true and correct pictures of what he sees and hears. Some of the phenomena called psychography (though more rarely) are also real. The spirit of the sensitive getting odylised, so to say, by the aura of the Spirit in the Devachan, becomes for a few minutes *that departed personality*, and writes in the handwriting of the latter, in his language and in his thoughts, as they were during his life time. The two spirits become blended in one; and the preponderance of one over the other during such phenomena determines the preponderance of *personality* in the characteristics exhibited in such writings and "trance speaking".

What we call *"rapport,"* is in plain fact an identity of molecular vibration between the astral part of the incarnate medium and the astral part of the disincarnate personality ... As in music, two different sounds may be in accord and separately distinguishable, and this harmony or discord depends upon the synchronous vibrations and complementary periods; so there is *rapport* between medium and "control" when their astral molecules move in accord. And the question whether the communication shall reflect more of the one personal idiosyncrasy or the other, is determined by the relative intensity of the two sets of vibrations in the compound wave of *Akasa*. The less identical the vibratory impulses, the more mediumistic and less spiritual will be the message. So then, measure your medium's moral state by that of the alleged "controlling" Intelligence, and your tests of genuineness leave nothing to be desired. *ML 16, pp.101-102*

(4) You want to know why it is deemed supremely difficult, if not utterly impossible, for pure *disembodied* Spirits to communicate

with men through mediums or *phantomosophy*. I say because: –

(a) On account of the antagonistic atmosphere respectively surrounding these worlds;

(b) Of the entire dissimilarity of physiological and spiritual conditions; and

(c) Because that chain of worlds I have just been telling you about is not only an *epicycloid* but an ellipse, not one but two points – two foci, which can never approach each other. Man being at one focus of it and pure Spirit at the other.

To this you might object. I can neither help it, nor change the fact, but there is still another and far mightier impediment. Like a rosary composed of white and black beads alternating with each other, so that concatenation of worlds is made up of worlds of CAUSES and worlds of EFFECTS, the latter – the direct result produced by the former. Thus it becomes evident that every sphere of Causes – and our Earth is one – is not only inter-linked with, and surrounded by, but actually separated from its nearest neighbour – the higher sphere of Causality – by an impenetrable atmosphere (in its spiritual sense) of effects bordering on, and even interlinking, never mixing with – the next sphere: for one is active, the other – passive, the world of causes *positive*, that of effects – negative. The passive resistance can be overcome but under conditions of which your most learned Spiritualists have not the faintest idea. All movement is, so to say, polar. It is very difficult to convey my meaning to you at this point; but I will go to the end. I am aware of my failure to bring before you these – to us – axiomatical truths in any other form but that of a simple, logical postulate – if so much – they being capable of absolute and unequivocal demonstration but to the highest Seers. But I'll give you food for thinking if nothing else. *ML 9, pp. 47-48*

(5) Ransack the Spiritualistic literature if you will, 'till the year 1877 (when *Isis Unveiled* was published – Ed.) Search and find in it – if you can, one single word about occult philosophy, or

esotericism or anything of that element, now so largely infused in the spiritual movement. Ask and enquire whether the very word of "occultism" was not so completely *unknown* in America, that we find Cora of the 7 husbands, the Tappan woman and talking medium, *inspired* in her lectures to say that the word was *one just coined* by the Theosophists – then dawning – that no one ever heard of elementary spirits and astral light – save the *petroleum* manufacturers and so on and on. **ML 47, pp. 271-272**

(6) Mediumship is abnormal. When in further development the abnormal has given way to the natural, the *controls* are shaken off, and passive obedience is no longer required, then the medium learns to use his will to exercise his own power, and becomes an adept. The process is one of development and the neophyte has to go to the end. As long as he is subject to occasional trance – he cannot be an adept. S.M. (Stainton Moses) passes two-thirds of his life in Trance. **ML 9, p. 43**

(7) Were the mediums and Spiritualists but to know, as I said, that with every new "angel guide" they welcome with rapture, they entice the latter into an *Upadana* (cause) which will be productive of a series of untold evils for the new Ego that will be born under its nefarious shadow, and that with every séance – especially for materialization – they multiply the causes for misery, causes that will make the unfortunate Ego fail in his spiritual birth, or be reborn into a worse existence than ever – they would, perhaps, be less lavish in their hospitality. **ML 16, p. 113**

(8) However ethereal and purified of gross matter they may be, the pure Spirits are still subject to the physical and universal laws of matter. They *cannot,* even if they would, span the abyss that separates their worlds from ours. *They can be visited in Spirit,* their Spirit cannot descend and reach us. They attract, they

cannot be attracted, their Spiritual polarity being an insuperable difficulty in the way. *ML 9, p. 45*

(9) But why should they (spirits) "communicate?" Do those you love communicate with you during their sleep objectively? Your Spirits, in hours of danger, or intense sympathy, vibrating on the same current of thought – which in such cases creates a kind of telegraphic spiritual wire between your two bodies – may meet and mutually impress your memories; but then you are *living*, not *dead* bodies. But how can an *unconscious* 5th principle (manas) … impress or communicate with a living organism, unless it has already become a *shell*? If, for certain reasons, they remain in a such a state of lethargy for several years, the spirits of the living may ascend to them, as you were already told; and this may take place still easier than in Devachan, where the *Spirit* is too much engrossed in his personal bliss to pay much attention to an intruding element. I say they *cannot*. *ML 20C, p. 133*

(10) But what is then "the nature of the remembrance and self-consciousness of a shell?" you ask. As I said in your note – no better than a reflected or borrowed light. "Memory" is one thing and "perceptive faculties" quite another. A madman may remember very clearly some portions of his past life; yet he is unable to perceive anything in its true light for the higher portion of his *Manas* and his *Buddhi* are paralysed in him, have left him. Could an animal – a dog, for instance – speak, he would prove to you that his memory, in direct relation to his canine personality, is as fresh as yours; nevertheless his memory and instinct cannot be called "perceptive faculties." A dog remembers that his master thrashed him when the latter gets hold of his stick – at all other times he has no remembrance of it.

Thus with a shell; once in the aura of a medium, all he perceives through the borrowed organs of the medium and of those in magnetic sympathy with the latter, he will perceive very clearly – but *not further* than what the shell can find in the perceptive faculties and memories of *circle* and medium – hence often the rational and at times highly intelligent answers; hence also a complete oblivion of things known to all but that medium and circle.

The shell of a highly intelligent, learned, but utterly unspiritual man who died a natural death, will last longer, and the shadow of his own memory helping – that *shadow* which is the refuse of the 6th principle left in the fifth – he may deliver discourses through trance speakers and repeat parrot-like that which he knew of and thought much over it during his life-time. But find me *one single* instance in the annals of Spiritualism where a returning shell of a Faraday or a Brewster (for even they were made to fall into the trap of mediumistic attraction) said one word more than it knew during its life-time. Where is that scientific shell, that ever gave evidence of that which is claimed on behalf of the "disembodied *Spirit*" – namely, that a free Soul, the Spirit disenthralled from its body's fetters, perceives and sees that which is concealed from living mortal eyes? *ML 23B, p. 173*

(11) Defy the best, the most reliable of mediums – Stainton Moses for one – to give you through that high disembodied shell, that he mistakes for the "Imperator" of the early days of his mediumship, to tell you what you will have hidden in your box, if S.M. does not know it; or to repeat to you a line from a Sanskrit manuscript unknown to his medium, or anything of that kind … *Spirits* they call them? Spirits with *personal* remembrances? As well call personal remembrances the sentences screeched out by a parrot … Indeed it will be worth your while to stimulate investigation in this direction. Yes, personal consciousness does leave everyone at death; and when even the centre of memory is re-established in the shell, it will remember and speak out its recollections but through the brain of some *living* human being.
ML 23B, pp. 173-174

(12) The Spiritual *Ego* goes on evolving personalities in which "the sense of identity" is *very complete* while living. After their separation from the *physical* Ego, that Spiritual Ego sense returns very dim and belongs wholly to the recollections of the *physical* man. The shell may be a perfect Sinnett when wholly engrossed in a game of cards at his club, and either losing or winning a large sum of money – or a Babu Smut Murky Dass trying to cheat his principal out of a sum of rupees. In both cases – ex-editor and Babu will, as shells, remind anyone who will have the privilege for enjoying an hour's chat with the illustrious dis-embodied angels, more of the inmates of a lunatic asylum, made to play parts in private theatricals as means of hygienic recreation, than of the Caesars and Hamlets they would represent. The slightest shock will throw them off track and send them off raving.
ML 23B, pp. 174-175

(13) "So then, the great bulk of the physical phenomena of Spiritualists," my dear brother, are *not* "due to these Spirits" but indeed – to "shells." *ML 20C, p. 133*

(14) Many of you thought that our appearing to E. (William Eglinton – a British medium – Ed.) would "save the situation" and force Spiritualism to recognise the claims of Theosophy. Well, we complied with your wishes. M. and I were determined to show to you that there was no ground for such hopes. The Bigotry and Blindness of the Spiritualists, fed by the selfish motives of professional mediums, are rampant and the opponents are now desperate. We must allow the natural course of events to develop and can only help on the coming crisis by having a hand in the increasing frequency of exposures. It would never do for us to *force* events, as it would be only making "martyrs" and allowing these the pretext for a new craze.
ML 95, p. 430

The Sun

(1) The fact is, that what you call the Sun is simply the reflection of the huge "storehouse" of our System wherein ALL its forces are generated and preserved; the Sun being the heart and brain of our pigmy Universe, we might compare its *faculae* – those millions of small, intensely brilliant bodies of which the Sun's surface away from the spots is made up – with the blood corpuscles of that luminary, though some of them as correctly conjectured by Science are as large as Europe. Those blood corpuscles are the electric and magnetic matter in its sixth and seventh state. What are those filaments twisted like so many ropes, of which the penumbra of the Sun is made up? What the central part that is seen like a huge flame ending in fiery spires, and the transparent clouds, or rather vapours formed of delicate threads of silvery light, that hang over those flames – what – but magneto-electric aura – the *phlogiston* of the Sun? *ML 23B, p. 164*

(2) Call it a chromosphere or atmosphere, it can be called neither; for it is simply the magnetic and ever present aura of the sun, seen by astronomers *only* for a brief few moments during the eclipse, and by some of our chelas whenever they like – of course while in a certain induced state. A counterpart of what the astronomers call the red flames in the "corona" may be seen in Riechenbach's crystals or any other strongly magnetic body.

The head of a man in a strong ecstatic condition, when all the electricity of his system is centered around the brain, will represent – especially in darkness – a perfect simile of the Sun during such periods. The first artist who drew the aureoles about the heads of his Gods and Saints was not inspired, but represented it on the authority of temple pictures and traditions of the sanctuary and the chambers of initiation where such phenomena took place.

The closer to the head or to the aura-emitting body, the stronger and the more effulgent the emanation (due to hydrogen, science tells us, in the case of the flames) hence the irregular red flames around the Sun or the "*inner corona.*" The fact these are not always present in equal quantity shows only the constant fluctuation of the magnetic matter and its energy, upon which also depend the variety and number of spots. During periods of magnetic inertia the spots disappear, or rather remain invisible. The further the emanation shoots out the more it loses in intensity, until gradually subsiding, it fades out, hence the "outer corona," its rayed shape being due entirely to the latter phenomenon, whose effulgence proceeds from the magnetic nature of the matter and the electric energy and not at all from intensely hot particles, as asserted by some astronomers.

All this is terribly unscientific. Nevertheless a *fact*, to which I may add another, by reminding you that the Sun we see is not at all the central planet of our little Universe, but only its veil or its *reflection*. Science has tremendous odds against studying that planet, which luckily for us we have not; foremost of all – the constant tremors of our atmosphere which prevent them from judging correctly the little they do see. This impediment was never in the way of the ancient Chaldee and Egyptian astronomers; nor is it an obstacle to us, for we have means of arresting, counteracting such tremors – acquainted as we are with all the akashic conditions. No more than the *rain* secret would this secret – supposing we divulge it – be of any practical use to your men of Science unless they become Occultists and sacrifice long years to the acquirement of powers.
ML 23B, pp. 162-163

(3) (Question) Is there any truth in the new Siemens theory of solar combustion, – i.e. that the sun in its passage through space gathers in at the poles combustible gas (which is diffused through all space in a highly attenuated condition) and throws it

off again at the equator, after the intense heat of that region has again dispersed the elements which combustion temporarily united? *ML 23A, p. 146*

(4) (Answer) I am afraid not much, since our Sun is but a reflection. The only great truth uttered by Siemens is that interstellar space is filled with highly attenuated matter, such as may be put in air vacuum tubes, and which stretches from planet to planet and from star to star. But this truth has no bearing upon his main facts. The sun gives *all* and takes back *nothing* from its system. The sun gathers nothing "at the poles" = which are always free, even from the famous "red flames" at all times, not only during the eclipses. How is it that with their powerful telescopes they have failed to perceive any such "gathering," since their glasses show them even the "superlatively fleecy clouds" on the photosphere? Nothing can reach the sun from without the boundaries of its own system in the shape of such *gross* matter as "attenuated gases."

Every bit of matter in all its *seven* states is necessary to the vitality of the various and numberless systems – worlds in formation, suns awakening anew to life, etc. and they have none to spare even for their best neighbours and next of kin. They are mothers, not stepmothers, and would not take away one crumb from the nutrition of their children. The latest theory of radiant energy, which shows that there is no such thing in nature, properly speaking, as chemical light, or heat ray, is the only approximately correct one. For indeed, there is but one thing – radiant energy which is *inexhaustible* and knows neither increase nor decrease and will go on with its self-generating work to the end of the Solar manvantara.

The absorption of Solar Forces by the earth is tremendous; yes, it is or may be demonstrated, that the latter receives hardly 25 percent of the chemical power of its rays, for these are despoiled of 75 percent during their vertical passage through the atmosphere at the moment they reach the outer boundary "of the aerial ocean." And even those rays lose about 20 percent in illuminating and caloric power, we are told. What, with such a *waste* must then be the recuperative power of our Father-Mother Sun? Yes, call it "Radiant Energy" if you will; we call it Life – all pervading, omnipresent life, ever at work in its great laboratory – the SUN. *ML 23B, p. 168*

(5) (Question) Is the Sun (*a*) as Allan Kardec says: – a habitation of highly spiritualized beings? (*b*) Is it the vertex (apex – Ed.) of our Manvantaric chain? And of all the other chains in this solar system also? *ML 23A, p. 148*

(6) (Answer) Most decidedly not. Not even a Dhyan Chohan of the lower orders could approach it without having the *body* consumed, or rather annihilated. (b) Not unless we call it the vertex of an angle. But it is the vertex of all the chains collectively. All of us dwellers of the chains – we will have to evolute, live, and run the up and down scale in that highest and last of the septenary chains (on the scale of perfection) before the Solar Pralaya snuffs out our little system. *ML 23B, p. 176*

(7) (Question) Could any clue be given to the cause of magnetic variations – the daily changes at given places ...? *ML 23A, p. 146*

(8) (Answer) None can ever be given by your men of Science, whose "bumptiousness" makes them declare that, only to those for whom the word magnetism is a mysterious agent, the supposition that the Sun is a huge magnet can account for the production by that body of light, heat and the causes of magnetic variations as perceived on our earth. They are determined to ignore and thus reject the theory suggested to them by Jenkins of the R.A.S. of the existence of strong magnetic poles *above* the surface of the earth. But the theory is the correct one nevertheless,

and one of these poles revolves around the north pole in a periodical cycle of several hundred years. Halley and Flamsteed – besides Jenkins – were the only scientific men that ever suspected it. *ML 23B, pp. 168-169*

(9) ... the Sun is full of iron vapours – a fact that was demonstrated by the spectroscope, showing that the light of the corona consisted largely of a line in the green part of the spectrum, very nearly coinciding with an iron line. Yet Professor Young and Lockyer rejected that, under the witty pretext, if I remember, that if the corona were composed of minute particles like a dust cloud (and it is this that we call "magnetic matter") these particles would (1) fall upon the sun's body, (2) comets were known to pass through this vapour without any visible effect on them, (3) Professor Young's spectroscope showed that the coronal line was not identical with the iron one etc. Why they should call those objections "scientific" is more than we can tell. *ML 23B, p. 163*

(10) Verily, when your astronomers, speaking of *sun-matter*, term those lights and flames "clouds of vapour" and "gases unknown to science" (rather!) chased by mighty whirlwinds and cyclones – whereas we know it to be simply magnetic matter in its usual state of activity – we feel inclined to smile at the expressions. Can one imagine the "Sun's fires fed with *purely mineral* matter" – with meteorites highly charged with hydrogen giving the "Sun a far-reaching atmosphere of ignited gas?" We *know* that the *invisible* Sun is composed of *that* which has neither name, nor can it be compared to anything known by your science – on earth; and that its "reflection" contains still less of anything like "gases," mineral matter, or fire, though even we, when treating of it in your civilized tongue, are compelled to use such expressions as "vapour" and "magnetic matter." To close the subject, the coronal changes have no effects on the earth's climate, though *spots* have – and Professor N. Lockyer is mostly wrong in his

deductions. The Sun is neither a *solid* nor a *liquid*, nor yet a gaseous glow; but a gigantic ball of electromagnetic Forces, the storehouse of universal *life* and *motion*, from which the latter pulsate in all directions, feeding the smallest atom, as the greatest genius, with the same material unto the end of the *Maha Yug*. *ML 23B, p. 164-165*

(11) Science makes too much and too little at the same time of "solar energy" and even of the Sun itself; and the Sun has nothing to do whatever with rain and very little with heat. I was under the impression that science was aware that the glacial periods, as well as those periods when temperature is "like that of the carboniferous age," are due to the decrease and increase or rather to the expansion of our atmosphere, which expansion is itself due to the same meteoric presence? At any rate, *we all know* that the heat that the earth receives, by radiation from the sun, at the utmost, *one third*, if not less of the amount received by her directly from the meteors. *ML 23B, p. 162*

Swabhavat, Eternal Essence and Force

(1) To comprehend my answers you will have first of all to view the eternal *Essence*, the Swabhavat, not as a compound element you call spirit-matter, but as the one element for which the English has no name. It is both passive and active, pure *Spirit Essence* in its absoluteness and repose, pure matter in its finite and conditioned state – even as an imponderable gas or that great unknown which science has pleased to call *Force*.

When poets talk of the "shoreless ocean of immutability" we must regard the term but as a jocular paradox, since we maintain that there is no such thing as immutability – not in our Solar System at least. Immutability, say the theists and Christians, "is an attribute of God," and forthwith they endow that God with every mutable and variable quality and attribute, knowable as unknowable, and believe that they have solved the unsolvable and squared the circle.

To this, we reply, if *that* which the theists call God, and science *"Force"* and *"Potential Energy,"* were to become immutable but for one instant, even during the Maha-Pralaya, a period when even Brahm the creative architect of the world is said to have merged into non-being, then there could be no manvantara, and space alone would reign unconscious and supreme in the eternity of time. Nevertheless, Theism, when speaking of mutable immutability, is no more absurd than materialistic science talking of *"latent* potential energy," and the indestructibility of matter and force. What are we to believe as indestructible? Is it the invisible something that moves matter or the energy of moving bodies! *ML 11, p. 60*

(2) Study the laws and doctrines of the Nepalese Swabhavikas, the principal Buddhist philosophical school in India, and you will find them the most learned as the most scientifically logical

wranglers in the world. Their plastic, invisible, eternal, omnipresent and unconscious Swabhavat is Force or *Motion* ever generating its electricity which is life.

Yes; there is a force as limitless as thought, as potent as boundless will, as subtle as the essence of life, so inconceivably awful in its rending force as to convulse the universe to its centre were it but used as a lever, but this Force is not God, since there are men who have learned the secret of subjecting it to their will when necessary.

Look around you and see the myriad manifestations of life, so infinitely multiform, of motion, of change. What caused these? From what inexhaustable source came they, by what agency? Out of the invisible and subjective, they have entered out little area of the visible and objective. Children of Akasha, concrete evolutions from the ether, it was Force which brought them into perceptibility and Force will in time remove them from the sight of man.

Why should this plant in your garden, to the right, have been produced with such a shape and that other one, to the left, with one totally dissimilar? Are these not the result of varying action of Force – unlike correlations? Given a perfect monotony of activities throughout the world and we would have a complete identity of forms, colours, shapes and properties throughout all the kingdom of nature. It is *motion* with its resulting conflict, neutralization, equilibration, correlation, to which is due the infinite variety which prevails. *ML 22, p. 140*

(3) The initiated Brahmin (Subbha Row) calls it (Swabhavat) Brahman and Sakti when manifesting as the force. We will perhaps be near correct to call it *infinite life* and the source of all life visible and invisible, an essence inexhaustible, ever present, in short, Swabhavat. (S. in its universal application, Fohat when manifesting throughout our phenomenal world, or rather the visible universe, hence in its limitations). It is pravritti when active, nirvritti when passive. Call it the Sakti or Parabrahma if

you like, and say with the Adwaitees (Subba Row is one) that Parabrahm plus Maya becomes *Iswar* the creative principle – a power commonly called God which disappears and dies with the rest when pralaya comes. Or you may hold with the northern Buddhist philosophers and call it *Adi-Buddi*, the all pervading, supreme and absolute intelligence, with its periodically manifesting Divinity .... *ML 15, p. 90*

Theosophy

(1) The sun of Theosophy must shine for all, not for a part. There is more of this movement than you have yet had an inkling of and the work of the T.S. is linked in with similar work that is secretly going on in all parts of the world. Even in the T.S. there is a division managed by a Greek brother, about which not a person in the Society has a suspicion, excepting the old woman (H.P.B.) and Olcott; and even he knows it is progressing and occasionally executes an order I send him in connection with it. *ML 47, p. 271*

(2) Then you will, of course, aim to show that this Theosophy is no new candidate for the world's attention, but only the restatement of principles which have been recognised from the very infancy of mankind. The historic sequence ought to be succinctly, yet graphically traced through the successive evolutions of philosophical schools and illustrated with accounts of the experimental demonstrations of occult power ascribed to various thaumaturgists.

The alternate breakings-out and subsidences of mystical phenomena, as well as their shifting from one centre to another of population, show the conflicting play of the opposing forces of spirituality and animalism. And lastly, it will appear that the present tidal-wave of phenomena, with its varied effects upon human thought and feeling, made the revival of Theosophical enquiry an indispensable necessity. The only problem to solve is the practical one, of how best to promote the necessary study and give to the spiritualistic movement a needed upward impulse. It is a good beginning to make the inherent capabilities of the inner, living man better comprehended. *ML 8, pp. 34-35*

(3) The doctrine we promulgate being the only true one, must, supported by such evidence as we are preparing to give, become

ultimately triumphant, as every other truth. Yet it is absolutely necessary to inculcate it gradually, enforcing its theories, unimpeachable facts for those who know, with direct inferences deducted from and corroborated by the evidence furnished by modern, exact science. That is why Col. H.S.O., who works but to revive Buddhism, may be regarded as one who labours in the true path of Theosophy, far more than any other man who chooses as his goal the gratification of his own ardent aspirations for occult knowledge. Buddhism stripped of its superstitions is eternal truth, and he who strives for the latter is striving for Theos-sophia, Divine Wisdom, which is a synonym of truth.

For our doctrines to practically react on the so-called moral code or the ideas of truthfulness, purity, self-denial, charity, etc., we have to preach and popularise a knowledge of theosophy. It is not the individual and determined purpose of attaining oneself Nirvana (the culmination of all knowledge and absolute wisdom) which is, after all only an exalted and glorious *selfishness*, but the self-sacrificing pursuit of the best means to lead on the right path our neighbour, to cause as many of our fellow creatures as we possibly can to benefit by it, which constitutes the true Theosophist.

K.H.'s *View of the Mahachohan Letter, Combined Chronology, p. 43*

The Theosophical Society

(1) The *Chiefs* want a "Brotherhood of Humanity," a real Universal Fraternity started; an institution which would make itself known throughout the world and arrest the attention of the highest minds. *ML 6, p. 24*

(2) What I meant by the "Forlorn Hope" was that when one regards the magnitude of the task to be undertaken by our theosophical volunteers, and especially the multitudinous agencies arrayed, and to be arrayed, in opposition, we may well compare it to one of those desperate efforts against overwhelming odds that the true soldier glories to attempt. You have done well to see the "large purpose" in the small beginnings of the T.S. Of course, if we had undertaken to found and direct it in *propria persona,* very likely it would have accomplished more and made fewer mistakes, but we could not do this, nor was it the plan: our two agents are given the task and left – as you are now – to do the best they could under the circumstances. And much has been wrought.

Under the surface of Spiritualism runs a current that is wearing a broad channel for itself. When it reappears above ground its effects will be apparent. Already many minds like yours are pondering the question of occult law – forced upon the thinking public by this agitation. Like you, they are dissatisfied with what has been hitherto attainable and clamour for better. Let this – encourage you. *ML 8, p. 35*

(3) I say that it is the vilification and abuse of the founders, the general misconception of the aims and objects of the Society that paralyses its progress – nothing else. There's no want of definitiveness in these objects, were they but properly explained. The members would have plenty to do were they to pursue reality

with half the fervour they do *mirage*. I am sorry to find you comparing Theosophy to a painted house on the stage, whereas in the hands of true philanthropists and theosophists it might become as strong as an impregnable fort. The situation is this: men who join the Society with the one selfish object of reaching power, making occult science their only or even chief aim, may as well not join it – they are doomed to disappointment, as much as those who commit the mistake of letting them believe the Society is nothing else. It is just because they preach too much "the Brothers" and too little if at all *Brotherhood* that they fail. **ML 38, pp. 251-252**

(4) Let it be made known "to all concerned" through the *Theosophist* and circulars issued to every branch, that hitherto they have looked too often and too unnecessarily to the Parent Body for guidance and as an exemplar to follow. This is quite impracticable. Besides the fact that the Founders have to show themselves and try earnestly to be *all* to everyone and all things – since there is such a great variety of creeds, opinions and expectations to satisfy, they cannot possibly and at the same time satisfy all as they would like to. They try to be impartial and never to refuse one what they may have accorded to another party. Thus they have repeatedly published criticisms upon Vedantism, Buddhism and Hinduism in its various branches, upon the *Veda Bashya* of Swami Dayand – their staunchest and at that time most valued ally; but because such criticisms were all directed against *non*-Christian faiths, no one ever paid the slightest attention to it....

Now in view to mending matters, what do you think of the idea of placing the Branches on quite a different footing? Even Christendom, with its divine pretensions to a Universal Brotherhood has its thousand and one sects, which, united as they all may be under one banner of the cross, are yet essentially inimical to each other, and the authority of the Pope is set to naught by the Protestants, while the decrees of the Synods of the latter are laughed at by the Roman Catholics. Of course, I would never contemplate, even in the worst of cases, such a state of things among the theosophical bodies.

What I want, is simply a paper on the advisability of remodelling the present formation of branches and their privileges. Let  them be all chartered and initiated as heretofore by the Parent Society, and depend on it nominally. At the same time, let every branch before it is chartered choose some one object to work for, an object, naturally, in sympathy with the general principles of the T.S. – yet a distinct and definite object of its own, whether in the religious, educational or philosophical lines. This would allow the Society a broader margin for its general operations; more real, useful work would be done; and every branch would be, so to say, independent in its *modus operandus*, there would remain less room for complaint and *par consequence* – for interference.
ML 54, pp. 317-318

(5) Of all our semi-chelas, you two are the most likely to utilise for the general good the facts given you. You must regard them received in trust, for the benefit of the whole Society; to be turned over and employed and re-employed in many and in all ways that are good. *ML 16, p. 115*

(6) If we look to Ceylon, we shall see the most scholarly priests combining under the lead of the Theos. Society, in a new exegesis

of Buddhistic philosophy and – at Galle on the 15th of September (1880), a secular Theosophical school for the teaching of Singhalese youth opened, with an attendance of over 300 scholars: an example about to be initiated at three other points in that island. If the T.S. "as at present constituted," has indeed no "real vitality" and yet in its modest way has done so much of practical good, how much greater results might not be anticipated from a body organized upon the better plan you could suggest! *First Letter of K.H. to A.O. Hume,*
Combined Chronology by M. Conger, p. 37

(7) Far from our thoughts may it ever be to erect a new hierarchy for the future oppression of a priest-ridden world. As it was our wish *then* to signify to you that one could be both an active and useful member of the Society, without inscribing himself our follower or co-religionist, so it is *now*. But it is just because the principle has to work both ways, that ... we feel and would have it known that we have no right to influence the free will of the members in this or any other matter. Such interference would be in flagrant contradiction to the basic laws of esotericism, that personal psychic growth accompanies *pari passu* the development of the individual effort, and is the evidence of acquired personal merit. *ML 87 p. 407*

(8) It's time that Theosophy should enter the arena. The sons of Theosophists are more likely to become, in their turn, Theosophists than anything else. No messenger of truth, no prophet has ever achieved during his life time a complete triumph, not even Buddha; the Theosophical Society was chosen as the corner stone, the foundation of the future religion of humanity. To achieve the proposed object a greater, wiser, and especially a more benevolent intermingling of the high and the low, of the alpha and the omega of society, was determined upon. The white race must be the first to stretch out the hand of

fellowship to the dark nations ... This prospect may not smile to all. He is *no* Theosophist who objects to this principle ....
K.H.'s View of the Chohàn Letter,
Combined Chronology by M. Conger, p. 44

(9) It is a universally admitted fact that the marvellous success of the Theosophical Society in India, is due entirely to its principle of wise and respectful toleration of each other's opinions and beliefs. Not even the President-Founder has the right directly or indirectly to interfere with the freedom of thought of the humblest member, least of all to seek to influence his personal opinion. It is only in the absence of this generous consideration that even the faintest shadow of difference arms seekers after the same truth, otherwise earnest and sincere, with the scorpion-whip of hatred against their brothers, equally sincere and earnest. Deluded victims of distorted truth, they forget or never knew that discord is the harmony of the Universe. Thus in the Theos. Society, each part, as in the glorious *fugues* of the immortal Mozart, ceaselessly chases the other in harmonious discord on the paths of Eternal progress, to meet and finally blend at the threshold of the pursued goal into one harmonious whole, the keynote in nature .... *ML 85, p. 401*

(10) I am sincerely afraid that you may have been perplexed by the apparent contradiction between the notes received by you from my Brother M. – and myself. Know, my friend, that in our world, though we may differ in methods, we can never be opposed in *principles of action,* and the broadest and most practical application of the idea of the Brotherhood of Humanity is not incompatible with your dream of establishing a nucleus of honest scientific enquiries of good repute, who would give weight to the T.S. organization in the eyes of the multitude, and serve as a shield against the ferocious and idiotic attack of sceptics and materialists. *ML 33, p. 244*

(11) But this consent, you will please bear in mind, was obtained solely under the *express* and *unalterable condition* that the new Society should be founded as a Branch of the *Universal Brotherhood*, and among its members a few elect men would – *if they choose to submit to our conditions*, instead of *dictating theirs* – be allowed to BEGIN the study of the occult sciences under the written directions of a "Brother." But a "hot-bed of magick" we never dreamt of. Such an organization as mapped out by Sinnett and yourself is unthinkable among Europeans; and it has become next to impossible even in India – unless you are prepared to climb to a height of 18,000 to 20,000 amidst the glaciers of the Himalayas. *ML 28, p. 209*

(12) We wish the London Society should preserve its harmony in division like the Indian Branches, where the representatives of all the different schools of Hinduism seek to study Esoteric Sciences and the Wisdom of old, without necessarily giving up for it their respective beliefs. Each Branch, often members of the same Branch – Christian converts included in some cases – study esoteric philosophy each in his own way, yet always knitting together brotherly hands for the furtherance of the common objects of the Society. *ML 85, p. 402*

(13) Could but your L.L. (London Lodge) understand, or as much as suspect, that the present crisis that is shaking the T.S. to its foundations, is a question of perdition or salvation to thousands; a question of the progress of the human race or its retrogression, of its glory or dishonour, and for the majority of this race – of *being or not being*, of annihilation, in fact – perchance many of you would look into the very root of evil, and instead of being guided by false appearances and scientific decisions, you would set to work and save the situation by disclosing the dishonorable doings of your missionary world. *ML 65, p. 365*

(14) Mrs. Kingsford's election (as president of the London Lodge – Ed.) is not a matter of personal feeling between ourselves and that lady but rests entirely on the advisability of having at the head of the Society, in a place like London, a person well-suited to the standard and aspirations of the (so far) ignorant (of esoteric truths) and therefore malicious public. Nor is it a matter of the slightest consequence whether the gifted president of the "London Lodge" Theos. Soc. entertains feelings of reverence or disrespect toward the humble and unknown individuals at the head of the Tibetan Good Law – or the writer of the present, or any of his brothers – but rather a question whether the said lady is fitted for the purpose we have all at heart, namely the dissemination of TRUTH through Esoteric doctrines, conveyed by whatever religious channel, and the effacement of cross materialism and blind prejudices and skepticism. *ML 85, p. 398*

(15) As the lady has rightly observed, the Western public should understand the Theosophical Society to be "a Philosophical School, constituted on the ancient hermetic basis" – that public having never heard of the Tibetan, and entertaining very perverted notions of the esoteric Buddhism System.

Therefore, and so far, we agree with the remarks embodied in the letter written by Mrs. K to Madam B. and which the latter was asked to "submit to K.H." and, we would remind our members of the "L.L." in this reference, that *Hermetic Philosophy* is universal and unsectarian, while the Tibetan School will ever be regarded by those who know little, if anything of it, as coloured more or less with sectarianism. The former nothing, neither caste, nor colour, nor creed, no lover of Esoteric wisdom can have any objection to the name, which otherwise he might feel were the Society to which he belongs to be placarded with a specific denomination pertaining to a distinct religion. Hermetic Philosophy suits every creed and philosophy and clashes with none. It is the boundless ocean of Truth, the central point whither flows and wherein meet every river, as every stream – whether its source be in the East, West, North, or South. As the course of the river depends upon the nature of its basin, so the channel for communication of Knowledge must conform itself to surrounding circumstances. *ML 85, pp. 398-399*

(16) If the Oriental group survives, something could yet be done for it. But never, henceforth, shall the Society in India be allowed to be compromised again by phenomena that are denounced wholesale as fraud. The good ship is sinking, friend, because the precious cargo has been offered to the public at large; because some of its contents have been desecrated by profane handling, and its gold – received as brass. Henceforth, I say, no such profane eye will see its treasures, and its outer decks and rigging must be cleansed of the impurity and dross that was accumulated on them by the indiscretion of its own members. Try to remedy the evil done. Every step made by one in our direction will force us to make one toward him. *ML 65, p. 366*

(17) ... the chief object of the T.S. is not so much to gratify individual aspirations, as to serve our fellow men; and the real value of this term "selfish," which may jar upon your ear, has a peculiar significance with us which it cannot have with you; therefore, and to begin with, you must not accept it otherwise than in the former sense.

Perhaps you will better appreciate our meaning when told that in our view the highest aspirations for the welfare of humanity become tainted with selfishness, if, in the mind of the philanthropist there lurks the shadow for self benefit or a tendency to do injustice, even when these exist unconsciously to himself. Yet you have ever discussed but to put down the idea of a universal Brotherhood, questioned its usefulness and advised to remodel the T.S. on the principle of a college for the special study of occultism. This, my respected friend and Brother – will never do! *ML 2, pp. 7-8*

(18) The Society will never perish as an institution, although branches and individuals in it may. *ML 34, p. 245*

Tibet

(1) For centuries we have had in Tibet a moral, pure-hearted, simple people, unblessed with civilization, hence – untainted by its vices. For ages has been Tibet the last corner of the globe, not so entirely corrupted as to preclude the mingling together of the two atmospheres – the physical and the spiritual. *ML 98, p. 434*

(2) We have to take measures for effectually protecting our country and vindicating the spiritual authority of our Priestly King. Perhaps never since the invasion of Alexander and his Greek legions have so many Europeans stood together under arms, so near to our frontiers *as they do now.* (Nov. 1880) *ML 106, p. 443*

(3) A crisis in a certain sense, is upon us now and must be met. I might say two crises – one, the Society's, the other for Tibet. For I may tell you in confidence that Russia is gradually massing her forces for a future invasion of that country, under the pretext of a Chinese war. If she does not succeed it will be due to us; and herein at least, we will deserve your gratitude. You see then we have weightier matters than small societies to think about; yet the T.S. must not be neglected. *ML 4, p. 11*

(4) Among the few glimpses obtained by Europeans of Tibet and its mystical hierarchy of "perfect lamas," there is one which was understood and described. "The incarnations of the Boddhisattva Padma Pani or Avalo-Kiteswara and of Tsong Kapa, that of Amitabha, relinquish at their death the attainment of Buddhahood – *i.e.* – the summum bonum of bliss and of individual *personal* felicity – that they might be born again and again for the benefit of mankind."

In other words, that they might be again and again subjected to misery, imprisonment in flesh and all the sorrows of life, provided that by such a self-sacrifice, repeated throughout long and dreary centuries, they might become the means of securing salvation and bliss in the hereafter for a handful of men chosen among them, but one of the many races of mankind. And it is we, the humble disciples of these perfect lamas, who are expected to allow the T.S. to drop its noblest title, that of the Brotherhood of Humanity, to become a simple school of psychology? No, no, good brothers, you have been labouring under the mistake too long already.

K.H.'s View of the Mahachohan Letter,
Combined Chronology by M. Conger, pp. 46–47

(5) If you care anything about our future relations, then you better try to make your friend and colleague, Mr. Hume give up his insane idea of going to Tibet. Does he really think that *unless we allow it,* he, or any army of Pelings will be enabled to hunt us out, or bring back news that we are, after all, but a "moon-shine"… Madman is that man who imagines that even the British Govt. is strong and rich enough and powerful enough to help him in carrying out his insane plan! Those whom we desire to know us will find us at the very frontiers. Those who have set against themselves the Chohans as he has – would not find us were they to go to L'hasa with an army. His carrying out the plan will be the signal for an absolute separation between your world and ours. His idea of applying to the Govt. for permission to go to Tibet is ridiculous. He will encounter dangers at every step and – will not even hear the remotest tidings about ourselves or our whereabouts. (Hume did not make this attempt – Ed.)
ML 100, p. 438

Time

(1) I may also remind you ... that *time is something created entirely by ourselves*; that while one short second of intense agony may appear, even on earth, as an eternity to one man, to another, more fortunate, hours, days. And sometimes whole years may seem to flit like one brief moment; and that finally, of all the sentient and conscious beings on earth, man is the only animal that takes any cognizance of time, although it makes him neither happier nor wiser. How then can I explain to you that which *cannot* feel, since you seem unable to comprehend it? Finite smiles are unfit to express the abstract and the infinite; nor can the objective ever mirror the subjective. To realize the bliss in *Devachan,* or the woes in *Avitchi,* you have to assimilate them – as we do. Western critical idealism ... has still to learn the difference that exists between the *real being* of super-sensible objects and the shadowy subjectivity of the ideas it has reduced them to.

Time is not a predicate conception and can, therefore, neither be proved nor analysed, according to the methods of superficial philosophy. And, unless we learn to counteract the negative results of that method of drawing our conclusions, agreeably to the teachings of the so-called "system of pure reason," and to distinguish between the matter and form of our knowledge of sensible objects, we can never arrive at correct, definite conclusions ... Space and time may be – as Kant has it – not the product but the regulators of the sensations, but only so far as our sensations on *earth* are concerned, not those in Devachan. There we do not find the *a priori* ideas of "space and time" controlling the perceptions of the denizen of Devachan in respect to the objects of *his* sense; but on the contrary, we discover that it is the *devachanee* himself who absolutely creates both and annihilates them at the same time. *ML 25, p. 194*

(2) One year has wrought a great change in your heart. The man of 1880 would scarcely recognise the man of 1881 were they confronted. Compare them, then, good friend and brother, that you may fully realize what time has done, or rather what you have done with time. To do this meditate – alone, with the magic mirror of memory to gaze into. Thus shall you not only see the lights and shadows of the Past, but the possible brightness of the future as well. Thus, in time you will come to see the Ego of aforetime in its naked reality. *ML 37, p. 249*

(3) New ideas have to be planted on clean places, for these ideas touch upon the most momentous subjects. It is not physical phenomena but these universal ideas that we study, as to comprehend the former we have to first understand the latter. They touch man's true position in the universe in relation to his previous and future births; his origin and ultimate destiny; the relation of the mortal to the immortal; of the temporary to the eternal; of the finite to the infinite; ideas larger, grander, more comprehensive, recognising the universal reign of immutable Law, unchanging and unchangeable, in regard to which there is only an ETERNAL NOW, while to uninitiated mortals, time is past or future as related to their finite existence on this material speck of dirt. This is what we study and what many have solved. *ML 6, p. 24*

(4) I feel even irritated at having to use these three clumsy words – past, present and future! Miserable concepts of the objective phases of the Subjective Whole, they are about as ill adapted for the purpose as an axe for fine carving. *ML 8, p. 29*

Universal Mind and Consciousness

(1) Did you ever suspect that Universal, like finite, human mind might have two attributes, or a dual power – one the voluntary and conscious and the other the involuntary and unconscious or the mechanical power? To reconcile the difficulty of many theistic and anti-theistic propositions, both these powers are a philosophical necessity. The possibility of the first or the voluntary and conscious attribute in reference to the infinite mind ... will remain forever a mere hypothesis, whereas in the finite mind it is a scientific and demonstrated fact. The highest Planetary Spirit is as ignorant of the first as we are, the hypothesis will remain one even in Nirvana, as it is a mere inferential possibility, whether there or here. *ML 22, p. 137*

(2) The book of *Kiu-te* teaches that space is infinity itself. It is formless, immutable and absolute. Like the human mind, which is the exhaustless generator of ideas, the Universal Mind or Space has its ideation, which is projected into objectivity at the appointed time, but space itself is not affected thereby. Even your Hamilton has shown that infinity can never be conceived by any series of additions. Whenever you talk of *place* in infinity, you dethrone infinity and degrade its absolute, unconditioned character. *ML 86, p. 404*

(3) The Lhas or adept alone possesses the real, his mind being en *rapport* with the Universal Mind. The Lhas has made the perfect junction of his soul with the Universal Mind in its fullness, which makes him for the time being a divine being, existing in the region of absolute intelligence, knowledge of natural laws or Dgyu (the real.) The profane cannot become a Dang-ma (purified soul) for he lacks means of perceiving Chhag, Genesis or the beginning of things. *Cosmological Notes, LBS – First Edition, p. 376*

(4) Volition and consciousness are at the same time self-determining and determined by causes, and the volition of man. His intelligence and consciousness will awake but when his fourth principle *Kama* is matured and completed by its (seriatim) contact with the *kamas* or energizing forces of all the forms man has passed through in his previous three rounds.
ML 13, pp. 76-77

(5) We do not bow our heads in the dust before the mystery of mind – for we *have solved it ages ago*. Rejecting with contempt the theistic theory, we reject as much the automatom theory, teaching that states of consciousness are produced by the marshalling of the molecules of the brain; and we feel as little respect for that other hypothesis – the production of molecular motion by consciousness. Then what do we believe in? Well, we believe in the much laughed at *phlogiston* (the principle of fire – Ed.) ... and in what some natural philosophers would call *nisus*, (impulse – Ed.) the incessant though perfectly imperceptible (to the ordinary senses) motions or efforts one body is making on another – the pulsations of inert matter – its life. *ML 10, p. 56*

Visions and Dreams

(1) In dreams and *visions* at least, when rightly interpreted there can hardly be an "element of doubt." ... I hope to prove to you my presence near you last night by something I took away with me. *ML 3A, p. 10*

(2) Methinks were you to have a vision nightly, you would soon cease to "treasure" them at all. But there is a far weightier reason why you should not have a surfeit – it would be a waste of our strength. As often as I, or any of us can communicate with you, whether by dreams, waking impressions, letters (in or out of pillows!) or personal visits in astral form – it will be done. But remember that Simla is 7,000 feet higher than Allahabad and the difficulties to be surmounted at the latter are tremendous. I abstain from encouraging you to expect too much, for, like yourself, I am loath to promise what, for various reasons, I may not be able to perform. *ML 4, p. 17*

(3) There is but one general law of vision (physical and mental or spiritual) but there is a qualifying special law, proving that all vision must be determined by the quality or grade of man's spirit and soul and also by the ability to translate diverse qualities of waves of astral light into consciousness. There is but one general law of life, but innumerable laws qualify and determine the myriads of forms perceived and of sounds heard. There are those who are willingly and others who are *unwillingly* – blind. Mediums belong to the former, sensitives to the latter. Unless regularly initiated and trained – concerning the spiritual insight of things and the supposed revelations made unto man in all ages, from Socrates down to Swedenborg and "Fern" – no self-tutored seer or clairaudient ever saw or heard *quite* correctly. *ML 40, p. 255*

(4) But for the attainment of your proposed object, viz. for a clearer comprehension of the extremely abstruse and at first incomprehensible theories of our occult doctrine, never allow the serenity of your mind to be disturbed during your hours of literary labour, nor before you set to work. It is upon the serene and placid surface of the unruffled mind that the visions gathered from the invisible find a representation in the visible world. Otherwise you would vainly seek those visions, those flashes of sudden light, which have already helped to solve so many of the minor problems and which alone can bring the truth before the eye of the soul. It is with jealous care that we have to guard our mind-plane from all the adverse influences which daily arise in our passage through earth life. *ML 11, p. 64*

(5) You have entirely mistaken my meaning in the telegram. The words "more at Adyar," related to the true explanation of your vision, not by any means to a promise of some further psycho-logical experiments made in that direction by myself. The vision was due to an attempt by DK., who is extremely interested in your progress. While he succeeded in getting you out of your body, he failed entirely in his effort to open your inner vision, for reasons correctly surmised at the time by yourself. I took no personal active part in the attempt. Hence my answer, "surmises correct – more at Adyar." *ML 58, p. 336*

(6) No adept has ever penetrated beyond the veil of primitive Kosmic matter. The highest, the most perfect vision is limited to the universe of *Form* and *Matter*. *ML 9, p. 47*

Wisdom

(1) I tell you a profound truth in saying that if you (like the fabled Shloma) but choose wisdom all other things will be added unto it – in time. *ML 43, p. 262*

(2) The truth is, my dear friend, that notwithstanding the great tidal wave of mysticism that is now sweeping over a portion of the intellectual classes of Europe, the Western people have as yet scarcely learned to recognise that which we term *wisdom* in its loftiest sense. As yet, he is only esteemed truly wise in his world who can most cleverly conduct the business of life, so that it may yield the largest amount of material profit – honours or money. The quality of wisdom ever was, and will be yet for a long time – to the very close of the fifth race – denied to him who seeks the wealth of the mind for its own sake, and for its own enjoyment and result without the secondary purpose of turning it to account in the attainment of material benefits. By most of your gold worshipping countrymen our facts and theorems would be denominated fancy-flights, the dream of madmen. *ML 54, p. 305*

(3) Thus, little by little, the now incomprehensible will become the self-evident; and many a sentence of mystic meaning will shine yet out before your Soul-eye, like a transparency, illuminating the darkness of your mind. Such is the course of gradual progress; a year or two back you might have written a more brilliant, never a more profound article.

Neglect then not, my good Brother, the humble, the derided Journal of your Society (*The Theosophist*) and mind not either its quaint, pretentious cover, nor the "heaps of manure" contained in it – to repeat the charitable and, to yourself, the too familiar remark used often at Simla. But let your attention be rather drawn to the few pearls of wisdom and *occult truths* to be occasionally discovered under that "manure." Our own ways and manners are, perchance, as quaint and as uncouth – nay more so. Subba Row is right; he who knows aught of the ways of the *Siddhas* shall concur with the views expressed on the third page of his incomplete letter: many of us would be mistaken for *Madmen* by your English gentleman. But he who would become a son of Wisdom can always see beneath the rugged surface.

So with the poor old Journal. Behold its mystically bumptious clothing! Its numerous blemishes and literary defects and with all that cover, the most perfect symbol of its contents: the main portion of its original ground, thickly veiled, all smutty and as black as night, through which peep out grey dots and lines and words, and even sentences. To the truly wise these breaks of grey may suggest an allegory full of meaning, such as the streaks of twilight upon the Eastern sky, at morning's early dawn, after a night of intense darkness; the aurora of a more "spiritually intellectual" cycle.

And who knows, how many of those, who undismayed by its unprepossessing appearance, the hideous intricacies of its style, and the other many failures of the unpopular magazine will keep on turning its pages, who may find themselves rewarded some day for their perseverance! Illuminated sentences may gleam out upon them at some time or other, shedding a bright light upon some old, puzzling problems. Yourself, some fine morning, while poring over its crooked columns with the sharpened wits of a well-rested brain, peering into what you now view as hazy, impalpable speculations, having only the consistency of vapour – yourself, you may, perchance, perceive in them the unexpected solution of an old blurred, forgotten "dream" of yours, which once *recalled* will impress itself in an indelible image upon your *outer* form, your inner memory, to never fade out from it again. All this is possible and *may* happen; for our ways *are* the ways of "Madmen"... **ML 48, p. 277**

Glossary

Abhidharma. (Sanskrit) Ancient Buddhist texts (3rd-century BC and later).

Ad. (Assyr.) The "Father." The only One.

Adept. (Latin) One who is "skilled." In theosophical writings, however, an "Adept" is one who is skilled in the Esoteric Wisdom and the teachings of life.

Adi-Buddha. (Sanskrit) The omniscient, infinite source of all things, having no beginning or end. The *One* or the *First*; Supreme Wisdom. A term used by mystic Northern Buddhists.

Adonai. (Hebrew) The same as Adonis. Commonly translated "Lord."

Advaita or Adwaitism. (Sanskrit) A Vedanta Sect. The non-dualistic school founded by Sankaracharya, the greatest of the historical Brahmin sages.

Advaitee or Adwaitin. (Sanskrit) A follower of the Advaita School of philosophy.

Akasha. (Sanskrit) "Brilliant," "shining." Subtle, supersensuous spiritual essence which pervades all space; also primordial spirit substance, the reservoir of being and of beings.

Alaya. (Sanskrit) The root and fountain of all beings, the Universal Soul. Mystically it is identical with *akasha,* and as the primeval root of all substance it is identical with *mulaprakriti.*

Amitabha. The Chinese perversion of the Sanskrit Amrita Buddha, or the "Immortal Enlightened;" also a name for Gautama Buddha.

Amrita. (Sanskrit) The ambrosial drink or food of the gods, giving immortality. The elixir of life in the Hindu Puranas.

Ananta-Sesha. (Sanskrit) Many-headed Cosmic Serpent in Hindu mythology.

Anaxagoras of Clazomene. (500-428 BC) The first philosopher to bring philosophy to Athens, Greece.

Arhat. (Sanskrit) Another term for an Adept and one who has passed the fourth initiation and has only one more incarnation.

Arupa. (Sanskrit) Formless, without form.

Ashta-vijnana. (Sanskrit) Knowledge of the spiritual Self.

Astral Light. An invisible "region" surrounding our earth; the most material excepting our physical universe; the carrier of prana or life-energy. Today the term "etheric" is used to describe this dimension or plane of being.

Attavada. (Sanskrit) The illusion that the personality or personal self is eternal.

Atma. (Sanskrit) The highest part of man – the Self: pure consciousness. The essential and radical faculty of man which gives knowledge or consciousness of Selfhood.

Augoeides. The luminous, divine radiation of the Higher Self which, when it re-incarnates, the personality is but its shadow.

Avaivartyas or Avaivartikas. (Sanskrit) Buddhas.

Avalokitesvara. (Sanskrit) "The on-looking Lord." In the exoteric interpretation he is Padmapani – the "lotus bearer" and the "lotus-born;" in Tibet, he is the first divine ancestor of the Tibetans, an avatar. In esoteric philosophy he is the Higher Self. The mantra "Om Mani padme hum" is specially used to invoke his help.

Avatara or Avatar. (Sanskrit) The descent or passing down of celestial energy or energies of an inspiring divinity, in order to overshadow and illuminate some human being for the helping of humanity. The one loaned for this purpose is always a highly evolved soul and possesses a pure physical body.

Avidya. (Sanskrit) Ignorance which proceeds from form and is produced by the illusion of the senses.

Avitchi. (Sanskrit) Literally: "waveless" suggesting the stagnation of life. It refers to a sphere or state of consciousness to which gravitate those who are suffering from evil passions. It is not punishment in the Christian sense and redemption from this state is possible. It can be experienced in between lives but also on earth.

Bacon, Francis. (1561-1626) Lawyer, courtier, statesman, philosopher and master of the English language. He advocated new ways by which men might establish a legitimate command over nature. During the reign of James I, he acted as Lord Chancellor. His final years were spent writing his most valuable works: *Novum Organum, Instauratio Magna* and *The New Atlantis.*

Bacon, Roger. (1220-1292) English Franciscan monk and adept in Alchemy and Magic Arts. He believed in the Philosopher's Stone in the way that all adepts of Occultism believe in it as symbolic of the transmutation of the lower animal nature into the highest and divine aspects of one's being. He was zealous in the pursuit of experimental science and was the author of several works: *Opus Magus, Opus Minus,* and *Opus Tertium.*

Bennett, D.M. (1818-1882) American founder and publisher of "The Truth Seeker," a periodical that espoused Free Thought and reform. Bennett was a devout Shaker for 13 years before evolving into a "free-thinker." He became a member of the *Theosophical Society.* He was framed by his enemies and jailed in New York for over a year. After his release, his supporters sent him on a world tour which included India where he met H.P. Blavatsky. The Master K.H. confirmed that Bennett was a disciple and agent of the Mahatmas.

Bhikkhus. (Sanskrit) Buddhist monks.

Bhikshu. (Sanskrit) Name given to the first followers of Sakyamuni Buddha.

Bodhisattva. (Sanskrit) Literally "he whose essence (sattva) has become intelligence" (bodhi) those who need but one more incarnation to become perfect Buddhas and to be entitled to Nirvana. However, the bodhisattva vow is to forego Nirvana and remain on earth to help humanity and all sentient beings.

Book of Kiu-te. (Tibetan) Very ancient Tibetan texts, pre-dating the Vedas and originally written in Senzar. *The Stanzas of Dzyan* of H.P. Blavatsky's *The Secret Doctrine* are based on these sacred scriptures.

Brahm, Brahma. (Sanskrit) The male Creator – existing periodically in his manifestation only – which is followed by a period of repose (pralaya).

Brahman. (Sanskrit) Impersonal, supreme uncognizable Principle of the Universe that is all pervading.

Brahmin. (Sanskrit) Highest of the four castes in India – the priest caste.

Buddhi. (Sanskrit) Universal Soul; also the spiritual Soul in man (the sixth principle) the vehicle of Atma, the seventh and highest principle.

Chatterjee, Mohini Mo hun. (1858–1936) An Attorney at law, Chatterjee was a personal student of the Master Koot Hoomi and one of the most brilliant Hindu members of the early Theosophical movement. He was of the Brahmin caste and a native of Calcutta. He lectured extensively in Europe and the USA. Adulation and fame, unfortunately, spoiled him and resulted in his exercising improper judgement in his relations. Eventually, he broke with H.P. Blavatsky and the Theosophical movement. He co-authored with Laura Holloway the book: *Man: Fragments of Forgotten History.*

Chohan. (Tibetan) "Lord" or "Master;" a chief. The chief of the Mahatmas Koot Hoomi and Morya is referred to as a Chohan, also as a "Mahachohan" (great Lord).

Crookes, Sir William. (1822–1919) English chemist and physicist noted for the discovery of the element thallium and for his cathode ray studies foundational in the development of atomic physics. Crookes also developed a theory of radiant matter and took up the study of atomic physics. During the 1870s he began a long series of studies in Spiritualism and Theosophy. He was a member of the *London Theosophical Lodge.*

Damodar K. Mavalankar. (1857-?) An early pioneer of the Theosophical movement. he was a tireless worker at the Headquarters both in Bombay and later in Adyar, Madras. He demonstrated great devotion to the Cause and the Mahatmas. He was business manager of the publications' department, an author of articles and an editor of *The Theosophist* magazine. A chela of the Master K.H., he abandoned his Brahmin caste and met with his Teacher, in his physical body, on numerous occasions. In 1885 he left for his Teacher's Ashram in the Himalayas but was never seen or heard from again. Later, letters arrived for Olcott from the Master K.H. indicating Damodar had reached the Ashram safely and had successfully undergone a major test.

Dee, Dr. John. (1527-1608) An Alchemist, astrologer, a mathematician contributing to the revival of interest in Mathematics in England in the 16th-century. He became the astrologer to Queen Mary Tudor and was imprisoned for being a magician but was later released in 1555. He also became the practicing astrologer in the court of Queen Elizabeth I.

Devachan. (Sanskrit) The "dwelling of the gods." A blissful state intermediate between two earth lives, in which there is no suffering and into which the Higher Self enters after its separation from the lower principles.

Devachanee. (Sanskrit) A dweller in Devachan.

Devas. Celestial beings – whether good, bad, or indifferent, of which there are many classes.

Dharma. (Sanskrit) The practice of righteousness; the fulfillment of one's natural duty.

Dharmakaya. (Sanskrit) "Vesture of Bliss;" a state of pure consciousness, free from personal thought. In Buddhism this is the third and highest of the three "bodies" or states of a high spiritual being such as the Buddha – the "Trikaya" – which consists of the *Nirmanakaya, the Sambhogakaya,* and *the Dharmakaya.* We can look on these three states, all of them lofty and sublime, as being vestures in which the consciousness of a high being clothes itself.

Dhyan Chohans. (Sanskrit) "The Lords of Light." The highest celestial beings, akin to the Roman Catholic Archangels. Divine Intelligences charged with the supervision of Cosmos.

Dikshita. (Sanskrit) Initiate teachings; dikshit – an initiate.

Eglinton, William. (1857-1933) A spiritualist and well known medium in England. In the early 1880s, Eglinton went to India and investigated the theosophical movement. For a short time he became the Secretary for The Theosophical Society in Simla. On return to England, he became a partner in the Ross publishing firm but was not successful and returned to mediumship for earning his livelihood. He became editor of a spiritual magazine entitled *The New Age Magazine.*

Elementals. Nature spirits or "sprites." Also beings who are beginning a course of evolutionary growth and who are in elemental states of their development. Also a general term for any being evolving below the minerals; yet the minerals are expressions of one host of elemental beings of a more evolved type. Medieval mystics taught there were four general kinds: fire (salamanders) air (sylphs) water (undines) earth (gnomes.) The term also refers to thought forms that human beings create with their minds.

Elementaries. This term signifies in general spooks or phantoms of disembodied persons and those whose temporary habitation is Kama-loka (purgatory or Hades of the ancient Greeks.)

Faraday, Michael. (1791-1867) English physicist, chemist, and one of the great experimentalists of all time. He discovered the principle of the electric motor and was the first to liquefy chlorine. He was convinced of the interrelationship between electricity and magnetism, and demonstrated the phenomena of electromagnetism.

Fifth Root Race (or "Developmental Stage of Humanity.") The present Root Race; it has seven sub-divisions or sub-races. The development of mind is significant for this Root Race.

Flammarion, Camille. (1842-1925) French astronomer and prolific author of more than 50 titles, including popular scientific works on astronomy; early sci-fi novels, and works on psychical research.

Flamsted, John. (1646-1719) The first astronomer royal of England. He founded the Royal Greenwich Observatory in 1675, where he was the first director.

Fohat. (Tibetan) The universal propelling vital force, the essence of cosmic electricity. In the manifested universe it is the ever present electrical energy and ceaseless formative and destructive power. In Occultism it is the active male potency of Sakti (the female reproductive power) in nature.

Fourth Root Race (or "Developmental Stage of Humanity.") This has seven major subdivisions or sub-races and is referred to as the "Atlantean." The development of the emotions was significant for this Root Race.

Halley, Edmund (1657-1742) Astronomer and mathematician. The first to calculate the orbit of a comet named after him. In 1705, he accurately predicted the return of the comet (1758) now known as his comet.

Hermes Trismegistus. "The thrice-great Hermes;" the Egyptian mythical person after whom the Hermetic philosophy was named. In Egypt he was the God Thoth or Thot. This was also a generic name for Greek writers on philosophy and alchemy.

Hermetic Writings. Any writing connected with the esoteric teachings of Hermes, who, whether the Egyptian Thoth or the Greek Hermes, was the God of Wisdom with the Ancients. The Hermetic Writings were highly prized by some of the early Christians and Church Fathers, such as St. Augustine, Cyril, and Origen.

Holloway, Laura Carter. (1843-1930) American author, journalist and lecturer who espoused women's rights. Her first book was *Ladies of the White House.* In the 1870s, she became committed to the Theosophical movement, meeting H.P. Blavatsky in 1884. She sponsored concerts for women only at Brighton Beach; published a children's book based on theosophical ideas entitled, Atma Fairy Stories, and also contributed articles for the Theosophical journal: *The Word.* Mohini Chatterji co-authored with her the theosophical book: *Man: Fragments of Forgotten History.* In addition to the theosophical movement, Laura Holloway developed a strong affinity for the Shaker Community and shared their beliefs in pacifism, vegetarianism, feminism, and cremation.

Hume, Allan Octavian. (1829-1912) Originally from England and a political family, Hume moved to India where he was employed with the East Indian Company. He was later a Civil

Servant and Magistrate at the city of Etawah. During the mutiny of Etawah in 1857, he showed a great deal of courage and was subsequently awarded the *Order of the Cross of Bath* for his outstanding courage. He also became Father of the Indian Congress party. Hume loved natural science and became renowned in Ornithological research. His ornithological collection is now housed in the Natural Science Museum, London, England. His interest in Theosophy culminated in his correspondence with the Masters, and contributions of articles to *The Theosophist*.

Iamblichus. (AD 245-325) A Syrian philosopher who along with Plotinus and Porphyry was a founder of Neoplatonism.

Isis. In Egypt Isis is both the goddess of Wisdom and the Virgin Mother. She is the female reflection of the god Osiris.

Iswara. (Sanskrit) Lord or personal god; the divine spirit in man. A title also given to gods in India.

Jnana. (Sanskrit) Knowledge of occult wisdom.

Jnata. (Sanskrit) The knower.

Jivamukti. (Sanskrit) An adept or yogi who has reached the ultimate state of holiness and separated himself from matter; a Mahatma or Nirvanee, a dweller in bliss and emancipation. One who has virtually reached Nirvana during life.

Jivatma. (Sanskrit) The ONE universal life, generally; but also the divine spirit in man; the seventh and highest principle of man.

Kama. (Sanskrit) Desire, passions; cleaving to existence.

Kama Loka. (Sanskrit) The semi-material plane, to us subjective and invisible, where the disembodied "personalities" go following the death of the physical. Today this is referred to as the Astral plane. The disembodied "personalities" remain in that state of existence until the effects of desire impulses are exhausted.

Kama Rupa. (Sanskrit) The seat of animal desires and passions. Man's fourth principle; the emotional body.

Kant Immanuel. (1724-1804) Foremost thinker of the Enlightenment and one of the greatest philosophers of all time. His comprehensive and systematic work in the theory of knowledge, ethics, and aesthetics greatly influenced subsequent philosophy. Originally a theological student, he was attracted to math and physics, especially the work of Sir Isaac Newton. He published a number of original works including: *Critique of Pure Reason* – a treatise on Metaphysics.

Karma. (Sanskrit) The law of cause and effect. Nemesis only in the one sense of bad karma. It is the power that controls all things, the result of moral action, the effect of an act committed for the attainment of something which gratifies a personal desire. Karma neither punishes nor rewards, it is simply the one Universal Law.

Khuddakapatha. Buddhist scripture containing the first discourses of the Buddha.

Kingsford, Anna. (1846-1888) English anti-vivisectionist and women's rights campaigner. One of the first English women to obtain a degree in medicine. She became very active in the Theosophical movement in England, becoming president of the London Lodge in 1883. With Edward Maitland, she co-authored the book *The Perfect Way*. Her book *Clothed With the Sun* was published after her death.

Kwan Yin. (Chinese) "Mother of Mercy." The female aspect of the Logos.

Kwan-shai-yin. (Chinese) The "manifested god" – the male aspect of the Logos of the Northern Buddhists.

Levi, Eliphas. (1810-1875) A learned Kabalist, his real name was Abbe Alphonse Louis Constant. He was author of a number of books on philosophical magic. At one time he was a priest, an abbot of the Roman Catholic Church, who was unfrocked due to his kabalistic interests.

Lha. (Tibetan) Spirits of highest spheres. Hence the name of Lhasa, the original residence of the Dalai Lama. The term also refers in Tibet to saints and yogi adepts.

Linga Sharira. (Sanskrit) The phantom body on which the physical is moulded; now referred to as the etheric or energy body. However, H.P.B. used to call it the astral body.

Logos. (Greek) The manifested Deity with every nation and people; the outward expression of the Cause or Source which is ever concealed. "The Word" of St. John's Gospel. The first born or manifested Deity emerging from the ultimate Source, the Absolute.

Mahakasha. (Sanskrit) Endless Space symbolized in Theosophy by the circle.

Mahapralaya. (Sanskrit) The great rest and night that follows a mahavantara and "Day of Brahma."

Mahatma. (Sanskrit) Literally "great soul." A Master and adept who has attained mastery over the physical, emotional and mental aspects of one's being.

Mahavantara. (Sanskrit) A great cycle of manifestation usually referred to as a "Day of Brahma."

Manvantara. (Sanskrit) A cycle or period of activity and manifestation. There are many kinds of manvantaras: universal; the manvantara of the solar system; terrestrial; related to our earth; and the manvanatara related to the period of activity of man.

Mara. (Sanskrit) The god of temptation, who tried to turn away Buddha from his Path when he was meditating under the bodhi tree.

Marcus Aurelius Antonnius. (AD 121-180) Roman emperor famous for his Meditations on Stoic Philosophy. Remembered as an exemplar of the stoic philosophy of Epictetus.

Massey, Charles Carleton. (1838-1905) An English barrister keenly interested in Spiritualism. He was present at the founding of the theosophical movement in New York, in November 1875. Also he was one of the founders of *The Psychic Research Society*, London, England.

Maya. (Sanskrit) All that which is temporary and subject to decay is regarded in the Hindu philosophy as maya – illusion.

Mesmer, Franz Anton. (1734-1815) German physician with an interest in astronomy. An exponent and pioneer experimenter in natural energetic transference between animate and inanimate objects, which he called "animal magnetism," but which was referred to later as "mesmerism" (but not to be confused with the practice of hypnotism).

Moksha. (Sanskrit) Liberation and freedom from the bonds of material existence and necessity to continue to reincarnate on earth.

Monad. (Sanskrit) The immortal part of man, the divine fragment or "pilgrim" which re-incarnates and evolves through many lives. In Theosophy, it means the Atma in conjunction with its vehicle, Buddhi, the seventh and sixth principles of man.

Moses, Rev. William Stainton. (1839-1892). An English clergyman and a spiritualist. Ordained a priest in the Church of England in 1870, he became interested in spiritualism and developed mediumistic abilities, including automatic writing. The Masters hoped he would evolve from being an unconscious passive medium into a conscious agent and mediator for the Himalayan Brotherhood.

Mulaprakriti. (Sanskrit) Undifferentiated, primordial substance. Root-matter.

Nag and Naga. Literally nag means serpent and is a symbol of eternity. In China and Tibet, the terms "Dragons" and Nagas, refer to adepts, wise-men, and yogis. The Nagas in the South and Central America tradition, as well as in India and ancient Egypt, are ever endowed with extraordinary powers.

Nidanas. (Sanskrit) The 12 fetters or causes of existence referred to in Buddhism.

Nirvana. (Sanskrit) Freedom from desires and everything connected with the physical world. Exemption from the necessity to reincarnate. A state of great bliss.

Occultism or Occult Science. The science of things hidden. Theosophists use the term to mean the study of the hidden things of being, the science of life or universal nature. The study of true Occultism means penetrating deep into the causal mysteries of Being.

Para-atman. (Sanskrit) Supreme Soul of the Universe.

Parabrahm. (Sanskrit) Supreme infinite Brahma – the Absolute Source – the "one without a second" who is attributeless and uncognizable.

Paracelsus. (1493-1591) Symbolic name of the greatest occultist of the middle ages. His real name was Philip Bombastes Aureolus Theophastus von Hohenheim. He was born in Austria and becoming the cleverest physician of his age, he was renowned for curing by the power of talismans. One of the most learned philosophers of the time, he was also a distinguished alchemist.

Paranirvana. (Sanskrit) Absolute Non-Being or Be-ness, equivalent to Absolute Being.

Phlogiston. (Greek) The matter or principle of fire.

Planetary Spirits. Primarily the rulers or governors of the planets. As our earth has its hierarchy of terrestrial planetary spirits, from the highest to the lowest plane, so has every other body in the heavens. The highest planetary spirit, ruling over any globe, is in reality the "Personal God" of that planet.

Plato. (428–348 BC) The greatest of the Greek philosophers, Plato lived 400 years before the current era. He was an initiate in the Mysteries and laid the foundation of Western culture. In 387 BC,

Plato established the Academy in Athens, an institute of philosophy and scientific research. He was a student of Socrates and a teacher of Aristotle.

Plotinus. (AD 205-270) Philosopher and religious genius who lived in Alexandria, Egypt, and who transformed the revival of Platonism, which was subsequently called "Neoplatonism." His own quest was for mystical reunion with the Divine.

Plutarch of Athens. (d. AD 432) Greek philosopher who became head of the Platonic Society of Athens and was one of the teachers of the philosopher Proclus. Plutarch wrote ordained *Commentaries* on some of Plato's *Dialogues* and Aristotle's work.

Popol Vuh. The Creation Story of the Maya. Most important text in the native languages of the Americas.

Poseidon. (Greek) The last remnant of the great Continent of Atlantis, referred to by Plato.

Prakriti. (Sanskrit) Nature as opposed to Spirit or Purusha – the two primeval aspects of the One Unknown Reality, the Absolute.

Pralaya. (Sanskrit) A period of repose – planetary, cosmic or universal. The opposite to a manvantara.

Priestley, Joseph. (1733-1804) English Clergyman, educator and scientist who discovered the element oxygen. His interest in science was encouraged by Benjamin Franklin and led to researches in electricity and later chemistry. He settled eventually in the USA and became a friend of Thomas Jefferson and John Adams.

Purusha. (Sanskrit) Spirit; heavenly man; spiritual Self.

Quietism. A doctrine of contemplation developed by a religious sect founded by the Spanish monk – Molinos. A practice focused on separating the mind from sense objects. It became a fashion in France and Russia in the early 19th-century.

Rishis. (Sanskrit) Adepts; the inspired ones. In Vedic literature the term is employed to denote those persons through whom the various Mantras were revealed.

Root Races. 7 Root Races or "developmental stages" form the evolutionary cycle of human life on this globe. Each is divided into 7 minor Races, which are further divided into sub-races and branchlets. The third Root Race was the Lemurian, the fourth was the Atlantean, and at the present we are in the middle of the fifth Root Race.

Round. This concerns our Planetary Chain, which consists of 7 globes (A, B, C, D, E, F, G/Z) existing simultaneously. Six are invisible, the only visible one of the earth chain being our globe (D.) The doctrine of the 7 Rounds refers to the Life Cycle Wave beginning its evolutionary course on Globe A and circulating around the 7 globes in turn, 7 times. The entire cycle is called a Planetary manvantara.

Row, T. Subba. (1856-1890) A Brahmin from a family of distinction, Subba Row was one of the most outstanding Hindu members of the early Theosophical movement. He was very learned in Vedanta philosophy and Occult Knowledge and also well-versed in ancient Indian scriptures. He was a representative of the Sringeri Matham (Monastery) at Madras and had considerable influence among orthodox Hindus. A chela of the Master Morya, he failed, unfortunately, to live up to the unique opportunities presented to him and eventually resigned from The Theosophical Society. He was author of *Esoteric Writings and*

Notes on The Bhagavad Gita.

Sakti. (Sanskrit) Universal energy. The active female energy of the gods in popular Hinduism – their wives and goddesses.

Samgha. (Sangha) (Sanskrit) A community of ordained Buddhists monks or nuns.

Sankaracharya, Sri. Dates are uncertain. Some scholars place him in the 8th-century AD. A great religious reformer of India and teacher of Vedanta philosophy, and a worker of miracles. He established many mathams or naths (monasteries) and founded the most learned sect amongst the Brahmans, called the Smartava. In his thirties, he went to Kashmir and reaching Kedaranath in the Himalayas entered a cave alone, from where he never returned.

Sannyasin. (Sanskrit) An ascetic. One who renounces all worldly bonds and attractions.

Second Death. This refers to the dissolution of the lower principles of man and withdrawing of the spiritual form from the desire body – known today as the astral. The first death refers to the casting off of the physical body, followed shortly by the casting off of the vital body (the etheric).

Shaberons. (Tibetan) A Tibetan term for Saints and Avatars. In Mongolia, Shaberons or Khubilkhans are considered by the lamaists to be the reincarnations of Buddhas.

Shammars. (Tibetan) Followers of the left-hand path.

Shastras. (Sanskrit) Treatises or books of divine or accepted authority, including law books. A shastri in India today means a man learned in divine and human law.

Shells. A Kabalistic term for the phantoms of the dead, the "spirits" of the Spiritualists, connected to physical phenomena. They are so named because they are simply illusive forms, empty of the higher principles.

Siddhas. (Sanskrit) Saints and sages who have almost become divine and have developed certain siddhis or powers.

Siddhis. (Sanskrit) Phenomenal powers acquired by yogis through holiness; also can be described as "attributes of perfection."

Sinnett, Alfred Percy. (1840-1921) A recipient of letters from the Indian Mahatmas, Sinnett was born in England and studied journalism. He moved to India where he was employed as the Editor of the Anglo-Indian newspaper, The Pioneer, in Allahabad. He was an early pioneer of the Theosophical movement and authored the books: *The Occult World* and *Esoteric Buddhism*. On return to England he was involved with the *London Lodge of the Theosophical Society*.

Siva. (Sanskrit) The third person of the Hindu Trinity. In his role as Destroyer he destroys only to regenerate. He is the patron of all the Yogis, being called *Mahadeva*.

Skandhas. (Sanskrit) Groups or bundles of attributes and tendencies which are part of man's temporary nature. According to Buddhism there are five – esoterically seven – skandhas or tendencies in every human being. These unite at the birth of a person and constitute his/her personality.

Solomon's Seal. The symbolical double, interlaced triangles with a point in the centre of them; one is turned upwards and the other downwards symbolizing evolution and involution. It has been adopted by The Theosophical Society and many theosophists. This double triangle in India is also called the "Sign of Vishnu" and may be seen on houses in villages as a talisman against evil. It has also been adopted by the Jews and called the "Star of David."

Spencer, Herbert. (1820-1903) Philosopher who insisted on a synthesis of knowledge from a close scientific investigation of biology and social phenomena. One of the early evolutionists prior to Darwin, He believed in the continuous development of the species from simple to complex. He wrote several works: *The Proper Sphere of Government, Social Statistics, The Man Versus the State* and *The Synthetic Philosophy.*

Spinoza. (1632-1677) Dutch philosopher of Portuguese origin, who lay the groundwork for 18th-century Enlightenment and modern biblical criticism. His main work – *Ethics* – earned him recognition as one of Western philosophy's most significant thinkers.

Surya. (Sanskrit) The Sun which is worshipped in the ancient Vedas as a god and named Surya.

Sutratman. (Sanskrit) "The thread of Spirit" also known as "the thread soul." The Individuality or Reincarnating Ego, which incarnates as a human being in one life after another and upon which are strung, like beads on a string, countless personalities.

Swabhavat. (Sanskrit) Literally – "that which is becoming." This is a state or condition of cosmic consciousness, where spirit and matter, which are fundamentally one, no longer are dual as in manifestation, but one; that which is neither manifested matter, nor manifested spirit alone, but both of the primeval Unity. When manifestation of the universe commences, the primeval unity begins to separate. The One becomes the Divine Masculine and the other the Divine Feminine. In esoteric philosophy Swabhavat is the Father-Mother.

Swabhavika. (Sanskrit) The oldest existing School of Buddhism in India, which assigns the manifestation of the universal and physical phenomena to Swabhava. Followers of this school of philosophy are called Swabhavikas.

Tathagatas. (Sanskrit) This can be used as a general term for Dhyan Chohans – the highest celestial beings and hosts, charged with the supervision of Cosmos.

Tanha. (Sanskrit) Thirst for life; clinging to the causes of re-birth or reincarnation.

Tantra. (Sanskrit) Religious treatises teaching mystical and magical formulae for the worship of the gods. Unfortunately, while there is much of interest in the tantric works, their tendency for ages has been directed toward sorcery. In many cases, tantric worship involves highly licentious and immoral practices.

Tathagata. (Sanskrit) One of the titles for Gautama Buddha, It also refers to the future Buddha or World Saviour.

Tantrikas. (Sanskrit) Those who study the Tantras and are engaged in tantric practices.

Tribhuvana. (Sanskrit) This term refers to the three main worlds or dimensions of consciousness with which humanity is concerned: the Spiritual, the Psychic (emotional-mental) and

Terrestrial dimensions.

Trishna. (Sanskrit) Thirst or longing for the things that the human being knew and which it desires to know again. It is this which draws the human soul of man back into incarnation on earth.

Tsong-Kha-pa. The 14th-century Tibetan reformer who introduced a purified Buddhism into his country. He was a great adept and was regarded as an Avatar of Buddha. He founded the Gelugpa Sect "yellow-cap" of Tibetan Buddhism, to which His Holiness the Dalai Lama belongs.

Tyndall, John. (1820-1893) English physicist who demonstrated why the sky is blue. He investigated gases and their ability to absorb and radiate heat and also studied the diffusion of light. A friend of the scientist Michael Faraday, he also wrote several books including: *Heat Considered as a Mode of Motion*; *Six Lectures on Light*; and *Forms of Water*.

Upadana. (Sanskrit) This term refers to the material cause which in time will bring about a certain effect.

Upadhi. (Sanskrit) The vehicle, carrier or bearer of something less material than itself. For example, the human body is the upadhi of its spirit.

Upasaka. (Sanskrit) Male chela, disciple or devotee.

Upasika. (Sanskrit) Female chela, disciple or devotee.

Vedas. (Sanskrit) The most ancient and sacred literary and religious works of the Hindus. There are four in number: the *Rig Veda*; the *Yajur Veda*; the *Sama Veda* and the *Atharva Veda*.

Vidya. (Sanskrit) A Sanskrit word connoting "knowledge," "philosophy," "science." Veda also comes from the same root – *vid*. This is a term that is used very generally in theosophical philosophy, having the three meanings given above. It is compounded with other words, such as *Atma-Vidya* (knowledge of the Atman or the Essential Self;) *Brahma-Vidya* (knowledge of Brahman;) *Guhya Vidya* signifying "Secret Knowledge," or the "Esoteric Wisdom."

Vishnu. (Sanskrit) The second person of the Hindu Trinity which is composed of the gods, Brahma, Vishnu, and Siva. His name is derived from the root *vid* which means to pervade. In the *Rig Veda*, Vishnu is a manifestation of the solar energy, described as "striding through the 7 regions of the Universe in three steps and enveloping all things with the dust of his beams." Later on he becomes a great god, the preserver and the renovator, he "of a thousand names."

Yoga. (Sanskrit) Literally means "union" and refers to the attaining of union with the divine spiritual essence within man. In India, it is the technical name for one of the six Schools of Philosophy and its foundation is ascribed to the Sage, Patanjali. There are a number of different forms of Yoga practice, such as *Karma-Yoga, Bhakti-Yoga, Jnana-Yoga,* and *Hatha-Yoga.* The Yoga practices taught and recommended by Patanjali come under the umbrella of *Raja-Yoga.* This Yoga emphasizes especially the controlling of the mind.

Yog Vidya. (Sanskrit) Knowledge of the practice of Yoga.

Yuga. (Sanskrit) An age of the world, according to Hindu philosophy, of which there are four. The *Krita* or *Sathya* Yuga (the Golden Age;) the *Treta* Age (Silver Age;) the *Dwapara* Age (the Bronze;) and the *Kali* Yuga (the Iron Age.) Of these four Yugas, it is believed that we are currently experiencing the Kali Age and have been doing so since the death of Krishna, approximately 3,000 years before the Christian era.

Sources for the Glossary: H.P. Blavatsky, *Theosophical Glossary*; The Theosophy Company, Los Angeles, California, 1952 – a photographic reproduction of the original edition, 1892; G. de Purucker, *Occult Glossary*; Theosophical University Press, Pasadena, California, 1953.

AXIS MUNDI
BOOKS

Axis Mundi Books provide the most revealing and coherent explorations and investigations of the world of hidden or forbidden knowledge. Take a fascinating journey into the realm of Esoteric Mysteries, Magic, Mysticism, Angels, Cosmology, Alchemy, Gnosticism, Theosophy, Kabbalah, Secret Societies and Religions, Symbolism, Quantum Theory, Apocalyptic Mythology, Holy Grail and Alternative Views of Mainstream Religion.